BEC Vantage
Masterclass
Upper Intermediate

Course Book

Nina O'Driscoll

Fiona Scott-Barrett

OXFORD
UNIVERSITY PRESS

contents

				vocabulary	reading
	introduction to the exam	4			
1	people and companies	6		Business sectors Types of company	Articles about companies and working practices
2	company structure	14		Departments Job roles and responsibilities	**Part 1** Job descriptions
3	business travel	22		Business travel	**Part 3** Article about business travel
4	company results	30		Finance Trends and results	**Part 2** Article about fashion retailer H&M
5	communication at work	38		Communication channels **Part 4** cloze	**Part 3** Article about e-mail
6	health and safety	46		Workplace accidents Health problems	**Part 1** Health and safety leaflet
7	recruitment and training	54		Recruitment methods and procedures	**Part 2** Article about on-line recruitment
8	advertising and promotion	62		Advertising and promotion methods	**Part 1** Small business guide to advertising methods
9	international business	70		Ways of entering new markets **Part 4** cloze	**Part 3** Article about doing business in Turkey
10	sales	78		Trade fairs and sales visits	Report on performance of a sales team
11	motivation	86		Motivational factors **Part 4** cloze	**Part 2** Article about motivation at work
12	customer service	94		After-sales service	**Part 1** Business guide to customer service
13	business ethics	102		Ethical issues	**Part 3** Article about ethics in business
14	new directions	110		New ways of organising work **Part 4** cloze	**Part 2** Article about flexible ways of working
	pairwork	118			
	exam information	122			
	grammar reference	130			
	tapescripts	139			
	glossary	149			

listening	language in use	speaking	writing
Interview about running your own business	Question forms	**Part 1** Interview	Opening and closing phrases for different types of correspondence
Part 2 People talking about working in different departments	Present simple and present continuous	Talking about your work or studies	**Part 1** Memo giving information
Part 1 Telephone calls to arrange an international meeting	Comparatives and superlatives	**Part 2** Short talk about choosing a hotel for a meeting	**Part 1** E-mail making a request
Part 3 Radio debate about Internet retailer boo.com	Past simple and present perfect	Information exchange about company performance	**Part 2** Report explaining findings
Part 1 Messages and a telephone call about arrangements	Countable and uncountable nouns **Part 5** error correction	**Part 3** Discussion about improving office communication	**Part 1** E-mail organising a training course
Part 2 People talking about safety issues	Modals	**Part 2** Short talk about office design	**Part 1** Memo reminding staff about safety procedures
Part 3 Interview with a candidate for a job	Connectors of contrast and addition **Part 5** error correction	**Part 3** Discussion about recruiting new staff	**Part 2** Report recommending action
Discussion about advertising strategy	Future forms	Presentation for an advertising campaign	**Part 2** Letter replying to an enquiry
Interview about expanding into new markets	Conditionals: 0, 1 and 2	Presentation about entertainment for foreign visitors	**Part 2** Report describing a business visit
Part 1 Telephone calls about an order and a trade fair	The passive **Part 5** error correction	**Part 2** Short talk about trade fairs and sales visits	**Part 1** Message summarising a phone conversation
Part 2 People talking about dissatisfaction with their jobs	The -ing form **Part 5** error correction	Interview and presentation on skills and motivations	**Part 2** Letter requesting information
Part 1 Telephone calls to call centres	Third conditional Past modals	**Part 2** Short talk about customer service	**Part 1** Memo reporting on a problem
Part 2 People talking about ethical issues	Articles	**Part 3** Discussion about an ethical problem	**Part 2** Report informing about progress
Part 3 Interview with a consultant about home-working	Degrees of future certainty **Part 5** error correction	Full Speaking test	**Part 2** Report making proposals

introduction to the exam

This paper consists of five parts and takes an hour.

Part	Task type	What does it test?	Number of items	What do you do?
1	Matching	Your ability to scan texts and understand the main ideas and specific details	7	Match statements with four short texts
2	Matching	Your ability to understand the meaning and structure of a text	5	Choose sentences to complete gaps in a text
3	Four-option multiple choice	Your ability to understand the main ideas, details and opinions expressed in a text	6	Answer each question by choosing an option from a set of four
4	Four-option multiple-choice cloze	Your vocabulary, e.g. correct word choice, collocations and fixed phrases	15	Choose one option from a set of four to complete each gap in a text
5	Proof reading	Your ability to identify errors and understand sentence structure	12	Identify unnecessary words in a text

Test of Writing

This paper consists of two writing tasks and takes 45 minutes.

Part	Task type	What does it test?	Number of words	What do you do?
1	Internal piece of communication, e.g. memo, e-mail, message or note	Your ability to write a short text, e.g. giving instructions, explaining a development, asking for information, agreeing to requests	40–50 words	Read the context and task instruction and write your memo, e-mail, message or note
2	Piece of business correspondence, e.g. letter, fax or e-mail, a report, or a proposal	Your ability to write: • business correspondence, e.g. explaining, apologising, complaining • a report, e.g. describing or summarising • a proposal, e.g. describing summarising, recommending	120–140 words	Read the task instruction and input material, e.g. business correspondence, chart or graph, and write your correspondence, report or proposal

Test of Listening

This paper consists of three parts and takes approximately 50 minutes.

Part	Task type	What does it test?	Number of questions	What do you do?
1	Gap filling / note taking	Your ability to identify factual information and write down missing details	12	Listen to three short telephone calls or messages and complete gaps in a text, e.g. on a form, or message pad
2	Multiple matching	Your ability to identify the topic, context or function of a short monologue	10	Listen to two sets of five short monologues. For each set you match the monologues with statements
3	Multiple choice	Your ability to understand the main ideas, opinions and feelings expressed in a long conversation	8	Listen to a longer passage, e.g. an interview or discussion, and answer questions by choosing one option from a set of three

Test of Speaking

The Speaking test consists of three parts and takes approximately 14 minutes. There will normally be two candidates and two examiners, one who will speak to you during the test and one whose role is to assess your English.

Part	Task type	What does it test?	Time	What do you do?
1	Conversation between the examiner and the candidate	Your ability to: • talk about yourself • give personal information about your home, interests and job or studies • talk about present circumstances, past experiences, express preferences and opinions	About 3 minutes	Answer the examiner's questions
2	Individual mini-presentation on a business theme	Your ability to: • organise a piece of extended speech • give information and express and justify opinions	About 6 minutes	Prepare and give a short talk on a chosen topic. When you finish speaking, the other candidate asks you a question about your talk
3	Two-way conversation	Your ability to express and justify opinions, compare and contrast, and agree and disagree	About 5 minutes	Discuss a given topic with the other candidate. The examiner then asks you further questions on the topic

unit 1 people and companies

Shell

Mercedes-Benz

vocabulary

1 Match the company logos above with the business sector each company operates in.

1 automotive
2 aviation
3 beverages
4 information technology

5 media
6 personal care
7 petroleum

8 pharmaceuticals
9 retail
10 telecommunications

2 Work with a partner. Together, think of the names of two or three other business sectors. Take turns to name your business sectors, while the rest of the class try to name companies that operate in that sector.

3 Some companies are known only by initials. How do you say these company names in English? What business sector do they operate in or what services do they offer?

4 Complete the quotes (a–e) with the words below.

entrepreneur   family firm/business   freelance
multinational   self-employed   state-owned

a The company I work for belongs to the country. People often say that .... companies are badly-run, but we're working hard to make the company as efficient as we can.

b What I like about working for a .... company is the chance to work abroad. I spent two years in Germany, and now I'm back at our head office in Japan.

c I'm .... I had my own company for a while, but I didn't enjoy managing other people. So now I work .... , doing projects for other companies.

d My grandfather started the company and now my father runs it. I'm studying management at a business college, and when I finish my course I'm going to join the ....

e I like starting companies, but when everything is going well, I sell them, move on and start another one. I'm much better at being an .... than a manager.

5 Work with a partner. Together prepare a short profile of a well-known company. Take turns to present your information about the company to the rest of the class, but do not say the company's name. The rest of the class must try to guess what company it is. Follow the example below.

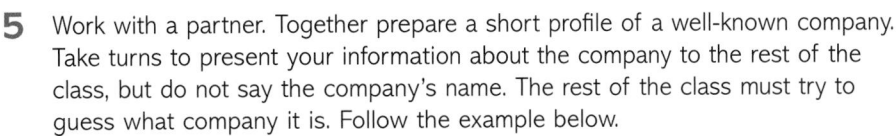

	Example	Your idea
Company name	Procter & Gamble	
Type of company	multinational	
Business sector	personal care / domestic cleaning products	
Type of products/services	toiletries, cleaning products	
Best-known product/service	Crest toothpaste, Ariel detergent	

Example

This is a multinational company. It operates in the personal care and domestic cleaning product sectors. It produces a lot of different toiletries, including toothpaste and soap, and cleaning products such as washing-up liquid. Its best-known products include Crest toothpaste and Ariel detergent.

reading

1 How do you think companies and working practices have changed since your grandparents' day. Think about these three areas.

- job security
- skills
- technology

2 Work with a partner. The six extracts below are from two different articles. One article is about changes in companies. The other is about people and changing working practices. Read each extract and mark it **C** (for companies) if you think it belongs to the first article and **P** (for people) if you think it belongs to the second.

1 A further reason for our increased interest in work is the ability – or need – to create our own careers, rather than having them organised for us by our employers. These days there are fewer company ladders to climb and so we have to make our own. Where security was once based on one employer, or at least one set of skills, security now comes from an ability to move with the times. The young have been the first to adapt to this situation. In the US, the average 32-year-old has had nine jobs. In the UK, one in four youngsters want to be self-employed. They have seen for themselves that no company can guarantee a job for life and have learned that a clever and skilful worker has the chance to choose the best employer. It is exhausting – but it can be liberating, too.

2 Nowadays it seems that work occupies a more central place in our lives than it used to do. Many people's sense of who they are now comes as much from their work as from their family and friends. That is why our first question at parties is not 'Where do you live?' or 'Do you have children?' but 'What do you do?' This trend creates a desire for work which brings personal fulfilment – for work we are proud of. If work means not just income but identity, then the choice of job becomes critical. Young people in particular are becoming more concerned about what they do and their employment choices are based on a desire for freedom, fulfilment and individuality.

3 Read the extracts again. With your partner, put the three extracts from each article in the correct order. Number them 1 to 3 for each article.

4 What words or phrases in the extracts helped you to put them in order?

5 Read the statements (a–h) below. Then mark each statement **Yes** if the idea is the same as an idea expressed in one of the articles, or **No** if it is not the same. (Some statements relate to both articles.)

a The main reason that people work is to earn money.
b Working life is more sociable than it used to be.
c Not many people nowadays work for one company all their lives.
d There will be no large companies in the future.
e People with lots of skills and ideas will find it easy to get jobs.
f Small companies are more profitable than large ones.
g Young people want the work they do to express their personal identity.
h Modern companies often ask other companies to do part of their work for them.

6 Work in small groups. Look again at the statements that you marked **Yes**. Do you think the situation is the same in your country too? Give examples from your own experience to support your ideas.

3 Look round the business section of any good bookshop and you will find dozens of books about the future of the company. There is little agreement about what exactly that future will be, and some analysts even suggest that the company as we know it will soon be a thing of the past. However, all the experts agree that companies are currently in a state of rapid change.

4 Changes in the nature of employment have also helped to make work more important to us. A recent survey suggests we spend more time communicating at work, either face-to-face or by phone, than ever before. This reflects a general shift away from manufacturing jobs and towards services – increasingly services that need a human touch. And while the working day is not filled with enjoyable interaction for everyone, there is no questioning the fact that for most people, most of the time, work is better now – which inevitably makes it more valuable.

5 Another area of agreement is that the human side of organisations will become more important. In the first half of the twentieth century, managers tried to take the human element out of business by turning people into machines. Nowadays, what makes companies different from each other is their ability to be creative. This means they need employees who have talent and new ideas. As most companies can no longer offer a job for life and a career ladder to climb, the big battle of the twenty-first century will be the fight to find new ways to attract and keep the best people.

6 To take the United States as an example, thirty years ago the American economy was dominated by a handful of big companies which produced large quantities of standardised products. The management structure of these firms consisted of many different levels, and the companies provided their workers with lifetime employment. That world is now dead. America's giant companies have ceased to exist or have been transformed by global competition. The survivors now produce smaller quantities of high-value customised products and have reduced the levels in their management structure to make themselves more efficient. Many firms now perform only the tasks they are very good at and hand everything else over to freelance workers or specialist suppliers.

listening

1 Work with a partner and discuss these points.

- Why do people become self-employed?
- What do you think people enjoy about being self-employed?
- What do you think people miss when they leave a company and become self-employed?

2 🎧 You will hear a journalist interviewing a woman for a newspaper article in a series about people who run their own businesses. Listen and complete the journalist's notes.

1 Name

2 Service she offers now

3 Former business sector

4 Reason for becoming self-employed

5 Length of time in business

6 How she communicates with her customers

7 What she enjoys about being self-employed

8 What she misses about working for a company

3 Compare the notes you have made with a partner. Listen again to the interview. Check your answers and complete any details you didn't catch before.

4 Look back at your answers to exercise 1. Did you think of any of the points that Maria mentioned?

language in use: question forms

1 🎧 You will hear the interview with Maria Maldini again. As you listen, complete the missing words in the questions below. Which questions are direct and which are indirect?

a Do you mind if .... our conversation as well?
b .... spell your family name?
c Could you tell me .... first .... the idea for the business?
d Where .... you .... at that time?
e .... give up your job then?
f What .... for becoming self-employed?
g How long .... in business?
h .... pleased with the way things are going?
i .... the treatment or training always .... place in the customer's home?
j What .... you .... most about working for yourself?
k .... anything you miss about working for a company?

2 Look at the direct questions in a–k above. What kind of questions are they?
a closed questions (ones which could be answered with just *yes* or *no*)
b open questions (ones which couldn't be answered with just *yes* or *no*)

3 What auxiliary verb is used in questions f, h and k? What do you notice about the order of the words in these questions?

4 When is it necessary to use *do*, *does* and *did* in questions? Where in the question do you put *do*, *does* or *did*?

5 Change the direct questions below to indirect questions. Follow the example.

Example   What time is it? (Could you tell me ...)
Could you tell me what time it is?

a Where's the manager's office? (Do you know ...)
b How does this machine work? (Could you explain ...)
c When did you join the company? (Could you tell me ...)
d Why did he leave his job? (Do you know ...)
e Is she efficient? (Do you think ...)
f Can I borrow your pen? (Do you mind if ...)

See grammar reference page 130

6 Think of a well-known company that operates in the country you are working or studying in now. The rest of the class try to guess which company it is.

The class may ask up to ten Yes/No questions.

Example

* Is it a multinational company?
* Does it work in the retail sector?
* Does the company produce goods?

If you don't know the answer to one of the Yes/No questions asked, the class wins a free open question.

Example

* What business sector does the company operate in?
* What kind of goods does it produce?
* What letter does the company's name begin with?

speaking

1 Interviews, either for jobs or during exams, often follow this pattern.

1 opening questions to get some information about you and help you relax
2 easy follow-up questions about what you do now
3 more difficult questions to find out about your ideas and opinions

Work with a partner. Look at the list of questions below and decide which category (1–3) to put each question in.

a Could you tell me something about a typical day at your work?
b What job would you like to do later?
c Do you think you would ever want to work abroad?
d Do you work or are you a student?
e How do you spell your family name?
f Is it easy to find interesting jobs in your country?
g What do you find most interesting about your studies/job?
h What skills do you think employers look for in young people nowadays?

2 With your partner, think of one extra question to go in each category.

Speaking Part 1

3 Work with a different partner. Take turns to interview each other. Ask some questions from each category. Before you start, read the Task procedure box on page 128, which contains instructions to help with the task.

> **tip**
> When you are answering closed questions or indirect questions, don't just say *Yes* or *No*.

writing: beginnings and endings

1 Look at the beginnings and endings of four different pieces of correspondence. Match each beginning (A–D) with an ending (1–4).

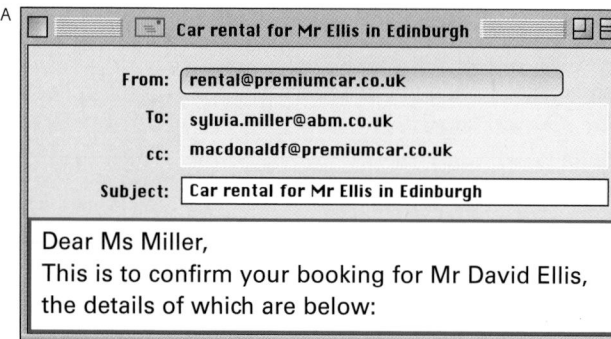

A

Car rental for Mr Ellis in Edinburgh

From: rental@premiumcar.co.uk
To: sylvia.miller@abm.co.uk
cc: macdonaldf@premiumcar.co.uk

Subject: Car rental for Mr Ellis in Edinburgh

Dear Ms Miller,
This is to confirm your booking for Mr David Ellis, the details of which are below:

B

From: Sylvia Miller, Office Manager
To: All staff
Subject: New front door entry system

Following last week's burglary, a new front door entry system is being installed tomorrow (26 March). Please make sure that

C

Temp Solutions
5 Gloucester Way
Basingham
BG1 2JA

The Office Manager
ABM
25 Weldon Road
Basingham BG1 2HB   25 March

Dear Sir or Madam,
Temp Solutions has been providing temporary office staff to top companies nationwide since 1995. We have just opened a new office here in Basingham and I am writing to

D

The Business Support Centre
Bishop's Court
Basingham
BG2 1PP

The Office Manager
ABM
25 Weldon Road
Basingham BG1 2HB   25 March

Dear Ms Miller,
Thank you for your recent enquiry about training courses for office staff.

2 Which of the types of correspondence in exercise 1 is used for these purposes?

   a mainly for communicating with other people in the same company (internal correspondence)

   b mainly for communicating with people who do not work in the same company (external correspondence)

   c in both situations

3 Complete the table below with phrases from this list. Follow the example.

Dear Mr/Ms + family name

Dear + first name

Dear Sir or Madam,

With best wishes / Best wishes,

Yours sincerely,

Yours faithfully,

Your first name (and possibly your job title)

Your first name, family name and job title (*use this twice*)

Opening and closing phrases for letters

You are writing to	You start with	You finish with	You identify yourself by
a person whose name you don't know			
a person whose name you know	Dear mr/ms + family name		
someone you know quite well			

4 Write appropriate beginnings, and endings if needed, for these three pieces of correspondence written by Sylvia Miller.

a

Thank you for your brochure.
I would like to enrol my assistant, Sharon Cook, on your next course on 'Working with Spreadsheets'.
I enclose a completed booking form.

b

I would like to remind all staff that everyone has a different entry code and that you must memorise your own personal one. Please contact me if you have forgotten it.

c

Could your Edinburgh office please deliver the car to Mr Ellis's hotel, (The Thistle Hotel, Charlotte Street) instead of Mr Ellis picking it up at the airport?

1

Yours faithfully,
Dawn Maguire
Manager

2

Yours sincerely,
Bruce Smith
Manager

3

Regards,
John Barnes
Sales agent

4

and personal entry code from me before you leave the office tomorrow.

unit 2 company structure

1 Read the short text below about Derrant Technologies and answer these questions.

a What does the company produce?
b Where is it based?
c Who are their customers?

2 Work with a partner. Look at the photos (1–7) above. Match the department names (a–g) with the photos.

a Finance
b Information Technology
c Sales and Distribution
d Human Resources / Personnel / Training
e Production and Quality Control
f Purchasing
g Marketing

DERRANT TECHNOLOGIES

Derrant Technologies is a small company which makes medical equipment. It has a very modern factory and warehouse near Sydney. It sells its products direct to hospitals and scientific research laboratories. The company wants to grow quickly, so finding new markets is very important.

3 Five of these departments are described briefly below. Match the descriptions (1–5) with the department names (a–g) in exercise 2.

1 This department <u>deals with</u> employees, for example, selecting and recruiting staff. It is also responsible for organising training to make sure the staff have the skills to do their work effectively.

2 This department is in charge of manufacturing the products and keeping the company's production facilities running efficiently. Another responsibility is checking and improving quality standards.

3 This department deals with the day-to-day running of the company's computer systems and solves problems when they go wrong. It also designs information systems for the different departments.

4 This department is in charge of sourcing (buying) any materials, equipment or components the production department needs to make the products. This involves finding suppliers and negotiating prices and delivery times.

5 This department's main responsibilities are finding out what products the customers want, how and where to promote them, and at what price. This involves carrying out market research – collecting and analysing data on their current and potential markets. They are also in charge of researching new ideas for products.

4 Underline the phrases in each text which introduce the tasks each department carries out, as in the example. Which phrase in texts 4 and 5 introduces more details about a task or responsibility?

5 Use appropriate phrases from exercises 3 and 4 to complete these descriptions of the other two departments at Derrant Technologies. Which department is being described each time?

This department (a) .... selling the finished products to customers. As well as negotiating contracts, (b) .... getting the products to the customers in the fastest, cheapest and most efficient way.

This department (c) .... the money coming into and going out of the business. It (d) .... the banks when the company needs to raise money. It also coordinates budgets for the different departments – their estimate of what they need to spend during a year.

6 Look at this organisation chart for the Human Resources department at Derrant Technologies. Match phrases from A and B to make sentences explaining the relationships between the people in the department. Follow the example.

HUMAN RESOURCES DEPARTMENT

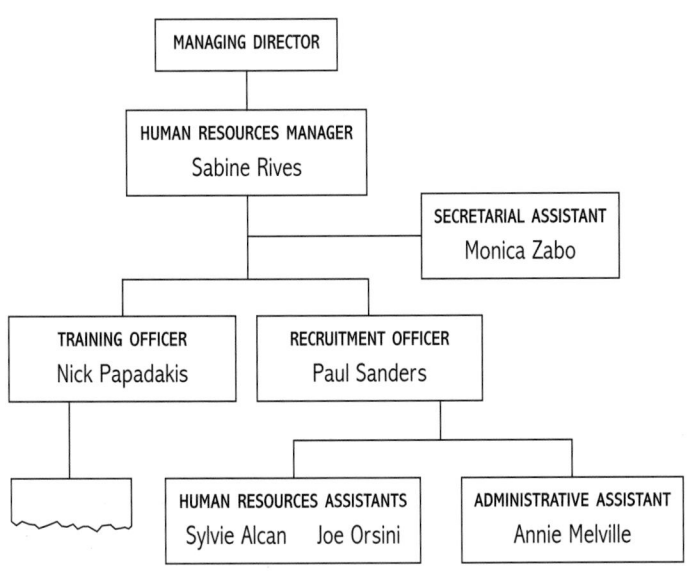

A
1 The Human Resources manager reports ƒ
2 Human Resources is headed
3 Paul is in charge
4 Nick is responsible
5 Annie is responsible
6 Monica works
7 Sylvie works

B
a with Joe to support Paul.
b to Paul.
c by Sabine Rives.
d of a team of three.
e for Sabine.
f to the managing director.
g for organising training.

A

TITLE: (1) ....

FULL-TIME ☑
PART-TIME ☐

DEPARTMENT: Marketing
SUPERVISOR: Marketing Manager

MAIN RESPONSIBILITIES

1 Co-ordinates the marketing team's activities to ensure that the team's projects stay on schedule.

2 Supervises the work of administrative/secretarial support staff in the team.

3 Makes all the travel arrangements for the marketing team.

4 Organises hospitality for customers and potential customers visiting the company.

B

TITLE: (2) ....

FULL-TIME ☐
PART-TIME ☑

DEPARTMENT: Marketing
SUPERVISOR: Marketing Administrator

MAIN RESPONSIBILITIES

1 Works with other administrative staff to provide support for the marketing team: word processing, dealing with general correspondence, answering the telephones, sorting the post.

2 Processes invoices to ensure that accounts are kept up-to-date, and information is passed to the Marketing Manager.

3 Under the direction of the relevant marketing team members, organises appointments, prepares department meetings, takes minutes of meetings and types up reports.

reading

1 Sonic NV is a Danish company which produces medical equipment. Look quickly through the texts (A–D) above which are job descriptions of posts in their Marketing Department. What type of information do they give about each job?

2 Read the job descriptions again and choose a title from the list below to complete the missing job titles (1–4) in the descriptions. Do not use any of the letters (a–f) more than once.

a Product Manager
b Market Research Analyst
c Marketing Manager

d Marketing Administrator
e Assistant Marketing Administrator
f Assistant Product Manager

Reading Part 1

tip
In tasks like this, you are unlikely to find the correct answer simply by spotting the same words in both a statement and a text. Instead, you usually need to find *the same idea* expressed *in different words.*

3 In the next task, you will be asked to match different statements to the job descriptions. First work through the example below and answer the questions.

*This job involves **a lot of travel abroad for the company**.*

There are two texts that contain references to travel abroad.

Text C ... *may involve **occasional travel abroad**.*
Text D *Supports the sales teams **in the company's foreign subsidiaries** by **regular visits**.*

a Which extract exactly matches the statement?
b Why is the other one not correct?

C

TITLE: (3) ....
FULL-TIME ✓
PART-TIME ☐

DEPARTMENT: Marketing
SUPERVISOR: Marketing Manager

MAIN RESPONSIBILITIES

1 Analyses data from market research studies.

2 Prepares reports and attends meetings to present market research findings to the marketing and sales teams.

3 Keeps up-to-date with competitor and market news by reading journals and attending conferences – may involve occasional travel abroad.

D

TITLE: (4) ....
FULL-TIME ✓
PART-TIME ☐

DEPARTMENT: Marketing
SUPERVISOR: Product Manager (Byron range)

MAIN RESPONSIBILITIES

1 Works together with advertising agencies to prepare product information and advertising material.

2 Provides the company management with regular breakdowns and analysis of sales figures and budgets for promotions and product launches for the Byron range.

3 Prepares meetings with the production, pricing and sales teams to review strategies for maintaining the brand's competitive position in different markets.

4 Supports the sales teams in the company's foreign subsidiaries by regular visits.

4 Which job description (A, B, C or D) do the statements below refer to? First read all the texts and highlight or underline any parts that might match statement 1. Then check which highlighted or underlined part matches it exactly. Do the same for each statement in turn. You will need to use some of the letters (A–D) more than once.

1 For this job it's important to know exactly what other companies are doing in your markets.

2 The person who does this job is in charge of other people.

3 Excellent secretarial and general office skills would be needed for this job.

4 The person who does this job needs to be good at interpreting financial data.

5 An important part of this job is dealing with visitors and organising business trips.

6 For this job good presentation and report writing skills are required.

5 Which words or phrases helped you to match the statements to the texts?

6 Work with a partner and discuss these points.

• Would you like to do any of the jobs described in the job descriptions? Which?
• What is it about this job that appeals to you?
• If none of the jobs appeals to you, what is it about them that you don't like?

listening

1 Look again at descriptions 2 and 4 in exercise 3 on page 15, which describe different departments' activities. Complete the table below with phrases from these descriptions. Follow the examples.

Production	Purchasing
manufacturing the products	sourcing materials, equipment or components

2 🎧 Listen to an employee at Sonic NV talking about his job. As you listen, tick any phrases you hear that appear in the table in exercise 1. Does the man work in the Production department or the Purchasing department?

3 Work in groups. Think of two or three phrases to describe tasks associated with these departments.

Information Technology (IT) ....

Marketing ....

Sales ....

Quality Control ....

Listening Part 2

4 🎧 You will hear four more people from Sonic NV talking about their work. Which department (A–D) does each one work in?

Speaker 1 ....   A IT
Speaker 2 ....   B Marketing
Speaker 3 ....   C Sales
Speaker 4 ....   D Quality Control

5 Did the speakers use any of the phrases you had thought of in exercise 3? Which words and phrases in the recordings helped you to make your choice?

6 The speakers described how different departments at Sonic NV work together. Work in groups. Look again at the department names in exercise 2 on page 14. Which departments do you think would work together in these activities (a–e)? What contribution would each make? When you have finished, compare your results with other groups.

a Recruiting staff for a new sales office in Paris.
b Choosing a new supplier for components for technical products.
c Handling complaints about faulty products.
d Attending an international trade fair.
e Redesigning the packaging for one of their products.

language in use: present simple and present continuous

1 🎧 Listen again to the employee in Sales at Sonic NV describe his work. As you listen, complete the missing verbs in the extracts.

Extract 1

'In my team we usually .... about 25% of our time here and the rest of the time on the road visiting customers.'

Extract 2

'Our customers .... mainly doctors and other health professionals. Apart from selling the products, a big part of our work .... to educate customers about the products. We .... closely with Marketing to produce product information and specifications.'

Extract 3

'Currently, we .... on specifications for the new Byron range. I .... the project.'

Extract 4

'We .... the Byron range in Asia next month, so tomorrow I .... the Product Manager to discuss product training for the sales team in Asia.'

2 Complete the table. Follow the examples.

	extract	tense
1 definite arrangements in the future	4	present continuous
2 usual activities and routines	1	present simple
3 current or temporary activities	....	....
4 general or permanent situations	....	....

3 Complete the comments (a–h) by people at Sonic NV with the verbs below. Use the same verb twice in each comment. Follow the example.

be   develop   have   see   stay
spend   think   take   work

Example

As part of my job I **develop** *new office systems. Currently I'm developing a new system for processing customer complaints.*

a I usually .... around 40 hours a week, but I .... longer hours this week to get everything finished.

b Our suppliers .... difficult about deliveries at the moment. It's strange, because usually they .... very good.

c Normally, my boss doesn't .... a lot of time travelling, but with the project in Austria, he .... more and more time out of the office.

d Most of the time I .... the bus, but because I'm running late this morning I .... a taxi to work.

e Normally on business trips to Paris we .... in the company's flat, but it needs some repairs, so we .... in a hotel this time.

f I .... of looking for a new position, possibly in marketing, because I really (not) .... this is the right job for me.

g Tom   I .... Derrant Technologies got that big contract we wanted in Brazil.

Hanne   Unfortunately, yes. In fact, I .... the Sales Manager today to discuss what went wrong.

h We .... two sales offices in Japan. A group of visitors from the Osaka office are here in Copenhagen now. We .... a reception for them in town this evening.

> tip
> Some verbs have a different meaning when they are used in the present simple (e.g. *I see* = I notice/understand) compared with the present continuous (e.g. *I'm seeing* = I'm meeting).

4 Apart from *see*, three other verbs in the comments in exercise 3 change their meaning, depending on the verb tense that is used. Identify them, and explain the differences in meaning.

5 Write a short paragraph about your work or studies. Include general information about the job/course, your usual activities, any current projects and definite future plans.

See grammar reference pages 130 and 131

speaking

1 🎧 Listen to two extracts from two different conversations in which Marco Benini talks about his job at Sonic NV. Match each extract with the impressions he gives (a–d).

a He wants to participate in the conversation.
b He doesn't really want to talk to the other person.
c He isn't enthusiastic about his job.
d He enjoys his job.

2 🎧 Listen to the extracts again. What is different about the way Marco does the following in each extract?

a answers questions   b expresses negative feelings

3 🎧 Listen to extract 2 again. How does Marco show his enthusiasm about his job and play down any negative points? Complete the missing words.

a … but actually I find the job .... It's .... that you're helping people to overcome difficulties.
b It is, and .... too. It's .... at the moment as I'm doing a lot of travelling and that's .... on my family, but otherwise I .... enjoy the work.

4 Work in pairs. Use the information in the profile below to improve this conversation so that B takes a more active part in the conversation and the tone is more positive. You may have to make changes to A's questions and responses.

COMPANY	Amtec, Singapore
	Produces hand-held computers Leading manufacturer worldwide Subsidiaries in four continents
JOB	Sales Manager. Co-ordinates large sales team
CURRENT PROJECT	Organising international sales conference for Amtec's subsidiaries
DISLIKES	Work can be stressful
LIKES	Plenty of variety, excellent rewards

A Where do you work?
B For a company called Amtec.
A Amtec? I don't think I've heard of them. What do they do?
B They make hand-held computers.
A That's interesting. And what do you do?
B I work in Sales here in Singapore.
A Really? So what are you working on at present?
B I'm organising a sales conference for Amtec's subsidiaries. It's very stressful.

5 Work in groups of three. Follow the instructions on page 118. Then change roles until each person in the group has had a chance to play all three roles.

writing: a memo giving information

1 Read two internal memos which have been circulated at Derrant Technologies. Complete the memos by adding these phrases (a–e).

  a Please let me know if   d Please note
  b Please contact   e Could you
  c For your information,

Memo 1

DERRANT TECHNOLOGIES

memo

To   Nick Papadakis, Training Officer
From Sabine Rives,
       Human Resources Manager
Date 25 May

(1)........................... the date for moving the office is now confirmed as Friday 10 June. (2)........................... make sure all your staff clear their desks before they leave work on Thursday evening? (3)........................... this is a problem for anyone in the team.

Memo 2

DERRANT TECHNOLOGIES

memo

To   **All department managers**
From **Nick Papadakis,**
       Training Officer
Date **26 May**

(4)........................... that the training department will be moving offices on Friday 10 June. All our computer and phone systems will be shut down from Thursday evening until Monday 13 June. (5)........................... me on my mobile 0409 456 384 if you need to speak to me urgently during this period.

2 Answer these questions about the two memos.

  a What is the purpose of writing?
  b What action is expected?

3 Memos in Part 1 of the exam need to be between 40 and 50 words. This memo from Nick Papadakis to his assistant has 80 words. Work in pairs. Rewrite it as three sentences. Your memo should have a maximum of 50 words.

> I would like to inform you that the office equipment and furniture are being installed in our new office on the 10th of June. I will be at the new office all day to supervise the work of installing the office equipment and furniture. If any of the team needs to speak to me while I am at the new office, they can contact me at the office on my mobile phone. The number is 0409 456 384.

Writing Part 1

tip When you write your memo, avoid repeating complete phrases from the instructions.

4 Before you start the exam task, look at the Task procedure box on page 124.

As part of the reorganisation at Derrant Technologies, a new customer service section is planned to handle all customer complaints. You are the Assistant Sales Manager and have to inform staff about the proposed changes.

Write a memo of 40–50 words to all staff:

- informing them about the new customer service section.
- telling them that they will get more detailed information next month.
- asking them to telephone your assistant Jenny Maguire with any queries (telephone number 9 468 3660).

unit 3 business travel

vocabulary

1 Look at the cartoon. Then choose titles from the list below.

a a title for the whole cartoon
b a title for pictures 1 to 4
c a title for pictures 5 to 8

A bad day for Mr Jones   The business trip   The dream
The joys of business travel   The reality   The risks of business travel

2 Match each noun (a–h) below with one picture (1–8) in the cartoon.

a a business class cabin
b a check-in desk
c a single room
d a hotel suite
e a meeting room
f a queue
g a restaurant
h an economy class cabin

3 Which of these adjectives and adverbs would you associate with the pictures?

basic   comfortable/comfortably   convenient   cramped   luxurious
rapid/rapidly   relaxing   spacious   squashed   stressful

4 Match the verbs (a–e) with the nouns (1–6). Some verbs may combine with more than one noun. Follow the example.

verbs		nouns	
a book *3, 4, 5, 6*	d reserve	1 business class	4 a hotel
b check in for	e travel (in)	2 economy class	5 a room
c check in to		3 a flight	6 a ticket

5 Tell the story illustrated in the cartoon. Use vocabulary from exercises 2, 3 and 4 above, and the grammatical structures below.

For pictures 1 to 4: Jones imagines/pictures himself + verb + -ing ...

Example   *Jones imagines himself checking in rapidly at a convenient check-in desk for business class passengers.*

For pictures 5 to 8: simple past tense

Example   *In reality, he waited in a long queue to check in for a flight in economy class.*

6 Which parts of the cartoon do you think are closest to the reality of business travel?

7 Work with a partner. Tell him/her about a bad experience of travelling you or someone you know has had on business or on holiday.

1 Would you enjoy a job which involved a lot of business travel? Why / Why not?

2 The article below is about business travel. Look quickly through it and decide what it is mainly about.

    a facilities for business travellers
    b the problems facing business travellers
    c companies' attitudes to business travel

Business travel today

1 Long-distance travel is now a routine part of many workers' lives, yet what was once considered a perk of the job is now seen as a headache by frequent fliers. Business travel isn't as exciting as it sounds. The reality for most travellers is that they rarely see anything beyond the airport, the office and the hotel. Even after a long overnight flight in a cramped seat without sleep, staff are frequently expected to be in the office next morning, ready to do a good day's work.

2 Despite alternatives such as fax, e-mail and teleconferencing, business travel continues to grow. Many companies have teleconferencing equipment, but do not know how to use it. In the global economy increasing numbers of people deal with more and more countries, and are required to travel for their jobs. Travel across the globe for business has also become much more cost-effective for companies. In the early eighties, a round-the-world ticket was at least £1,250. Now it's £700.

3 Stephen Joy, a marketing director at US toy maker Mattel, has been a frequent traveller during his sixteen-year career. He believes business travel has become more stressful. 'As your life gets fuller, with children and so on, it becomes a lot more difficult,' he says. 'But, it's not just to do with age. Modern communications mean that the only time you're truly out of reach is on the plane. When you get to the hotel you log on and get your e-mail. In the past when you were away, you were away. Now you're expected to take the in-tray with you, and managing your work from afar can be very difficult, especially if you're in a different time zone.'

4 As the volume of business travel has grown, companies have begun to pay increasing attention to its impact on costs. 'Now I don't travel in as much comfort as I did as a junior years ago,' says Joy. Today, costs are scrutinised and many companies are concerned with little more than cheap travel.

5 There may also be as many health risks associated with long-distance flights as there are passengers in economy class. Because most airlines re-circulate the air inside planes, mixing half-fresh air with half-recycled air, flu and colds are among the most frequent problems for travellers. New research suggests that jet lag, once seen as a minor inconvenience, may be far more upsetting to travellers' health and routines than earlier thought. More worryingly, a recent study identified a possible link between long-distance travel and an increased risk of heart attacks, especially amongst older passengers. Is it time for companies to reassess attitudes to travel and show a little more concern for their travelling staff?

3 In the next exercise, you will do a multiple-choice task. First work through this example.

Paragraph 1 Why are many business travellers unhappy about long distance travel?

A It can cause headaches.
B They usually have to fly at night.
C Aircraft have become very uncomfortable.
D They often don't get time to recover from their journeys.

a *A headache* is mentioned in the paragraph, but does the text say that it is *caused by* long distance travel?
b *A long overnight flight* is mentioned in the paragraph, but does the text say that business travellers *usually* fly at night?
c A phrase in the paragraph implies that aircraft can be uncomfortable – which one? Does the sentence this phrase appears in also say that aircraft *have become* very uncomfortable or are more uncomfortable than they used to be?
d Is *time to recover* mentioned in the paragraph? Does any sentence in the paragraph imply, in different words or by examples, that business people don't get time to recover from journeys?
e Which option A, B, C or D would you choose?

• Don't choose an option just because you see the same, or similar, words or phrases as in part of the text. Check carefully if the meaning of the whole sentence in which the words or phrase appear matches the meaning of the option.
• Sometimes an idea in the text is suggested, rather than stated directly, as in the example 3d.

4 Answer the questions, checking each option in turn against the text.

Paragraph 2 According to the writer, what is the expansion in business travel due to?
A employees' unwillingness to use alternative methods of communicating
B companies' ignorance about new communications technology
C the overall growth in international business
D the fact that long-distance flights cost less than half of what they used to

Paragraph 3 Stephen Joy thinks the main reason business travellers suffer more stress these days is because
A typically people who travel for business have young children.
B many of them are too old to travel regularly.
C they receive too many mobile phone calls.
D while they are abroad they still have to carry out their normal duties.

Paragraph 4 How are companies dealing with the increase in business travel?
A by keeping travel costs as low as possible
B by sending younger staff on business trips
C by using less comfortable airlines
D by reducing the number of days employees spend out of the office

Paragraph 5 Which of these points is made about long distance air travel?
A It leads to breathing problems.
B It is no longer thought to cause jet lag.
C It may be dangerous for elderly people.
D It causes serious health problems for everyone who flies regularly.

5 Work with a partner and compare your answers. Discuss the reasons you chose each option and why you rejected the other options.

6 Find words in the text which have these meanings.
a Paragraph 1 an extra benefit in addition to your salary (noun)
b Paragraph 2 giving good results for the amount of money spent (adjective)
c Paragraph 4 a strong effect (noun)
d Paragraph 4 examined closely (verb)

language in use: comparatives and superlatives

1 How do you form comparatives and superlatives with the adjectives and adverbs below? Look at the table, then write the correct letter **A**, **B** or **C** next to each one. Which three adjectives have irregular endings in the comparative and superlative form?

cramped	....	hot	....
dangerous	....	large	....
easy	....	old	....
efficiently	....	slowly	....
expensive	....	stressful	....
frequently	....	upsetting	....

A

adjective + -er or
adjective + -est
(high → higher → (the) highest)

B

more + adjective or
the most + adjective
(careful → more careful → (the) most careful)

C

more + adverb
the most + adverb
(quickly → more quickly → (the) most quickly)

2 These adjectives and adverbs have irregular comparative and superlative forms. What are they?

bad   badly   good   well

3 The article on business travel on page 24 contains many examples of comparisons. Look through the article and find phrases with a similar meaning to the words in italics.
   a Business travel is *less exciting than* it sounds. (paragraph 1)
   b Now I *travel in less comfort than* I did as a junior years ago. (paragraph 4)
   c There may be *the same number of* health risks associated with long distance flights *as* there are passengers in economy class. (paragraph 5)

4 Sometimes a comparative form has another word (a modifier) before it. Modifiers are used to make a comparison more accurate. Look through the article again and find the words which are used to modify these comparisons.
   a .... more cost-effective (paragraph 2)
   b .... more difficult (paragraph 3)
   c .... more upsetting (paragraph 5)
   d .... more concern (paragraph 5)

5 Put the words in brackets in the correct place in the sentences.
   a When you're single, it's often easier to travel for business. (much)
   b On most short-haul flights travelling business class is more comfortable than travelling economy class. (a little)
   c Even junior staff are expected to travel more frequently. (far)
   d Today business travel upsets people's lives and routines more regularly because of frequent delays at airports. (a lot)

6 Compare the job or course you are doing at the moment with one you have done in the past. Use the comparative forms below.

Examples

It doesn't take me as long to get to my work.
I don't have nearly as much time to go out in the evenings as I did before.

... *(nearly) as* + adjective + *as* ...
... *not (nearly) as* + adjective + *as* ...
... *as many / much as* ...
... *a little / a bit / a lot / far more* ...

See grammar reference page 131

listening

1 Enrica Grasi works in Human Resources at a multinational company, Vevier Engineering. She is organising a two-day international meeting to discuss personnel policy within the company. The team consists of three people from HQ in Geneva, two from New York, one from Canada and one from Mexico.

a Where would you hold the meeting to be convenient for all the team?
b Make a list of things Enrica will need to do to arrange the meeting.

2 You will hear Enrica Grasi phoning Alicia Gomez, who works in New York. First look at some notes summarising their conversation that Alicia made after the call. Match the types of information (a–d) with the gaps (1–4).

a a day or date
b an ordinal number, e.g. first / second
c a feature of a city, e.g. the centre / the main station
d the name of a town or city

Conversation 1

> Alicia OK for both the (1)........................ week of October and the 1st week of November.
> Agrees that (2)........................ is a good place to hold the meeting. Suggests finding a hotel near the (3)........................ .
> Phone her late on (4)........................ to confirm dates and venue.

3 🎧 Listen to Enrica and Alicia's conversation. Write one or two words or a number in the numbered spaces on the note above.

4 Work with a partner. Together, anticipate what kind of information is missing from the two notes below. Mark your ideas in pencil beside each gap.

5 🎧 You will hear two more conversations about the meeting Enrica Grasi is arranging. Write one or two words or a number in the spaces on the notes below.

Conversation 2 Someone leaves a message for Enrica

> ## Phone message
>
> To: Enrica
>
> Date: 26 September
>
> Message: While you were out Patricia (5)........................ from the Crowne Hotel called with some prices:
> - participants' rooms: $2,180 in total (special (6)........................ rate)
> - meeting room: (7)........................ per day. This includes a (8)........................ and non-alcoholic drinks.

Conversation 3 Enrica Grasi leaves a message for Martyn Best in Toronto

> Message from Enrica, 26 September
>
> Meeting in NY confirmed.
> – dates: 25 and 26 (9)........................
> – starting time: (10)........................
> – venue: the (11)........................ Hotel.
> Action:
> Call Karl Davidson (Enrica's (12)........................)
> about my accommodation!

speaking

1 Work in small groups. Which factors do you think would be important when choosing a hotel for an international meeting for twenty middle-ranking sales staff? Choose four of the points below and rank them in order (1 = most important).

a Convenience for airports
b Size and availability of meeting rooms
c Quality and availability of rooms for the delegates
d Hotel amenities, e.g. bars, restaurants and sports facilities
e Availability of equipment, e.g. video
f Availability of business support, e.g. photocopying, e-mail facilities
g Cost per delegate per day

2 Below you can see the plan a speaker made for a short talk on the topic you have just discussed. Listen to the talk and answer the questions.

a Does the presenter cover all four of the points in her plan?
b What does she say to introduce her first point?
In .... , the .... when choosing a hotel for an international meeting is the meeting room or rooms.
c What does she say to show when she's starting a new point in the talk?
1 .... , if people are coming from different countries you need to find out about rooms ...
2 My .... amenities for ...
3 .... , for an international meeting where ...

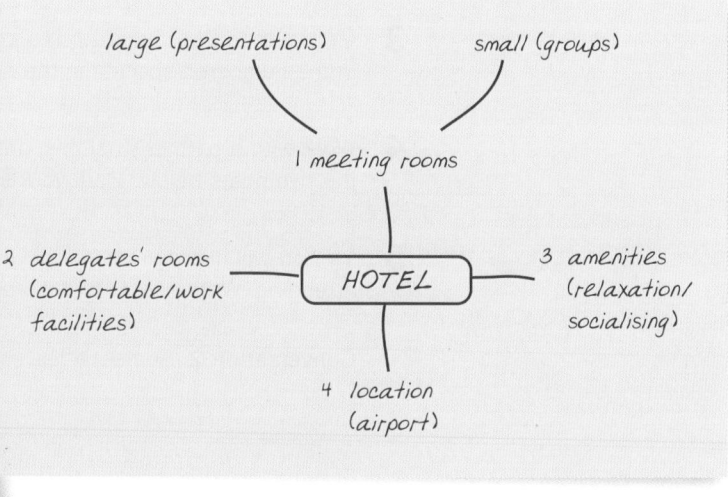

large (presentations)   small (groups)

1 meeting rooms

2 delegates' rooms
(comfortable/work
facilities)

HOTEL

3 amenities
(relaxation/
socialising)

4 location
(airport)

Speaking Part 2 **3** Now plan your own talk on the same subject. Use the four points you chose in exercise 1 and add reasons for your choices. Make a plan like the one in exercise 2 to help you organise your talk.

4 Find a partner who was not in the same group when you did exercise 1. Take turns to give your talk. You should each try to speak for about one minute.

writing: making requests and writing concisely

tip
How to stay within the 40–50 word limit:
- Use no more words than are absolutely necessary.
- Where possible use a shorter equivalent e.g.
  ~~make a telephone call~~ = call
  ~~make contact with~~ = contact

1 In Paper 2, Part 1 it's important to keep your writing concise. Complete the second sentence so that it has an equivalent meaning to the first sentence. Use words from the list below.

arrange   book   contact   explaining   faxed   give   rearrange   reserve

a If these dates are not convenient, could you get in touch with my secretary to arrange another date for the meeting.
   If these dates are not convenient, please .... my secretary to .... the meeting.

b Could you please let me have your arrival time so that I can make arrangements for someone to meet you at the airport?
   Please .... me your arrival time, so I can .... for someone to meet you at the airport.

c I've sent you a fax giving you an explanation for the changes we've made to the agenda.
   I've .... you .... the changes we've made to the agenda.

d Can you call the hotel and make a booking for a conference room for eighteen people? Can you also make a reservation at the hotel for eighteen single rooms?
   Can you call the hotel and .... a conference room for eighteen? Please also .... eighteen single rooms.

2 Complete this list with shorter equivalent verbs.

a make a telephone call   *telephone, phone, call*
b make contact with / get in touch with   *contact*
c let me know   ....
d make arrangements   ....
e make a reservation   ....
f make a booking   ....
g give an explanation   ....
h send an e-mail / send a fax   ....
i organise again   ....

3 Look at the draft of an e-mail which Enrica Grasi of Vevier Engineering wants to send to her assistant Karl Davidson about an international meeting she's organising in New York.

a What is the purpose of the e-mail?
b Write a shorter version in no more than 50 words by using shorter equivalents for the expressions in bold.

> **New York meeting**
>
> Carlos Rivas **made a phone call** to say he won't be arriving until 1.30 on Tuesday, so **could you please let** the hotel **know** that we won't need the meeting room until 2.30 p.m. **Could you also ask them to make arrangements for** sandwiches for people when they **get to the hotel**? Can you then **make contact with** everyone to tell them about the changes?

Writing Part 1

4 You and your colleague, Tom Banks, are organising a two-day international sales meeting on 1–2 June.

Write an e-mail of 40–50 words to Tom:

- informing him that you're working on an agenda for the meeting and that you will send it by e-mail tomorrow.
- asking him to get in touch with any comments – you need them by Friday.
- asking him to make arrangements for a reception and come back to you with ideas for it tomorrow morning.

unit 4 company results

vocabulary

1 What do you know about these fashion retailers? What do they have in common?

Benetton   boo.com   Gap   H&M   Zara

2 Match each of these extracts with one of the names above.

1 Results for the Swedish retailer of low price, high fashion clothing were better than expected. Their turnover for the year was 3.9 billion Euros, an increase of 9% on the previous year. The company is now present in thirteen markets in Europe as well as in the US.

2 Profits fell as the American clothing company struggled with a slowdown in consumer spending and a decline in sales of its once popular T-shirts, jeans and khakis. In response, the company cut 1,000 jobs in the summer.

3 Part of the Spanish Inditex Group, this successful, high fashion women's clothing chain generates 78% of the group's sales despite a very low marketing budget. The chain is growing fast. Last year, it entered six new markets, including Puerto Rico and the Czech Republic, where it opened a store in one of the best shopping districts in Prague.

4 The Italian retailer, famous for its colourful casual clothing and its controversial advertising, has stores in 120 countries, and is currently expanding operations in Japan including upgrading many of its smaller stores.

5 The high profile Internet fashion retailer failed to find the further funding it needed to survive and went bankrupt less than a year after the site was first launched. All the company's 300 staff were made redundant when the company collapsed.

3 Match each of these definitions with a word in the texts in exercise 2.

a The areas or countries where a product is sold. (extract 1)

b The total value of the products or service sold during a particular period of time. (extract 1)

c The money you gain from selling something after you take away all your costs. (extract 2)

d The total number of products a company sells in a given period of time. (extract 2)

e The amount of money that a department has available to spend. (extract 3)

f The money which is given for a specific purpose, e.g. starting up a business. (extract 5)

4 Answer these questions.

a Which verbs from the texts have similar meanings to the words below?

1 produces (extract 3)

2 went into (extract 3)

3 increasing the amount of activity (extract 4)

4 improving (extract 4)

5 set up (extract 5)

b Which two expressions in extract 5 tell you a company failed?

c Which expression tells you that staff lost their jobs?

5 Complete the table.

verb	opposite	noun
1 *generate*	fail to generate	sales/profits
2	close	a store
3	withdraw from	a market
create	4	jobs

6 What typically happens when a business start-up fails? Add these words to the list of things that can go wrong. Then, in pairs, put the steps in a logical order. Three have been done for you.

lose   costs   generate   high   funding   staff   redundant   bankrupt

A They don't .... enough income.   ....1....

B Nothing works and eventually they go ....

C So they fail to get more .... to keep the business going.   ....

D Investors .... confidence in the business.   ....3....

E They find they can't pay their suppliers or ....

F Their level of spending is too ....

G For example, they make some staff ....6....

H They try everything they can to reduce their ....

7 Complete the table with words from the extracts in exercise 2. Add any other words you know to describe these trends.

↗ upward movement	↘ downward movement
an increase	

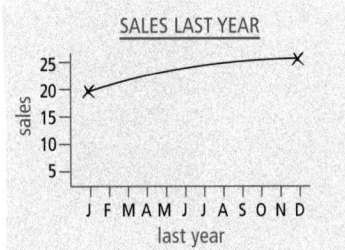

SALES LAST YEAR

last year

8 Look at the graph and complete these sentences with the prepositions.

by   from   in   of   to

a The company reported an increase .... sales.

b Sales increased .... 20,000 .... 25,000.

c They increased .... 5,000.

d That represents an increase .... 25%.

1 Think of a successful clothing retailer in your country.

  1 Prepare a short description about the retailer including this information.
- the kind of clothing it sells
- how it differs from its competitors
- the reasons why you think it's successful

  2 Work with a partner. Take turns to talk about the company you chose.

2 The article below is about Swedish fashion retailer Hennes and Mauritz (H&M). Read it and match each paragraph to one title below. Do not pay any attention at this stage to the numbered gaps in the text.

  a Tackling the American market
  b The company then and now
  c How the clothing market has changed
  d The company's recent performance

A Swedish success story

1 When Hennes & Mauritz launched its first store in London in 1976 there was little interest among passers-by. (1) .... It is an extraordinary transformation that has seen H&M become one of the world's leading international clothing retailers, seemingly able to cross borders effortlessly in a business where such moves often end in failure. The UK was the group's first step outside Scandinavia but, by the time of the US launch, H&M had 600 stores in eleven countries, spreading its concept of fashionable clothes at low prices throughout northern Europe.

2 For Stefan Persson, H&M's majority owner and former chief executive, it is not just the company that has changed but also global fashion. Back in the 1970s, styles differed strongly from market to market. (2) .... Markets are becoming more and more similar all over the world. 'People read more or less the same magazines, watch the same films and listen to the same music,' Mr Persson explains. 'Maybe it's a little bit boring that all countries become the same but it's an advantage for a global business such as ours.'

3 Of course, H&M is not the first European retailer to think it can repeat its formula on the other side of the Atlantic. (3) .... Mr Persson is optimistic, however, and says he believes that the company's strong emphasis on fashion differentiates H&M from the competition. 'It is this that has been lacking in the US. I think customers are ready for something more fashionable, a bigger variety and a wider range than our competitors offer – and our prices are very attractive.'

4 Since H&M entered the US market, it has opened twenty-one stores and has also grown rapidly in other new markets such as France and Spain. (4) .... Results in the second quarter have improved and the company remains optimistic about the US, where sales are good and the company has not been affected by the downturn in the US economy. In fact, any slowdown in the US and European economies may be good news for H&M – an economic weakening has historically made value retailers such as H&M more attractive to customers.

When matching sentences with gaps in paragraphs check that:
- the sentence you choose fits the meaning of the whole paragraph.
- the sentence you choose fits the meaning of the ones that come immediately before and after it.
- the sentence fits grammatically with the ones immediately before and after it.

3 Find two sentences from the list (A–H) which fit the topic of each paragraph (1–4).

A In Britain, however, sales have slowed down.

B Last year, the opening of the first New York store attracted such massive crowds that the doors had to be closed to prevent accidents.

C Many have tried to crack this very competitive market but so far few have succeeded.

D Nobody seemed to notice that a new store had come to town.

E Now the company's range of clothing is 95 per cent the same wherever you go.

F The company blamed the 15 per cent fall in profits in the first quarter on the high cost of expansion in these markets.

G The competitor tried to crack the American market, but failed.

H It was also an era when a youth culture emerged.

4 Read paragraph 1 again. Pay special attention to the sentence before gap 1 and the sentence immediately after the gap. Of the two possible sentences you identified in exercise 3 above, which would fill the gap better, and why? Discuss your choice and your reasons with the rest of the class.

5 Follow the same procedure for gaps 2 to 4.

6 Look at the completed paragraph 3 and find three words based on the verb *compete*. Use the words you found to complete this short text.

> The retail fashion sector is **highly** (1)........................... . In the US, H&M is in (2)........................... with local department stores and retailers as well as its **major** (3)........................... , Gap. In Spain, a new market for H&M, it faces **fierce** (4)........................... from the successful Zara chain.

7 Which words have a similar meaning to the words in bold in the text above?

strong   extremely   principal   tough   intensely   main

8 Write three sentences about companies or sectors you are familiar with, using words and phrases from exercises 6 and 7.

9 Work with a partner and discuss these points.
- Do you agree that fashions and lifestyle are becoming more similar all over the world. Is there a difference in this respect between younger and older people?
- Do you think globalisation provides more choice and better quality for consumers?

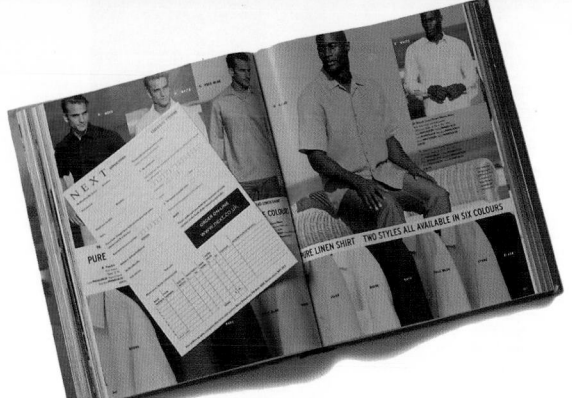

amazon.co.uk
and you're done.™

listening

1 Where do you normally buy these products? Complete the survey.

	a high street shop	an on-line store	a catalogue
CDs			
books			
clothes			
software			

2 🎧 You will hear a radio debate in which retail analysts Marlene Preiss and Frank Tam discuss the failure of boo.com, an on-line clothing retailer. Some of the reasons they give are listed below. Number them in the order they are mentioned and write the name of the speaker. Follow the example.

lack of funding

poor management   *1 Marlene*

overspending

technical problems

Listening Part 3

3 🎧 Read the questions (1–5) below. At this stage, pay more attention to the question itself, rather than the three options. You will hear the recording again. Identify the words you hear which tell you that the answer to each question will be given soon.

1 According to Marlene, what was the biggest financial mistake boo.com made?
  A They spent too much money too soon.
  B Their advertising budget wasn't big enough.
  C They wasted money on entertainment.

2 Initially people didn't like boo.com's website because
  A the order processing system didn't work.
  B it wasn't simple enough to use.
  C it didn't look attractive.

3 What was the result of the changes boo.com made after Christmas 1999?
  A The website worked better.
  B Their spending decreased by forty per cent.
  C Their sales improved slightly.

4 How much more money did boo.com try to raise in May?
  A £80m   B £20m   C £100m

5 Frank doesn't think today's investors would invest in such a company because
  A it didn't have the right kind of staff.
  B it didn't have a good business idea.
  C it didn't have a good business strategy.

tip

Do not choose an option just because it contains some words you hear in the recording. The correct option usually expresses the same idea in different words.

4 🎧 Read the questions again and look at each option carefully. You will hear the recording a third time. For each question, mark one letter (A, B or C) for the correct answer.

5 Work with a partner. Draw up a list of four or five tips to help Internet start-up companies avoid the kind of problems boo.com experienced.

language in use: past simple and present perfect

1 Look back at the text on page 32 and sentences A–H on page 33. Complete the sentences below with the verbs and time phrases used in the article.

   1 _In 1976_ Hennes & Mauritz _opened_ its first store in London.

   2 .... , the opening of the first New York store .... massive crowds.

   3 .... , styles .... strongly from market to market.

   4 _So far_ .... few European retailers .... in the US.

   5 .... the American launch, H&M .... twenty-one stores and .... rapidly in France and Spain.

2 Answer these questions.
   a Which of the sentences use the past simple and which the present perfect?
   b Which of the sentences indicate the following?
      • an activity at a specific time or period in the past
      • an activity or trend which started in the past and still continues

3 Which of the time phrases in exercise 1 normally go with the past simple and present perfect? Put them in the correct place in the table and then add the time phrases below.

past simple	present perfect
In 1976	So far

three months ago
for the last twelve months
over the last three years
this year
throughout the 90s
since 2000

4 Use these verbs to complete extracts from TRI Sports' annual report. Make sure the verb is in its correct form.

be   be able to   double   enter   increase
make   perform   open   see

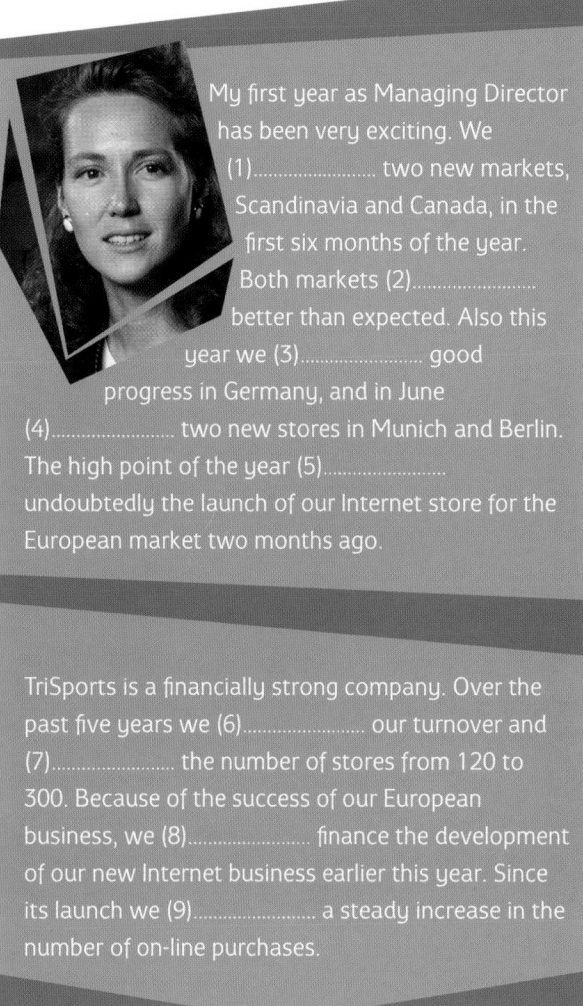

My first year as Managing Director has been very exciting. We (1)........................ two new markets, Scandinavia and Canada, in the first six months of the year. Both markets (2)........................ better than expected. Also this year we (3)........................ good progress in Germany, and in June (4)........................ two new stores in Munich and Berlin. The high point of the year (5)........................ undoubtedly the launch of our Internet store for the European market two months ago.

TriSports is a financially strong company. Over the past five years we (6)........................ our turnover and (7)........................ the number of stores from 120 to 300. Because of the success of our European business, we (8)........................ finance the development of our new Internet business earlier this year. Since its launch we (9)........................ a steady increase in the number of on-line purchases.

5 Work with a partner. Talk about how things have changed in your work and your life.

   Examples

   I didn't take a holiday last year because I was too busy. This year I've been on holiday twice, once to Hong Kong and the other time to Bali.

   Last year we faced a lot of competition in France, so at the beginning of the year we withdrew from the market. Since then our results have improved.

   See grammar reference page 132

speaking

1 Mariposa is a US retailer selling children's clothing. Work in two groups to find out about the company's performance. Students in group A, look at this page. Students in group B look at page 118.

A

B
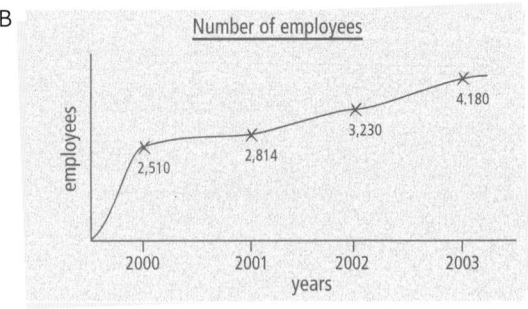

C
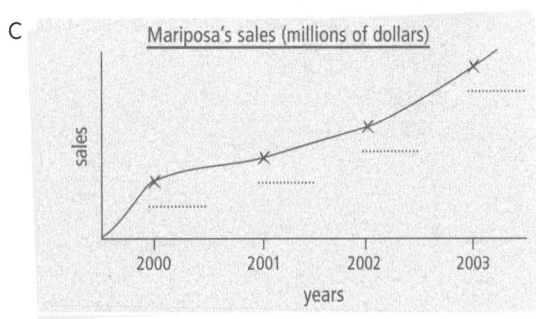

D
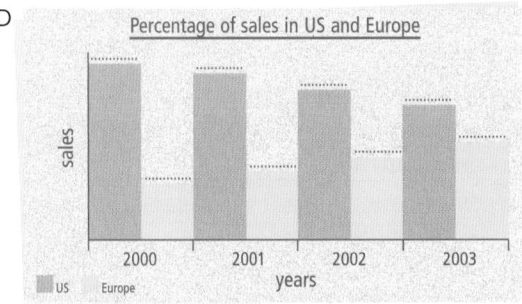

2 With the other students in your group, complete a–d below to make useful questions related to graphs C and D.

a ....*what were*............. Mariposa's sales in ...*2000/2001/2002*..... ?

b What percentage .... were from the US in
.... ?

c .... this ratio change the year after that?

d Sorry, I didn't catch that. Could you .... ?

3 Form a pair with one student from group B. Answer their questions about graphs A and B. Then ask questions about graphs C and D and complete the missing information.

4 Mariposa wants to expand in Europe where its range of colourful children's clothing is particularly popular. At present it has stores in most of the big European cities. What could the company do to target customers in the smaller towns and rural areas?

writing: a report explaining findings

1 Mariposa's expansion plans are underway. Read the report on page 37 and answer the questions.

a What's the purpose of the report?

b Who is it written for?

2 Add these headings to the report and decide on a title.

Conclusion   Findings   Background

3 Find examples of the past simple and the present perfect and explain why the writer has chosen that particular tense.

Report

1 ....

Last month we set up a team to investigate mail order shopping for the Greek market. We have completed the results.

2 ....

During the last three years, we have seen a steady increase in the market for mail order children's clothing in our main European markets. This is mainly because of its convenience for busy professionals and the competitive prices.

Turnover in our stores in Athens and Thessaloniki increased by 25% last year. However, these two cities represent only 50% of the population. Introducing mail order will give us access to a wider customer base, and we estimate a 15% increase in sales over the next two years.

3 ....

In conclusion, with other European markets reporting good results for mail order, and the potential for growth in Greece, we suggest introducing mail order there next year.

Writing Part 2

4 You work for Mariposa. You are part of a team set up last month to investigate launching an on-line store for the European market.

Look at the extracts from newspaper headlines and information about the project on which you have already made some notes. Use your notes to write a report of between 120–140 words. Use the same headings as the report in exercise 3.

Shop from the comfort of your home

Fashion retailer Mariposa proves that mail order can work in Europe

ON-LINE SUCCESS STORY

10% increase in sales for Mariposa following the launch of their US Internet site last month

Mention launch as background

Internet site for Europe

Facts

Reason for figure of 8 million

- Internet access in Europe getting cheaper
- Forecast: 8 million on-line buyers within 3 years
- Sales of clothing on the Internet represent just 1% of retail sector

Low figure, but performance of some new fashion sites in Scandinavia / Germany good

Recommend

first set up Internet site for Germany and Scandinavia

Scandinavian e-tailer chic.com reports good first quarter results

unit 5 communication at work

vocabulary

1 Match these comments (a–f) with the photos (1–3).

a The great thing is you can save money on paper and distribution costs.

b When there's bad news, I always tell them about it in person.

c I like to keep copies of documents we need to refer to again.

d When you need to get people on your side, your voice and body language can help to get your message over.

e You can send or receive messages at any time so it's ideal for working with colleagues in different locations or time zones.

f Confidential documents, such as proposals, are always sent to customers in writing.

2 Work with a partner. Which of the three communication channels – face to face, written or electronic – would be the most appropriate for these situations. Why?

a Requesting the latest production figures from your factories in Malaysia and Mexico for a report you're writing.

b Telling staff about the closure of the sales office where they work and offering them work in other offices.

c Making a complaint to a supplier about the poor quality of their products.

3 Some words naturally go together. Look at these examples from the comments in exercise 1.

- combinations of verbs and nouns: *save money*. You can also *save time*, but not *save problems*.
- combinations of adjectives and nouns: *confidential document*, e.g. you might send a *confidential report* or *letter*, but you would not talk about a *confidential colleague*.
- combinations of nouns and nouns: *time zone*. You can also talk about a *time limit*, but not about a *time area*.

4 Each adjective below commonly goes with all but one of the nouns listed with it. Draw a line through the noun it does not usually go with.

a official   complaint / colleague / letter / report

b final   draft / report / information / decision

c immediate   attention / action / memo / response

d urgent   message / phone / document / request

5 Match the verbs (a–g) with the words. The verbs may be used more than once.

a check   c exchange   e post   g write
b delete   d pass on   f send

an e-mail   a letter   a draft   a copy   a message   information

6 Look back at exercises 1 and 2 on page 38. Find examples of noun + noun combinations and complete the table below.

| .... costs | production .... |
| body .... | .... office |

Reading Part 4

7 Read through the text below. What is the general theme of the text? Can you think of a title for the text? Do not pay attention to the numbered gaps at this stage.

Sending information electronically has many benefits, but company e-mail systems aren't always used appropriately. You shouldn't (1).................... your company's time and money by sending (2).................... of every e-mail you write to everyone you know. You also need to remember that (3).................... an e-mail does not automatically remove it from the company's computer network, so this is not a suitable channel for exchanging (4).................... information. However, it is a good choice for (5).................... up meetings or providing updates on projects, and is very useful for communicating (6).................... colleagues in other countries.

Face to face communication is a good option when you have to (7).................... with sensitive topics. It is also useful when you need to (8).................... on information that requires (9).................... action.

Written communication is appropriate when a response is not required immediately. Always plan your key points before you write the first (10).................... of your letter or report and remember to (11).................... the final one carefully for errors before sending it.

tip To check your answers, write the words you've chosen in the gaps. Then read through the whole text again and check that the words you've selected sound and look right in the completed text.

8 First reread the sentences the gaps appear in, then choose the best word to fill each gap from A, B, C or D below. Gaps 1–4 and 9 check your knowledge of words that commonly go together. Gaps 5–8 check your knowledge of prepositions that follow certain verbs.

	A	B	C	D
1	miss	waste	lose	pass
2	copies	replicas	extras	reproductions
3	cutting	sending	posting	deleting
4	unknown	limited	confidential	urgent
5	arranging	making	setting	getting
6	to	at	for	with
7	talk	deal	handle	discuss
8	pass	inform	exchange	communicate
9	immediate	urgent	straight	soon
10	model	draft	copy	sample
11	correct	print	check	confirm

1 Work with a partner. Discuss what you think these phrases mean.

- snail mail   • flame mail

2 Skim the article below until you find the phrases in the text. Read the sentences they appear in. Were you right about their meanings?

Can snail mail beat e-mail?

When e-mail first came into general use about fifteen years ago, there was a lot of talk about the imminent arrival of the paperless office. However, it seems that e-mail has yet to revolutionise office communication. According to communications analyst Richard Metcalf, some offices have actually seen an increase in paper as a result of e-mail. 'Information in the form of e-mail messages now floods our computer screens. These messages can be sent so quickly that memos tend to be distributed in the hundreds. For those secretaries whose bosses ask them to print out all their e-mails and leave them in their in-trays, this means using up a great deal of paper every month.'

Metcalf has found that because e-mails have a tendency to get lost in cyberspace, PAs are increasingly likely to be asked by clients and colleagues to send all important documents both by e-mail and by fax or snail mail – through the post. 'This highlights a further potential problem with e-mail in today's office – it is taking up time rather than saving it.'

With e-mail, communication is much easier, but there is also more room for misunderstandings, says psychologist Dr David Lewis. Generally, much less care is taken with e-mails than with letters or faxes where the sender will probably print the document and reread it before putting it in an envelope or on to the fax machine.

'The nature of the medium means that e-mails are frequently poorly and hastily composed and consequently often unclear. It's little wonder that there are so many misunderstandings. It is a problem which people need to be particularly aware of when using e-mail.'

More worrying still is the increasing misuse of e-mail for sending 'flame-mail' – abusive or inappropriate e-mail messages. Recent research in several companies suggests that aggressive communications like this are on the increase. E-mail has become the perfect medium for letting out workplace frustration because it is so instant.

E-mail can be problematic in other ways. Staff all too often make the mistake of thinking that the contents of an e-mail, like things said over the phone, are private and not permanent. But it is not only possible for an employer to read all your e-mails, it is also perfectly legal. E-mail messages can be traced back to their origin for a period of at least two years, so you might want to rethink e-mailing colleagues your frustrations about your job. The advice is to keep personal e-mails out of the office.

It goes without saying that e-mail exists to make life easier and if used correctly is an invaluable tool for businesses of all sizes. But perhaps, for the time being, the fact that in the business world 70% of all documents are still in paper form is not such a bad thing after all.

3 Read quickly through the whole article and decide which sentence below best sums it up.

a It presents a very positive view of electronic communication.
b It expresses some reservations about electronic communication.
c It presents a very negative view of electronic communication.

Reading Part 3

4 Read the questions (1–6) below, then read the article again, in more detail this time. Highlight or underline the sentences or phrases you think contain the answer to each question. Write a short phrase or sentence answering each question in your own words.

1 Why has the promise of the paperless office not come true in some offices?
2 What does Richard Metcalf say about e-mail in paragraph 2?
3 What does David Lewis say about many e-mail messages?
4 Why is e-mail the preferred channel for abusive messages?
5 Why should employees not use company e-mail systems for personal messages?
6 What does the writer conclude about e-mail in the last paragraph?

> **tip** The strategy you have just practised is particularly useful when dealing with multiple-choice questions which test your understanding of opinions and ideas, rather than facts. Remember:
> • to read the question.
> • to highlight/underline the relevant section of the text.
> • to try to find an answer to the question in your own words.
> • to match your response to the closest option.

5 Look at the options (A–D) for each question in exercise 4. For each question (1–6), mark one letter (A, B, C or D) for the answer you choose.

1 A People write more memos than they used to.
  B Secretaries keep paper copies of everything they send.
  C Many managers prefer to read their messages on paper.
  D Staff leave messages lying around in the office.

2 A It is not an appropriate channel for sending important information.
  B It increases the amount of paperwork done in offices.
  C It is not popular with many secretaries.
  D It is a less efficient channel than fax.

3 A They are badly written.
  B They are too long.
  C They are never printed out.
  D They are never read.

4 A Because it's so easy to use.
  B Because the other person can't respond immediately.
  C Because it allows you to express your anger at once.
  D Because it's a good way to reduce levels of frustration in the office.

5 A It is illegal to do so.
  B Companies have access to any e-mails that are sent.
  C Companies don't like staff doing this.
  D Other employees may read them.

6 A That it has already made life a lot easier for companies.
  B That it is not being used enough in companies today.
  C That it will never replace written communication.
  D That it will only become really useful when people use it properly.

6 Interview a partner about his/her use of electronic mail. Find out this information.
  • how often he/she uses it
  • what he/she finds it useful for
  • what he/she likes and dislikes about it

language in use: countable and uncountable nouns

1 Countable nouns have both a singular and a plural form, uncountable nouns only have a singular form.

a These nouns have appeared so far in this unit. Mark them **C** (countable) or **U** (uncountable).

advice ....*U*..........

document ....

information ....

message ....

misunderstanding ....

research ....

b Do the same for these nouns.

article	....	progress	....
computer	....	security	....
data	....	seminar	....
draft	....	stress	....
equipment	....	suggestion	....
fact	....	survey	....
legislation	....	training	....
news	....		

2 Some nouns can be used both as uncountable and countable nouns, but with slightly different meanings. Look at these extracts from the text. What is the difference in meaning between the countable and uncountable uses of the words in bold?

Paragraph 1   *... **e-mail** has yet to revolutionise office **communication**.*

Paragraph 2   *... because **e-mails** have a tendency to get lost ...*

Paragraph 4   *... aggressive **communications** like this are on the increase.*

3 What is the difference between these pairs of words?

experience / an experience
contact / a contact
paper / a paper

See grammar reference pages 132 and 133

Reading Part 5

tip
When you think you have spotted an extra word, always read *the whole sentence* as well as the line the word appears in, to check that it does not relate to a later part of the sentence.

1 Read the extract below from the first draft of an internal memo. In each full line there is one extra word which should not be there. Three lines include mistakes related to grammar points you have studied above. Two lines contain unnecessary prepositions following a noun or a verb.

1 Work with a partner. Read through the text and underline the nouns. Are they countable or uncountable? Are there any extra words that appear before these nouns that should not be there? Put a circle round these words.

2 Look for nouns and verbs which have prepositions after them. Are any of these prepositions unnecessary? Put a circle round these words.

Memo

It has come to our attention that each of employee in the company receives up to 190 written or spoken messages a day. That represents a lot of an information to read or listen to, think about and answer every day. We also found that how many of these communications were quite unnecessary. The result of is an overload of information which, combined with poor time management, is having a negative impact on to the company's morale and productivity.

2 Follow the same procedure for the second extract below. There are the same number and type of mistakes as in the first extract.

One of the biggest complaints amongst some of staff is the amount of time they spend dealing with day-to-day communications. In fact, it is now each one of the most frequently mentioned causes of many stress. At the same time, our information technology systems are pushed up to the limit by the volume of non-essential communications. We have therefore invited the consultants AS&T to review over our communication systems.

listening

1 Work with a partner. Find out what he/she likes and dislikes about answer machines and mobile phones.

Listening Part 1

2 James Riley works in the Marketing Department for Caramia, an Irish company which produces skin care products. Read the notes below which he made after listening to two messages on his voice mail. Who do you think each message was from: a colleague or a supplier?

Message 1

Things to do for Katie.
1 Phone Martin Jarvis at CFI Training and register her on a course in Time Management, in the last week of June.
2 Fax her the minutes of yesterday's department meeting.
- She'll phone me before lunch to check progress.

Message 2

Jacques Barbier from Packaging Solutions in Brussels phoned to cancel meeting on Wednesday a.m.
Wants to re-schedule meeting for next Thursday at 10 a.m.
If OK, call his office before 3 p.m. From tomorrow contact him at the Plaza Hotel, New York. Telephone number: 212-939-5500

3 🎧 Listen to the two messages and answer the questions.
   a Were you right about your answers to exercise 2?
   b James has made three mistakes in his notes for each message. As you listen underline the incorrect information.

4 🎧 Listen again and correct James's mistakes.

5 🎧 You will hear James phone Martin Jarvis at CFI training. Write one or two words or a number in the numbered spaces on the form below.

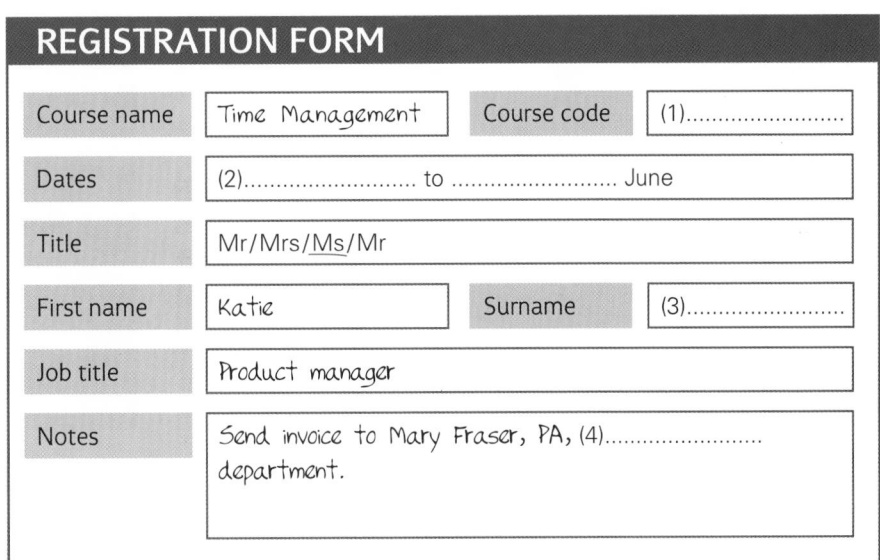

REGISTRATION FORM

Course name	Time Management	Course code	(1).........................
Dates	(2).......................... to .... June		
Title	Mr/Mrs/Ms/Mr		
First name	Katie	Surname	(3).........................
Job title	Product manager		
Notes	Send invoice to Mary Fraser, PA, (4)......................... department.		

speaking

1 Look at this plan for a short discussion about a company problem. Match the phrases (1–12) with the part of the discussion (A–F) you would use them in. Follow the example.

1 What do you think?   C
2 Good, that's agreed then. We'll …
3 I think … would be good, because …
4 I'm not sure. It sounds rather …
5 OK, let's start.
6 Shall I begin?
7 Shall we go on to the next point?

8 So we've agreed that …
9 That's true, but …
10 Well, we could …
   The advantage would be that …
11 Do you have any other ideas?
12 Yes, I like that idea.

Start the discussion. (A)

Talk about the first point.
• Make suggestions (B)
• Ask for your partner's ideas (C)
• React to your partner's suggestions (D)

Summarise what decision you've reached. (E)

Move on to the second point. (F)

Talk about the second point.
• Make suggestions (B)
• Ask for your partner's ideas (C)
• React to your partner's suggestions (D)

Summarise what decision you've reached about the second point. (E)

Speaking Part 3

2 Read the problem on the task sheet below. You have 30 seconds to think of some ideas about this problem. The photos may help you.

> ## Staff problem
>
> As a result of expansion, your company has recently hired a lot of new people for all levels of the company. However, the original staff do not mix or communicate well with the new staff. You have been asked to organise some events to help the new staff and the original staff work better together.
>
> Discuss the situation together and decide:
> • what kind of event to organise for the managers.
> • what kind of event to organise for the office staff.

3 Work with a partner. Discuss the problem on the task sheet. Follow the discussion plan in exercise 1 and use the suggested phrases as appropriate. You have about three minutes.

writing: getting the style right

1 Work in groups. Look at the task for Writing Part 1 and the three possible answers. Evaluate each answer using the checklist below and decide which one is best.

CHECKLIST	
content	Must cover all the points in the bullets in the task instruction.
length	Between 40 and 50 words.
style	Neutral business style. Concise and clear.
vocabulary choice	Should avoid using exactly the same words as in the instruction.

You are Sales Manager at Caramia in Holland. You are planning a team-building seminar for your sales team. Katie Whitely, a colleague at your company's Head Office in Dublin has given good reports about a company called CFI Training.

Write an e-mail of 40–50 words to Katie:
- asking her to contact Kevin Lynch at CFI Training to find out if he could run the seminar for 30 people in July.
- informing her that you need his proposal by Friday.
- suggesting Kevin telephones you at 9 a.m. tomorrow to find out more.

1
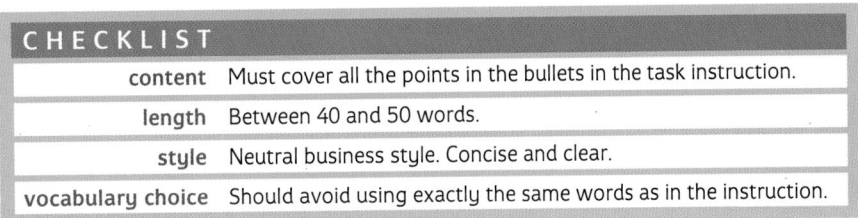

I would be most grateful if you would contact Kevin Lynch at CFI Training with regard to organising a team-building seminar for the 30 people in our sales team in July. Please inform him that it is most urgent and we require his proposal by Friday. I therefore suggest that he telephones me tomorrow at 9 a.m. for further information concerning the project.

2

Could you ask Kevin Lynch at CFI Training about running a team-building seminar for 30 of our sales staff in July? If he is interested, tell him it's urgent and I need his proposal by Friday. He can contact me tomorrow at nine for more details.

3
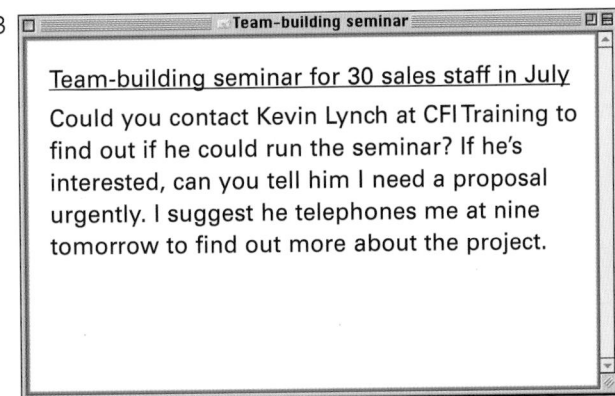

Team-building seminar for 30 sales staff in July

Could you contact Kevin Lynch at CFI Training to find out if he could run the seminar? If he's interested, can you tell him I need a proposal urgently. I suggest he telephones me at nine tomorrow to find out more about the project.

2 Write a reply from Kevin Lynch to the Sales Manager at Caramia Holland. Write an e-mail of 40–50 words to the Sales Manager:
- expressing your interest in running the seminar.
- explaining that you won't be able to call at 9 a.m. – out of the office all day – and suggesting two other times, 6 p.m. tomorrow (Tuesday) or 9 a.m. Wednesday.
- asking her to inform you which time is better.

unit 6 health and safety

vocabulary

1 Guess the answers to questions 1–4. Check the correct answers with your teacher. Work with a partner. Discuss the possible reasons for the answers to 4.

1 What do you think is the main cause of injuries at work in the UK?
   a falling while walking
   b lifting heavy objects
   c operating dangerous machinery

2 What percentage of European workers do you think suffer from work-related back problems at some time in their lives?
   a less than fifty per cent
   b between fifty and seventy-five per cent
   c over seventy-five per cent

3 In which of these countries or areas do you think the highest percentage of people say their job is very stressful?
   a Europe   b Japan   c the United States

4 Which *three* of these groups of young British workers do you think have the most accidents?
   a agricultural labourers   d fast food restaurant staff
   b assembly workers in factories   e motor cycle couriers
   c construction workers   f shop staff

2 Look at the picture below of an office interior which shows several hazards and health risks. Match these descriptions with the hazards (A–G).

1 inadequate lighting   5 inadequate ventilation
2 trailing cables   6 wet floor surface
3 an obstruction   7 unsuitable furniture
4 damaged/uneven floor surface

3 Match the hazards in exercise 2 with the potential problems (1–6). Some hazards may cause more than one problem.

This/These could cause someone to:

1 trip and fall.
2 slip and fall.
3 be trapped in the room.
4 feel hot and unable to breathe.
5 have sore eyes.
6 suffer from back pain.

4 Match the health problems (1–3) with a definition (a–c).

1 eye strain   2 a fracture   3 repetitive strain injury

a a crack or break in a bone
b muscle pain caused by repeating the same movement frequently
c pain caused by using a part of your body for too long or with inadequate lighting

5 Complete the table below with words from exercises 2 to 4.

verb	noun	adjective
fracture		fractured
light		(well-/badly-) lit
obstruct		(un)obstructed
	repetition	
	a slip	slippery
ventilate		(well-/badly-) ventilated

6 Complete the gaps in these extracts with words or phrases from exercises 2 to 5.

Good office design can save your company money and improve efficiency. Simple measures like installing ceiling fans or windows which open ensure that rooms are (1).................................... and make your staff healthier and more productive. Appropriate office furniture can reduce days off work due to staff suffering from (2)................................... or (3)................................... .

Accident Report

Ms Lopez was carrying some packets of paper from the storeroom to the photocopy room when she (4)...................................... over a broken floor tile, fell and (5)...................................... her arm. She was admitted to hospital twenty minutes later. Subsequent examination showed that the corridor was inadequately (6)...................................... and that other parts of the (7)...................................... were uneven or damaged.

During our inspection we noted that five of your seven fire exits were (8)...................................... by boxes, cartons or items of furniture. In most rooms there are not enough power points, resulting in (9)...................................... which could (10)...................................... trips and falls.

1 Read quickly through the text below. Which of these themes does it *not* cover?

a dangers from office equipment
b health problems
c work-related stress
d safety legislation and legal requirements

A guide to office health and safety: your rights and responsibilities

A Most injuries in the office are caused by slips or trips. By law, your employer must ensure that floor surfaces are safe and that areas in which people move around are unobstructed and adequately lit. As an employee, you must comply with your company's safety regulations and mustn't do anything which could endanger your own or other people's safety. You should report any possible hazards, such as obstructions, trailing cables, slippery floors or uneven surfaces, to your supervisor as soon as you notice them.

B All office equipment gives off heat and dries the air. Laser printers and some photocopiers also emit ozone, which can cause dry eyes, sore throats and breathing problems. Ideally, photocopiers should be placed in a separate, well-ventilated room. If this is not possible, they should be at least 2.5 metres away from the nearest workstation. Computer screens emit some electromagnetic radiation, but the levels are below the safe limits set by international standards so your employer doesn't have to supply special protective devices for use with computer screens.

C Long periods of work at computer screens can lead to eye strain, however. By law, your employer must allow you to take frequent short breaks to avoid this problem. As the regulations do not state how long these breaks have to be, you should discuss your individual needs with your supervisor. You may also ask your company to pay for an eye test. An employer has to pay for your glasses if they are prescribed specifically for the distance at which you view the screen, but not if you use these glasses in other situations too.

D Prolonged work at a keyboard or using a mouse may also result in repetitive strain injury. Your employer has a legal duty to provide a suitable workstation with appropriate lighting and an adjustable chair. Try different arrangements of your chair, desk and computer equipment to find the most comfortable position for your work. As a broad guide, your forearms should be approximately horizontal and your eyes the same height as the top of the screen. A document holder may help you avoid awkward neck and eye movements. Again, frequent breaks or changes of activity are recommended.

2 In the next task, you will be asked to match statements to the different paragraphs of the text. First work through this example.

    a Look back at the list of themes in exercise 1 above. Which one does the following sentence relate to?
      This problem is covered by legislation, but not in detail.
    b Read the text and underline all references to the theme you identified in a.
    c Now you need to decide which of the references you've found is relevant. Look again at the example sentence and decide which of the references you underlined in b matches this specific point.
    d Write the letter of the paragraph this appears in.

Reading Part 1

3 Which paragraph of the text (A, B, C or D) does each statement 1–6 refer to? Follow the same procedure as in exercise 2.

    1 Reassuring information about the safety of a piece of office equipment is given.
    2 A range of health problems suffered by office workers is mentioned.
    3 Employees' legal obligations are explained.
    4 This advice would be helpful when deciding where to put a new piece of office equipment.
    5 These practical tips will help employees improve their posture when using office equipment.
    6 A company's legal obligations to staff with vision problems are explained.

4 Find words or phrases in the text which have these meanings.

    a Paragraph A do what you have to or are asked to do (verb + preposition)
    b Paragraph C recommended by a doctor (passive verb)
    c Paragraph D continuing for a long period of time (adjective)
    d Paragraph D able to be changed or moved (adjective)
    e Paragraph D difficult or uncomfortable (adjective)

5 Work with a partner. Student A: Read the text again and complete the table with short notes about obligations mentioned in the text. Student B: Read the text again and complete the table with short notes about recommendations mentioned in the text. Follow the examples. When you have finished, exchange information about the notes and complete the rest of the table.

Employers' obligations	• make sure floor surfaces are safe and corridors are well-lit and unobstructed • • •
Employees' obligations	•
Recommendations for employers	• place photocopiers in separate room
Recommendations for employees	• report any possible hazards • • • •

6 Look back at the picture of an office on page 46. Which hazards shown are the employer's fault? Can you identify any further hazards now that you have read the text? What should the employee do to improve the health and safety of the workplace?

language in use: modals

1 Look back at the table you completed in Reading exercise 5 (page 49) and the reading text on page 48. Which modal verbs were used to explain obligations and recommendations? Put them in the table below. Follow the example.

function	modal verb(s)
expressing a possibility	
expressing a stronger possibility	
explaining an obligation	must
explaining a lack of obligation	
making a recommendation	
explaining what is allowed	
explaining what is forbidden	

2 Look again at the text and find the sentences which contain the modal verbs below. The letter of the paragraph is given in brackets to help you. Put the modal verbs in the correct part of the table. Be careful – one of the modal verbs is used in the text to express two different functions.

can (B)   could (A)   doesn't/don't have to (B)
may (C, D)   mustn't (A)

3 Where in the table above would you put these modals?

don't need to   shouldn't

4 In which other part of the table could the modal verb *can* go?

5 Look at the leaflet on the right explaining a company's policy on smoking in their offices. Rephrase the underlined parts of each sentence using an appropriate modal verb from the table. Make any other grammatical changes necessary. Follow the example.

Example

*Employees **mustn't** smoke anywhere except in the designated areas. **Anyone who consistently breaks this rule could/may** lose his/her job.*

6 Does your workplace or the place where you study have a smoking policy? If so, write a short notice explaining the policy, using appropriate modal verbs from the chart in exercise 1 above. If not, invent an appropriate policy that respects the needs of non-smokers and smokers, then write a short notice explaining the policy, using appropriate modal verbs from the table.

See grammar reference page 133

COMPANY SMOKING POLICY

a Employees <u>are forbidden to</u> smoke anywhere except in the designated areas. <u>It is possible that anyone who consistently breaks this rule will</u> lose his/her job.

b Smokers <u>are allowed to</u> use rooms 4B and 6C for cigarette breaks or coffee breaks. They <u>are permitted to</u> take up to four five-minute breaks a day to smoke, excluding lunch and coffee breaks. They <u>are not obliged to</u> tell their supervisors when they go for an approved cigarette break but <u>are not allowed to</u> take more than four breaks without special permission.

c Smokers <u>are strictly forbidden to</u> empty ashtrays into wastepaper bins as <u>there is a possibility that this will</u> cause a fire. You <u>are advised not to</u> leave the doors of the smoking rooms open, as this interferes with the ventilation system.

d Clients and visitors to the company <u>are also obliged to</u> comply with the smoking regulations. To avoid causing embarrassment to visitors, <u>it is recommended that you</u> explain our policy to them on arrival and ask if they are smokers. If so, use the special meeting room provided for smokers; for small, informal discussions <u>it is also possible for you to</u> use the smoking section of the reception hall.

1 Look at the list of eight options (A–H) in exercise 3 below. With which of these options would you associate the phrases (1–8) below? Follow the example.

1 A lot of the time I feel ... *D*
2 The reason was ...
3 Remove the clip at the top then ...
4 It was all (sb's) fault ...
5 This could lead to serious problems ...
6 I would advise you to ...
7 You must send a written account of ...
8 There's absolutely no risk of ...

2 Work with a partner and think of one other phrase you might hear in each of these situations. Share your ideas with the rest of the class.

Listening Part 2

tip
• Often two or more options are quite similar (e.g. B and C in this exercise). You need to listen carefully to make sure that you have chosen the correct one.
• In the recording you will not hear exactly the same words that appear in the options (e.g. in a monologue that goes with option E you will probably not hear the speaker say the words *warn* or *warning*).

3 🎧 You will hear five short recordings. For each recording, decide what the speaker's intention is. Write one letter (A–H) next to the number of the recording. Do not use any letter more than once. Before you start, read the Task procedure box on page 126, which contains instructions to help with the task.

1 ....
2 ....
3 ....
4 ....
5 ....

A to reassure somebody about the safety of a piece of equipment
B to explain how an accident happened
C to blame somebody for causing an accident
D to complain about a work-related health problem
E to warn someone of a potential hazard associated with a piece of equipment
F to give instructions on operating a piece of safety equipment
G to make recommendations to improve safety features/reduce risks
H to explain the official procedure for reporting an accident

4 Look at the tapescript on page 142 and underline the phrases which helped you to choose the correct answers.

5 🎧 You will hear another five short recordings. For each recording, decide what improvement relating to health and safety the speaker recommends for his/her workplace. Write one letter (A–H) next to the number of the recording. Do not use any letter more than once.

1 ....
2 ....
3 ....
4 ....
5 ....

A replacing some of the existing furniture
B increasing the frequency of safety training sessions
C installing a new ventilation system
D displaying more notices about safety procedures
E introducing a different shiftwork system
F upgrading the lighting in the offices
G providing protective clothing
H extending the amount of cupboard space

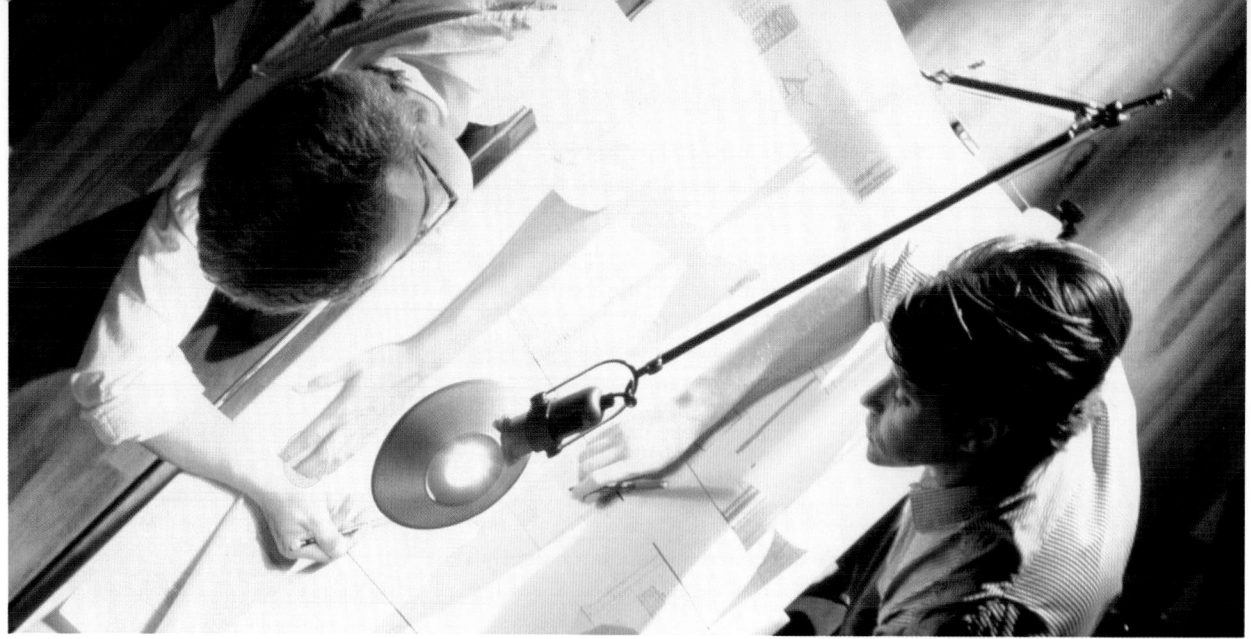

speaking

1 You are going to practise Speaking Part 2. Before you start, read the Task procedure box on page 129, which contains instructions to help with the task.

2 Student A: Look at the topic card below.
Student B: Look at the topic card on page 119.

Topic card A

> **WHAT IS IMPORTANT WHEN ...?**
>
> Considering the safety features of a new office
> * lighting
> * layout
> *
> *

3 Think of two extra points that are relevant to the topic. Then think of one or two examples or reasons to support or illustrate your points. Look back at the plan on page 28 to help you prepare and organise a short talk.

4 Student A: Talk for a minute and try to cover all the points in your plan. At the end of your talk, answer the question your partner asks.
Student B: Make a note of the time your partner starts and finishes his/her talk. If a minute has passed, and your partner is still talking, raise your hand. If he/she talks for less than a minute, say nothing now. Listen carefully and at the end of the talk, ask your partner a relevant question.

tip

One of the areas you are assessed on in Paper 5 is your ability to organise your ideas and speak for an appropriate length of time.
* Try to say something on each of your points in the minute.
* Make sure what you say is relevant to the topic.

5 Assess your performance.

Student B: Tell your partner exactly how long he/she spoke for. Tell your partner if there were any parts of his/her talk that were difficult to understand.
Student A: Did you manage to say what you wanted to say in the minute? If not, what parts could you have made shorter? Did you run out of things to say before a minute had passed? If so, what extra points could you have added? Tell your partner if you thought his/her question was relevant and, if not, why not.

6 Now change roles so that Student B can give his/her talk. Follow exactly the same procedure as in exercise 4 and 5.

writing: a safety notice (memo)

1 Read the memo below from a company health and safety officer, then answer these questions.

a What words would you put in the line that starts 'To'?
   1 Everyone in the distribution department
   2 All staff
   3 All heads of departments
   4 The manager of the distribution department

b What pronoun is used in the memo when referring to the person or people who will read it?

c How would you describe the style of the memo?
   1 informal   3 impolite
   2 unfriendly   4 impersonal

M E M O

To:

From: Ted Rawlings, Health and Safety Officer

Date: 29 November

Following a small fire in the distribution department last week, I would like to remind all employees that they may smoke in the designated areas only. Smokers must use the special ashtrays provided in these areas and must not extinguish their cigarettes in wastepaper baskets.

---

2 Underline the phrases used in the memo which have the following functions.

a to introduce a reminder about the safety regulations
b to explain the background to the memo

3 You are the Health and Safety Officer at a large company. The Maintenance Manager left you this note. Use these shorter phrases to replace the underlined words.

further notice   minor   due to   under repair

> We had an accident on staircase B _which_
> _happened because of_ some broken steps.
> Thank goodness it was _not_ a _very serious_
> accident. The stairs are _being fixed by_
> _workmen_ at the moment, so until _I let_
> _you know you can use it again_, nobody
> must use this staircase at all.

Writing Part 1

4 Write a memo of 40–50 words to all staff:
   • explaining what has happened.
   • reminding them to inform you or their supervisor if they see any possible hazards.
   • informing them what is happening now.

Use phrases from exercises 2 and 3 to help you.

unit 7 recruitment and training

Mark Giddens D

Qualifications
BA Economics, University of California, Berkeley 1990–1994

Job Experience
F&B Recruitment, London, Recruitment Manager 1999–now

Responsibilities:
- Setting up London branch of F&B Recruitment
- Recruitment strategy for banking and finance sectors
- Recruitment process

F&B Recruitment, California, Recruiter 1996–1999

vocabulary

1 Match the captions (a–e) below with the photos (1–5).

a sorting through job applications
b searching for a job on an electronic job board
c recruiting staff at a graduate job fair
d looking for a job at a recruitment agency
e interviewing to fill a job vacancy

2 Match the words below with the labels (A–D) in the photos above.

candidate   curriculum vitae (CV)   job listings   recruiter

3 Complete the table with the words below.

application	candidate	employee	graduate	interview	opening
personnel	recruiter	reference	staff	trainee	vacancy

A nouns (people)	B nouns (not people)

4 Which three words in column A in exercise 3 have almost the same meaning? Which two do not have a plural form? Match the other four words in column A to the definitions below.

   a someone who has successfully finished university
   b someone who is learning a new job
   c someone who might be considered for a job
   d someone whose job is to find new employees for a company

5 Which two words in column B in exercise 3 have the same meaning? Which word in column B can also be used as a verb? Use words from column B to complete the sentences below.

   a The company has a/an .... for a qualified and experienced accountant.
   b You are invited to attend a/an .... on Friday 6 March at 10.00 a.m.
   c In my view, Mr Davis is the best candidate for the job and he has an excellent .... from his last company.
   d Your .... for the position of Sales Manager has not been successful.

6 Complete the recruitment checklist below by adding verbs from this list. Follow the examples.

Check	~~Choose~~	Circulate	~~Hire~~	Interview
Invite	Place	Select	Sort	

ROMTECH
HUMAN RESOURCES DEPARTMENT

Recruitment procedure checklist

1 .... job advertisements in the newspaper or post job openings on a job board.

2 .... through CVs and applications.

3 .... CVs and applications to the relevant manager(s) in the company.

4 _Choose_ .... potential candidates by consulting with the relevant manager(s).

5 .... candidates for interviews.

6 .... candidates.

7 .... potential candidates' references.

8 .... the best candidate(s).

9 _Hire_ .... successful candidate(s).

7 Complete the recruitment survey form below. Then compare and discuss your answers in small groups.

RECRUITMENT SURVEY

If you wanted to find a job, which two methods below do you think would be the best? Why?

			Reason
replying to an advertisement in a newspaper?	Yes ☐	No ☐	....
searching through listings on a job board?	Yes ☐	No ☐	....
registering yourself with a recruitment agency?	Yes ☐	No ☐	....
attending a job fair?	Yes ☐	No ☐	....
using personal contacts (friends or relatives)?	Yes ☐	No ☐	....
another method (how/what?)			....

1 The text below is about methods of recruiting new staff. Read the text quickly. How many recruitment methods are described? Do not pay any attention at this stage to the numbered gaps in the text.

Finding the Right People

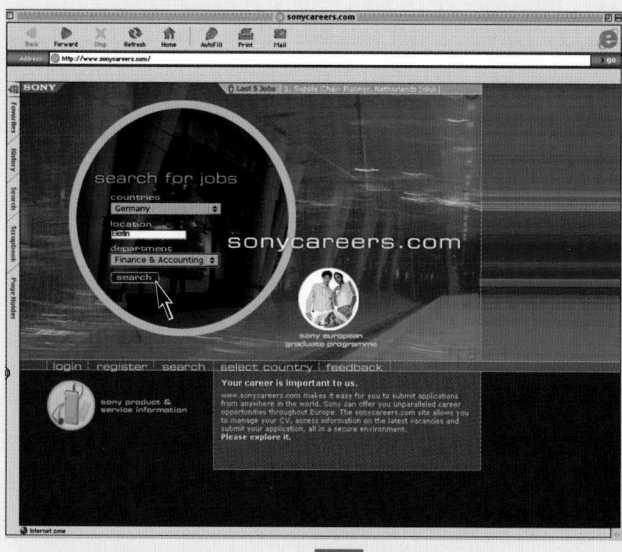

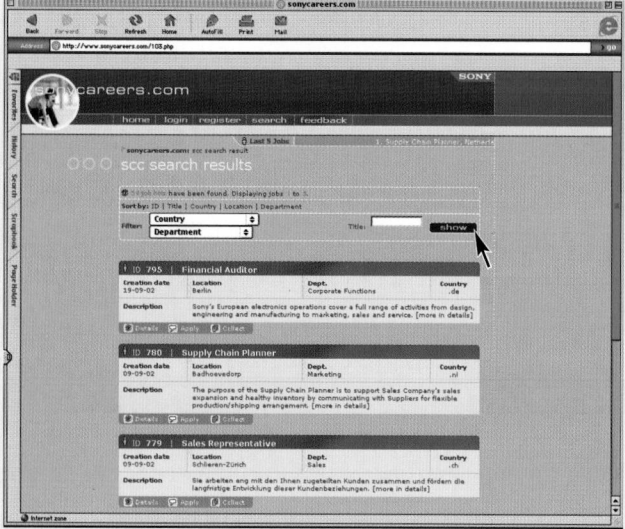

Faced with increasing shortages of labour, especially personnel with specialist expertise, companies throughout the world are turning to new methods of attracting talented and qualified job candidates.

Thousands of companies are experimenting with electronic recruitment and a few on the leading edge have fully integrated it into their human resources strategy. While corporate websites are now commonplace, few are used to their full potential. In recruiting, a company website should be used not only to post job openings, but also to market the company to prospective employees and to accept job applications. (0)...*G*... These can then be circulated to specific recruiters within the company if they match the requirements of existing job openings. They can also be stored in a database so that they can be considered for future job openings.

If creating a state-of-the-art website seems too complicated, or a company wants to reach people who might not ordinarily visit their website, some of the Internet's commercial job-listing services may provide the answer. There are literally hundreds of these job boards, including many specialising in specific skills or industries. (1)........ The cost of these services compares favourably with placing job advertisements in newspapers. A minimum package allowing ten postings per month plus access to the CV database costs about $400 to $500 a month. (2)........

The Internet is undoubtedly a powerful tool for attracting and locating potential new employees. However, it does not solve all the problems recruiters face. Many companies simply do not have the time to sort through dozens of CVs, in electronic form or otherwise, nor do they necessarily have the expertise to pick the right people. Accordingly, although the costs are higher, many firms are turning to recruitment agencies to find the right people for them. (3)........ 'We recruit specifically for the engineering and petrochemical industries,' says Jacqui Thompson, operations manager of the Human Resource Bureau. 'We have a database of personnel from all over the country, from which we put forward candidates that we feel meet the client's requirements. (4)........ What's more, we often find that those companies which do try to go it alone come to us six months later when they still haven't found the type of candidate they want.'

Ms Thompson's experience is borne out in other areas. 'Traditionally, companies only used agencies for top jobs,' says Sharon Pinner of FSS, a company which recruits for the financial and IT sectors. '(5)........ Companies are facing a shortage of good candidates in areas such as accountancy and IT, and they don't have the recruitment resources to ensure they make the right choice.'

2 Look at sentence G in exercise 3 below and the relevant gap in the text. Read the sentences immediately before and after the gap, and find the words in the text which form a link with the underlined words in sentence G.

3 Read the text again and choose the best sentence from the list (A–G) to fill each of the gaps. Do not use any letter more than once. Find the same kind of links for each of the gaps.

A In contrast, a newspaper might charge the same price, or more, to run a job advertisement for only one or two days.

B Many firms are still happy to recruit junior personnel themselves, but some companies find this too time-consuming.

C Ninety per cent of companies in the industries we deal with now recruit externally as they cannot access the staff they need without outside help.

D Now we are regularly asked to recruit middle-managers.

E The largest ones also offer companies extra services, such as access to their databases of CVs.

F This is particularly true of companies which need specialist or technical staff.

G The most successful of these sites allow candidates to submit their CVs either by filling out an on-line form or by pasting an existing electronic CV file into the form.

4 Complete the table with the notes (a–i) about the advantages and disadvantages of each recruitment method.

a all the paperwork is dealt with
b applications can be kept for future reference
c companies may access databases of CVs
d difficult to design
e expensive
f experts in finding the right people
g informs potential employees about the company
h applications and CVs still have to be processed (*use this twice*)
i very cost-effective

Recruitment method	Advantages for employers	Disadvantages for employers
The company website	• •	• •
Electronic job boards	• •	•
Recruitment agencies	• •	•

5 In what ways could an on-line recruitment agency help people who are looking for jobs?

language in use: connectors of contrast and addition

1 Look back at the reading text on page 56 and the sentences (A–G) on page 57. Underline any sentences which contain the following connectors.

also	although	however	in contrast
not only … but also		what's more	while

2 Complete the table below with the connectors from exercise 1. Then add *in addition* and *moreover*.

contrasting two aspects of the same subject
contrasting two different subjects
linking two similar aspects (addition)

3 Look again at the connectors in the table.
  a Which five are used at the start of a sentence and followed by a comma?
  b Which two are used at the start of a clause, with a comma at the end of that clause?

4 Look again at the reading text on page 56.
  a What do you notice about the position of *also* in sentences?
  b What is the structure of the sentence containing *not only … but also*?

5 Rewrite the sentences below, using the connector given in brackets.

Example
Although Romtech UK uses its own trainers to deliver much of its training, its subsidiaries only use external training suppliers. (however)
Romtech UK uses its own trainers to deliver much of its training. However, its subsidiaries only use external training suppliers.

  a Using internal trainers reduces the cost per head for training. It also allows Romtech to offer training which really meets the needs of its employees. (moreover)
  b Most of the internal trainers are experts in their field. However, some of them lack experience in training techniques. (while)
  c Working with external suppliers brings new ideas into the company. In addition, it allows the company to train more staff more quickly. (not only … but also)
  d Ten years ago Romtech employees rarely received any training but nowadays each employee gets at least three weeks' training a year. (in contrast)

6 Look back at the completed table in exercise 4 on page 57. Write six sentences about the different recruitment methods. Three sentences should include connectors of contrast, and three connectors of addition.

See grammar reference pages 133 and 134

Reading Part 5   In most lines of the text about training there is one extra word. If a line is correct, write CORRECT. If there is an extra word in the line, write it in CAPITAL LETTERS.

Organising training in small companies

0	There are many training consultants and organisations which companies can be use to	*BE*
00	train their staff. Although many such training specialists usually have a high level	*CORRECT*
1	of training skills, but they often only have limited knowledge of the company's real	....
2	business or products and services. In addition to, using external training suppliers is	....
3	often a costly solution. Organising training internally, in contrast, helps with the	....
4	company to keep training costs under control, and allows the company to	....
5	train more people as well. The disadvantage of this type of training is that staff	....
6	frequently lack of the necessary training techniques and knowledge about how	....
7	adults learn. However, if this is the preferred solution, companies can develop their	....
8	trainers' skills by sending them on courses on the training methods.	....

listening

1 Read the job advertisement below. What kind of person is F&B Recruitment looking for? Make notes about the ideal candidate's background, experience and personal qualities.

Recruitment Consultant

F&B Recruitment specialises in placing IT and banking personnel. We are looking for somebody to join our team.

Your role will involve managing the entire recruitment process from advertising to placement and developing business with new and existing clients.

You will need:
- excellent interpersonal and communication skills.
- top skills in telephone and face-to-face interviewing.
- strong administrative and written skills.

You will have a minimum of three years' experience in recruitment consultancy or Human Resources, and ideally a background in Information Technology and Banking.

2 Mark Giddens of F&B Recruitment will be interviewing candidates for this position. With a partner, think of five questions he might ask them.

3 Listen to Mark Giddens interviewing Margot Rice, who recruits graduates for the computer company, Romtech. How many different jobs has Margot had at Romtech? Were Mark's questions similar to yours?

Listening Part 3

tip
If you miss the answer to a question, leave it and move on to the next one or you may miss that one too! You will have another chance to hear the recording.

4 Listen again. For each question 1–5, mark one letter (A, B or C) for the correct answer. Before you start, read the Task procedure box on page 127, which contains instructions to help with the task.

1 In her job as HR Assistant, Margot's main duty was to
   A give help and advice to staff on human resource policy.
   B organise staff training courses.
   C provide administrative support for the recruitment process.

2 What Margot most disliked about her job as HR Assistant was
   A the amount of administration she had to do.
   B telling candidates they hadn't got the job.
   C making telephone calls to candidates.

3 In her current job Margot spends most of her time
   A managing the two people who work for her.
   B dealing with people from outside the company.
   C on routine administration.

4 Margot attends recruitment fairs at universities
   A at certain times of the year.
   B once a year.
   C all through the year.

5 How did Margot feel about setting up the job swap programme?
   A that she was too busy to cope with it well
   B angry, because she had to work extra hours at the weekend
   C that she learnt a lot from doing it

5 Look back at the advert and the notes you made in exercise 1. Would you offer the job to Margot? Explain why / why not, giving evidence from what you heard.

speaking

1  Customers of Romtech UK are complaining about poor service. Listen to two extracts in which two Romtech managers discuss the problem. As you listen, complete the gaps in the extracts on page 119.

Speaking Part 3

2 Work in groups of four. Students A and B: Discuss the points on the task sheet below for about three minutes. Students C and D: Listen and make notes about these points.
- Did the speakers use any of the phrases in exercise 1? Which ones?
- What other appropriate phrases did they use during the discussion?
Then give feedback to Students A and B.

Before you start, read the Task procedure box on page 129, which contains instructions to help with the task.

New staff

You work for a British electronics company. As a result of expansion, this company now urgently needs to hire five new general office staff and three well-qualified electronic engineers. You have been asked to advise on the best way of recruiting these new staff.

Discuss the situation together and decide:

- the best and most cost-effective way of finding the new office staff.
- the best way of finding well-qualified electronic engineers quickly.

---

3 Look at the task sheet on page 119 and exchange roles.

writing: a report recommending action

1 A software developer is setting up an office in Swindon in the UK. Read the report on page 61, produced by the company's HR department. Who is it written for?

a administrative assistants in the HR department
b the management of the company
c somebody outside the company

2 Match these labels with the numbers on the report.

a Heading   b Section   c Title   d Sub-heading   e Sub-section

How many main sections does it have and what topic does each deal with?

3 Underline the words the writer uses to introduce the following parts of the report.

a the reason for writing the report   b her recommendations

What other expressions could she use?

1 .... → # Recruiting staff for Swindon

2 .... → ## Introduction
The purpose of this report is to recommend ways of recruiting staff for the new Swindon office.

Findings
We have investigated using both local and specialist IT recruitment agencies.

3 .... → ### Local recruitment agencies
We have been in contact with a number of local recruitment agencies. They report that there are plenty of skilled office staff in the area, but a shortage of people with specialist IT skills.

IT recruitment agencies
We have also contacted the IT recruitment agency, Fastband. They will deal with the entire application and screening process.

4 .... → Although their costs are high, it would reduce the administrative work for HR. Moreover, it would enable the company to recruit more quickly.

Recommendations
Because of our urgent need for new staff, we recommend that local

5 .... → agencies are used to recruit administrative staff and Fastband for IT personnel.

4 Circle any connectors the writer uses to introduce additional points or contrast advantages and disadvantages.

Writing Part 2

tip
- Check you have included all the points in the memo and the handwritten notes.
- Be careful not to use exactly the same words as in the notes.

5 Your company is planning a training programme for customer care staff to be completed before the end of the year. You have been asked to write a report recommending a training supplier.

Look at the memo from your assistant and use the information and your handwritten notes to write the report. Write 120–140 words.

1 Plan your report. Decide on a title, the number of sections and the headings.
2 Remember to use connectors to link your arguments.

---

telephoning and time management courses for our graduate training programme

Memo

From: David Brown, HR assistant

I have talked to two training providers about customer care training.

Excellence Training
- Previous experience with us.
- Can't start programme until October.

not able to meet the end of the year deadline

Bannerdown ← *I think we should use them*
- No previous experience with them.
- Lots of experience in training courses.
- Can start in August.
- Cost 10% lower.

unit 8 advertising and promotion

vocabulary

1 Match the pictures (1–6) with the advertising methods (a–f) below.

a outdoor advertising

b phone directory advertising (yellow pages)

c printed media advertising

d direct mail

e a point-of-sale promotion

f Web marketing

2 Which method of advertising or promotion would you associate these words with? Rewrite them in the table. Some words may go in more than one row. Follow the examples.

banner ad   ~~billboard~~   commercial   consumer magazine   coupon
display ad   free gift   full page ad   letter   ~~listing~~   poster
reply card   special offer   trade magazine

direct mail	
outdoor advertising	billboard
point-of-sale promotion	
printed media advertising	
radio advertising	
TV advertising	
yellow pages advertising	listing
Web marketing	

3 Some methods of advertising or promotion are more suitable to certain products or services than others. In your country, what kinds of products or services are usually advertised or promoted using the following methods?

- on local radio stations
- in national newspapers
- by direct mail
- on the Web

- outdoors
- in local newspapers
- at the point of sale
- on national TV

4 Think of a product or service which you have bought within the last couple of months, but which you do not buy regularly. Work with a partner. Take turns to interview each other, using the survey form below.

CUSTOMER SURVEY

1	What was the product or service you bought?
2	Did you learn about this particular product or service because:
	you saw / heard it advertised? (where / by what method?)
	someone you know recommended it?
	a sales assistant recommended it?
	you looked it up in the yellow pages?
	you found out about it another way (what?)
3	What influenced your choice of product or service?
	the price
	the quality
	a special offer or free gift
	the style of the product/service
	the way the product/service had been advertised (If so, in what way?)
	something else (what?)

5 Compare your answers with the rest of the class.

a Find out the following information.
- How many people learnt about a product or service through advertising?
- How many people chose a product or service as a result of the way it had been advertised?
- How many people chose a product or service as a result of a promotional offer (e.g. special offer or free gift)?

b When members of your class were influenced by advertising or promotional offers, what was the most successful method?

6 Think of a TV commercial which has interested or amused you. Describe the commercial to a partner, without saying exactly what product or service it was advertising. Can your partner guess what the product or service was?

7 What do you think the following quotation means? Do you agree with it?

> ' Advertising may be described as the science of arresting human intelligence long enough to get money from it. '

SOURCE: *THE GARDEN OF FOLLY* BY STEPHEN LEACOCK

reading

1 The four short texts below are extracts from a guide to advertising methods for owners of small businesses. Read through the texts quickly. Which method of advertising is each referring to? Choose from this list.

1 TV
2 outdoor
3 yellow pages
4 newspaper
5 direct mail
6 radio
7 the Web

A This method is convenient because you can insert an advertisement at short notice and your ad can contain details, such as prices and telephone numbers or special offer coupons giving discounts. Another advantage is the large variety of sizes available and so, even on a tight budget, you can place a series of small ads. Position is exceedingly important, so specify in what section you want your ad to appear. Request an outside position for ads that have coupons to make them easier to cut out.

B This offers the greatest possibility for creative advertising, can give a product or service instant validity and allows you to target specific audiences, such as children and their parents during afternoon cartoons. Despite some recent criticism, when used properly, this is still the most effective advertising medium there is, but you shouldn't attempt it unless you have enough money in your budget to do it right. It is advisable to employ an advertising agency to help you create a commercial that will be effective for the goods or service you are offering.

C This is a relatively inexpensive way of selling an image or idea, but is a poor medium for transmitting details such as prices or telephone numbers. Using it in conjunction with printed advertising makes it twice as effective – you can say in your commercial 'See our ad in the *Sunday Times*'. As so many stations exist nationwide, the total audience for any one station is limited, therefore it's important to know which stations your potential customers listen to and at what times of the day.

D This form of advertising allows you to place your business listing or ad in selected classifications, so that when people need your product or service, they look up the appropriate section and contact you. Since those who have looked up your classification are already in the market to buy, your ad does not have to convince people of the desirability of purchasing your product or service. What it does need to emphasise is the reasons why the reader should select your firm over the competition.

Reading Part 1 **2** Look at the statements (1–7) on page 65 and read the texts above again. Which advertising method (A, B, C or D) does each statement refer to? For each statement, choose one letter (A, B, C or D). You will need to use some of the letters more than once. Before you start, read the Task procedure box on page 122, which contains instructions to help with the task.

Example

0 *This form of advertising reaches people who are already interested in what you are selling.* D

1 Combining this method with another one is likely to get better results.
2 You can offer your customers an easy way to save money if you advertise by this method.
3 This method lets companies focus their advertising on groups of people with similar interests.
4 Before placing this kind of advertisement you need to think about what makes your company better than others in the same field.
5 This method works best if handled by somebody with expertise in this area.
6 You need to do careful research before you choose this method so that you can reach a sufficient number of people.
7 You should use this method if you don't have much money to spend on advertising.

3 Which verbs from the text go with the nouns or noun phrases below?

.... a coupon
.... an ad / business listing
.... a section / classification in the yellow pages
.... specific TV / radio audiences

4 Make notes in the first four rows of the table below using information from the texts (A–D). The first row has been done as an example.

advertising method	advantages	disadvantages
newspapers	• can place ads at short notice • can include details • large range of sizes	———
radio	•	• •
yellow pages	•	———
TV	• •	•
outdoor advertising		
direct mail		
Web marketing		

5 The notes below relate to outdoor advertising, direct mail and Web marketing. Work with a partner and decide which part of the table to put each note in. Some of the notes may apply to more than one of the advertising methods.

a attracts no more than two or three seconds of a reader's time
b allows you to target your message to specific groups of people
c can't be switched off or thrown away unread
d people usually see the same message a number of times
e may be thrown away unread
f some people do not have access to this medium

6 Which method or combination of advertising methods do you think would be best for these organisations?

a a multinational soft drinks company
b a local dry-cleaning company
c a national chain of florist's shops
d a charity that is organising a local fund-raising pop concert
e a car manufacturer that is launching a new model
f an insurance company

listening

1 🎧 You will hear two extracts from a meeting between Sandra Chen, who runs a small business called The Rite Bite, and Paul Dewar, who works for an advertising agency. Listen to the first extract and mark the statements about their conversation **True** or **False**.

a Sandra chose this advertising agency because someone recommended it to her.
b She currently runs a food delivery service.
c The low calorie hot meals are bought mainly by working people.
d She has approached the agency because she needs help in promoting a new shop.

2 🎧 Listen to the same extract again. This time, complete the table below.

The Rite Bite's products	• *Hot lunches*
	•
their current customers	•
	•
their new service	•
their potential new customers	•
their current method of advertising	•

3 What method(s) do you think would be the most appropriate to advertise The Rite Bite's new service?

4 🎧 Listen to the second extract and answer these questions.

a What features of The Rite Bite's products appeal to their customers?
b What three features will the agency use to promote the new service?
c What advertising and promotional methods does Paul Dewar suggest?

5 🎧 Listen to extract 2 again and then look at the tapescript on page 144. Find words or phrases in the dialogue which match these definitions.

a features and benefits that make your product different from the competition
b the type of customer a company wants to attract
c the text that actors will read for a radio or TV commercial
d the text that will appear in a printed advertisement
e the job of booking air time and advertising space

6 Is there a market for this type of product and service in your country? What features and benefits would you need to emphasise?

language in use: future forms

1 🎧 You will hear five short extracts from the listening passages again. As you listen, complete the missing words in each extract.

Extract 1
... they work too far away to get to us, so
.... take our products to them.

Extract 2
We think the delivery service ....
popular, but ...

Extract 3
Tell me, when exactly .... the
delivery service?

Extract 4
.... back to you in the middle of
next week and ...

Extract 5
... we can arrange another meeting at which
.... our ideas.

2 Match each extract in exercise 1 to the function (a–e) expressed by the words you filled in. What structures were used in each case?
   a making an offer or decision at the time of speaking
   b talking about an event which has already been arranged for a specific time in the future
   c making a prediction or expressing an opinion about what will happen in the future
   d talking about a plan or intention for the future
   e talking about a future fact

3 Match the following sentence patterns with one of the functions in exercise 2.
   a *am/is/are planning to* + verb
   b *hope/expect/imagine (that)* + noun phrase + *will* + verb

4 Sandra Chen has now had a second meeting with Paul Dewar and approved his proposal for her advertising campaign. She's explaining the details to her partner, Maggie. Complete the gaps in their conversation below with the appropriate future form of the verb in brackets. Follow the example.

Sandra   So, the radio advertising (0) *is going to start* (start) two weeks before the launch. It (1) .... (be) a 60-second commercial and the local station (2) .... (broadcast) it six times a day each weekday.

Maggie   That doesn't seem like very often. Do you think enough people (3) .... (hear) it?

Sandra   Well, as far as I know, Paul (4) .... (book) three slots each day between eight and nine a.m. and three between five and six. That's when our target buyers listen to the radio – in the car driving to and from

work. He hopes we (5) .... (maximise) our audience by using those times.

Maggie   I see. Well that seems sensible. And the print ads?

Sandra   The first one (6) .... (appear) on 24 September and the agency's booked space for every day that week. What we haven't finalised yet is what form the promotional offer (7) .... (take). He's made three different suggestions, but I wanted to discuss them with you first.

Maggie   OK. Has he put them in writing?

Sandra   Yes – it's all in this folder.

Maggie   And when (8) .... (you see) him again?

Sandra   I've got another meeting with him tomorrow at 4.30.

Maggie   Right, then I (9) .... (take) the folder home with me this evening and look through his suggestions and we can discuss them tomorrow morning. Is that OK?

Sandra   Yes, good idea.

See grammar reference pages 134 and 135

5 Think about the next six months in the company or department where you work. Write a total of at least six sentences about the following points.
   • future events that have been arranged
   • plans or intentions
   • hopes or expectations
If you don't have a job yet, write about future events in your own life and your personal plans, intentions, hopes and expectations for the next six months.

speaking

1 You are part of the creative team at the advertising agency, Seymour Media. Your company has been asked to prepare a radio commercial and some promotional ideas to launch The Rite Bite's new delivery service. Work in groups and complete the information to help you plan your campaign.

Target customers	
Special features of the service	
Main image for the campaign to put across	

2 Hold a meeting to discuss your ideas for a 60-second radio commercial. Include information about: type of commercial, e.g. a simple description of the service or a conversation between two people; sound effects; music.

3 Brainstorm some promotional ideas which you can use at the start of the campaign. Then choose the best three.

4 Prepare a short spoken presentation of your ideas for the radio commercial and promotional ideas. Your aim is to persuade the managers from The Rite Bite to choose your campaign.

5 Present your ideas. While each group is presenting, the other groups play the role of the managers from The Rite Bite. Before you start, look at page 120.

writing: replying to an enquiry

1 Shirley Francis, the Advertising Sales Manager at *Superhealth* magazine received an enquiry from Jason Black at Vitatone about advertising their health products in the magazine.

The paragraphs A–E in Shirley's reply are not in a logical order. Work with a partner and decide on a more logical order.

SUPERHEALTH magazine,
PO Box 653,
Bath
BA1 2AA

Dear Mr Black,

A The deadline for accepting copy for the October issue is 25 August.

B I enclose our media package folder for your information. This includes:
  • information about our readership, analysed by gender, age, interests and purchasing preferences
  • a card detailing our advertising rates
  • publication dates for the next six issues of the magazine

C Please contact me if you need any further information.

D I hope you will find the information in the folder useful and relevant to your needs. As you will see, many of our readers regularly purchase food supplements.

E Thank you for your recent enquiry about advertising in our monthly magazine Superhealth.

Yours sincerely,

Shirley Francis

SHIRLEY FRANCIS
ADVERTISING SALES MANAGER

2 Which paragraph (A–E) of the letter performs the functions below?

a refers to the potential client's letter

b offers extra help if it is wanted

c describes what is enclosed with the letter

d gives a specific answer to a question asked in the potential client's letter

e highlights a point that may be of special interest to this potential client

3 Underline the phrases or sentences Shirley Francis uses for the following functions.

a to draw Jason Black's attention to a point that may be of special interest to him

b to offer extra help if it is wanted

c to refer to Jason Black's letter

d to refer to the folder that is enclosed with the letter and the information in it

Writing Part 2

tip
- Remember to include an appropriate opening and closing phrase. See Unit 1, pages 12 and 13.
- In the exam there is no need to include addresses and dates.

4 You are an advertising sales assistant at *DIY Round-up* magazine. Your boss has passed you the letter below and asked you to reply to it.

Look at the letter and the hand-written notes your boss has made on it. Then, using all these notes, write your letter. Write 120–140 words.

RED TIGER TOOLS

RED TIGER TOOLS,
PO Box 11734,
London
WC1 6PP

Advertising Sales Manager
DIY Round-up Magazine
BDP Magazines plc
PO Box 653
Bath BA1 2AA

Dear Sir or Madam,

point out that ours are more than 60% DIY enthusiasts and the rest small business owners (joinery, construction, etc.)

We are a Korean company which produces power drills and other hand-held tools. Our European customers are mainly DIY enthusiasts and small businesses in the construction trade.

We are launching a new lightweight power drill in the UK market later this year and may be interested in placing a series of advertisements in your *DIY Round-up* magazine.

Could you please send me information about the readership of your magazine and your advertising rates for different sizes and styles of ads?

send some examples from former issues: she may find this helpful

Yours faithfully,

Send our usual 'ad kit' (statistics about our readers, advertising rates card, current issue of the magazine)

Vickie Moon

Vickie Moon
Assistant to the UK Sales Manager

unit 9 international business

vocabulary

1 The map shows part of the distribution network for an Australian company that manufactures and sells security systems. Look at the map and answer the questions.

  a How many companies are named?
  b Which of these companies do you think are part of the same group? Why?

2 Match the words (a–e) below with the numbers (1–5) on the map.

  a distributor   b exports   c head office   d sales outlet   e sales subsidiary

3 In which country, Indonesia or New Zealand, do you think Triton Systems makes a bigger profit on its products? Why?

4 Read the quotes on page 71 about two companies' experience of expanding internationally. How many ways of entering new markets are mentioned? What are they? Do not pay any attention at this stage to the numbered gaps in the text.

Company 1

66 Expanding into (0) ....B........ markets involves decisions about which markets to (1) .... into and the best way to do business in each market. In Europe, for example, we decided to sell (2) .... We (3) .... up our own sales subsidiary and now have a team of 40 working there. In Japan, on the other hand, we (4) .... out a deal with a(n) (5) .... distributor and now sell through them. 99

Company 2

66 We find that buying up the right local company can really (6) .... up entry and growth in a new market. It is much easier than (7) .... your own operations. So far we've bought companies in 20 new markets. We (8) .... for businesses that are well (9) .... financially and have a good team of managers. To avoid confusion, it's also important to make sure everything is (10) .... down in writing – so no verbal agreements. 99

5 Choose the best word to fill each gap from A, B, C or D below. For each question 1–10, mark one letter (A, B, C or D). There is an example at the beginning (0). Before you start, read the Task procedure box on page 123, which contains instructions to help with the task.

read the Task procedure box on page 123

0 A abroad	B foreign	C home	D outside
1 A enter	B come	C move	D open
2 A quickly	B direct	C straight	D immediately
3 A launched	B began	C introduced	D set
4 A negotiated	B worked	C did	D discussed
5 A internal	B international	C nearby	D local
6 A accelerate	B quicken	C speed	D hurry
7 A setting	B making	C establishing	D placing
8 A look	B ask	C request	D seek
9 A set	B done	C run	D made
10 A put	B written	C placed	D confirmed

tip: Some gaps in the cloze test your knowledge of phrasal verbs. Make sure you read the options carefully because they often include one or more single verbs with a very similar meaning as the phrasal verb but which do not combine with a preposition, e.g. *look into* but not *investigate into*.

6 Look at the completed text in exercise 4 and complete the table below. Follow the example.

verb	verb and preposition	goes with
enter	move into	a new market
establish	....	a subsidiary/operation
negotiate	....	a deal
acquire	....	a company
accelerate	....	entry/growth
seek	....	companies/new markets

7 When companies research new export markets, there are various ways they can get information. Match each of these sources of information (1–4) with a definition (a–d).

1 chamber of commerce
2 embassy
3 trade delegation
4 trade fair

a an event where companies from the same business sector show their newest products to prospective customers
b an official group of business people in a particular town or area who work together to improve trade and pass on business information
c a group of people who represent their country or company and go to another country to set up business connections
d a group of officials who represent their government in a foreign country, and the name of the building where they work

1 Look at the title of the article below. What do you think the article is about? The words below are key words from the six paragraphs of the article. Work with a partner. Discuss what you think is the main idea in each paragraph. Then read the article and check your ideas.

Paragraph 1   starting business, right contacts, trade fairs, international banks
Paragraph 2   local business person, knowledge, permits, translators
Paragraph 3   hospitality, chat, small talk, talk business.
Paragraph 4   decision-making, take longer, leave time, delays
Paragraph 5   Istanbul, Ankara, western businesswoman, male colleagues
Paragraph 6   formality, suits, dress

Contacts that make or break Turkish ventures

1 When starting business in Turkey, you need to take two things into consideration: it helps to have the right contacts and you need to maintain them. But what do you do if you don't have good contacts to build business relationships? Good starting points are trade fairs where you can meet potential clients, partners, agents and distributors. Another useful route is to join trade delegations organised, for example, by an international chamber of commerce. International banks and accountancy firms are also helpful, especially for advice on how to set up and do business in Turkey.

2 A local business person who can act on your behalf, however, is always the best bet. As well as having access to good business contacts, he or she should have a good knowledge of the relevant authorities as government permits can be an important part of business. A local contact can also save time because of links to business services such as interpreters and translators.

3 Turkish hospitality is renowned and your business partner is likely to put business on a personal level. Deals are rarely done without a preliminary chat over a glass of Turkish tea – or even an invitation to your host's home. Small talk plays a vital role. Topics include your arrival, your accommodation and how you find the country. It can sometimes be difficult to gauge when it would be appropriate to talk business, but as a general rule you should wait until your contact mentions it. In time your Turkish counterpart will ask you in detail about your company, products and services and competitors. That is when it becomes appropriate to switch to business.

4 Time can appear to be elastic in Turkey. Meetings and decision-making may take longer than elsewhere, so it is wise not to try to push things too hard as that may prove to be counter-productive in the long run. You should not expect everything to happen as you planned, so leave enough time to manage delays and unexpected

issues or changing circumstances. This is especially important when dealing with public authorities that issue permits to conduct business.

5 Most business is conducted in Istanbul, Turkey's commercial metropolis. Ankara is more important when dealing with public authorities or the government. A western businesswoman will be accepted as a negotiating partner in either of these cities and more widely in the country amongst the younger generation of managers. However, she will be more effective if she can negotiate as part of a team that includes male colleagues.

6 Finally, business in Turkey requires a certain degree of formality. Men should wear suits, women a suit or dress. This applies even if your Turkish partner is casually dressed.

The multiple-choice questions follow the same order as the text.

2 Read the article again. For each question 1–5, mark one letter (A, B, C or D) for the answer you choose. Before you start, read the Task procedure box on page 123, which contains instructions to help with the task.

1 The advice in the first paragraph is intended mainly for people who:
   A want to improve their business relationships with Turkish companies.
   B want to set up their own businesses in Turkey.
   C have never done business in Turkey before.
   D are planning to attend trade fairs in Turkey.

2 One of the main reasons why it's important to have good local business contacts is that they
   A provide translation services.
   B act as an interpreter in your negotiation.
   C issue any permits you need.
   D can help you obtain any permits you require.

3 In paragraph 3, when does the writer say you should start the serious business part of a discussion?
   A in an informal setting, for example over tea
   B only when your potential business partner introduces the subject
   C after you spend a few minutes on general and social topics
   D when you are invited to a potential business partner's house

4 How does the writer suggest dealing with delays?
   A allow time for them
   B push hard to make sure they don't happen
   C only accept them when dealing with public authorities
   D use your contacts to speed up the issue of permits

5 According to the article, a female negotiator would not get the best results if she were
   A in negotiations where the management team were young.
   B in negotiations outside the main cities of Istanbul and Ankara.
   C negotiating on her own.
   D the only woman in the team.

3 Find words or phrases in the text which have these meanings.
   a Paragraph 2 the best option (phrase)
   b Paragraph 2 an official written statement giving somebody permission or the right to do something (noun)
   c Paragraph 3 evaluate (verb)
   d Paragraph 3 change (verb)
   e Paragraph 4 flexible (adjective)
   f Paragraph 4 have the opposite effect from the one you want (be + adjective)
   g Paragraph 6 an informal way of dressing (adverb + adjective)

4 In the article, the writer talks about the importance of small talk for developing the business relationship. *'Small talk plays a vital role. Topics include your arrival, your accommodation and how you find the country.'* Work with a partner. You are going to act out the small talk phase before a meeting with a potential foreign partner.

   1 Complete the conversation plan details.

Purpose of meeting	....
Place	in the offices of the potential foreign partner
Relationship	it's the first face-to-face contact
Accommodation	....
Country/City	....

   2 Act out the conversation. Take turns to be the potential partner.

speaking

1 🎧 Jenny Burns, Managing Director of FDC, has recently signed a distribution agreement with a Japanese company. You will hear a discussion in which she and two colleagues talk about what gifts to take on a visit to the company.

a What kind of gifts do you think would be appropriate?

b Listen to the discussion. What gifts do they consider? What do they decide on?

2 🎧 Look at the list of phrases (a–i) below and try to fit them in the correct spaces. Follow the example. Listen again and check your answers.

Alex	Well, I know Mr Wada plays golf, so (1) ...*h*... give him a set of golf clubs.
Patrick	Golf clubs? (2) ....
	(3) .... some top quality malt whisky?
Jenny	Alcohol. No, (4) .... , but (5) .... something that's representative of Glasgow ...
Alex	(6) .... something that represents us as a modern ...
Patrick	(7) .... an original piece of art?
Jenny	(8) .... , Patrick.
Alex	(9) .... get it done in time?

a I agree, but if we do that I think it should be
b I do like the idea of
c I don't think that would be right
d I really like that idea
e I've got another idea. How about
f It's certainly unusual, but do you think we could
g that might not be appropriate
h we could
i What about

3 Look back at the completed phrases in 1–9 above. Mark each one with a letter.

- **S** (suggests an idea)
- **A** (accepts it)
- **R** (rejects it diplomatically)
- **U** (shows he/she is unsure about the idea)

4 Your company has signed a joint venture with FDC. Work in groups. You are the members of a project team which has been set up to arrange a day's entertainment for visitors from FDC.

1 Look at the information about the visitors.
2 Brainstorm three or four ideas for the entertainment programme and discuss each one in turn. Try to use phrases from exercise 2 above.
3 Present your programme for the visit to the rest of the class.

Jenny Burns,
MANAGING DIRECTOR

Likes to get on with the business and not keen on small talk. Enjoys adventure sports.

Alex McKinsey,
FINANCIAL MANAGER

Interested in travel and the culture of different countries. Has spent many years living and working abroad.

Patrick O'Connor,
INTERNATIONAL SALES MANAGER

Family man with two young children. Likes good food and drink.

writing: a report describing a visit

1 Charlie Goodyear, the International Marketing Manager at Triton Systems, made a business trip to Istanbul in Turkey between 15 and 17 April. He visited the embassy and two potential distributors, Kaya Ltd. and Soyak Ltd. Work with a partner and decide on a title and headings for the sections in his report.

....	
Introduction	The purpose of the trip was to meet two prospective distributors.
1	I had a meeting with the commercial attaché, Anita Richards. I also attended a reception at the embassy and was introduced to Alpay Yolmaz, a local businessman with excellent contacts. If we need any help, he will be happy to act as our local advisor.
2	I met Kaya's owner Mustafa Kazan. It appears to be a very dynamic company and already acts as a distributor for other companies in the home security sector.
3	I had discussions with the Sales Manager, Osman Ersoy. Soyak Ltd. is well run and has a good distribution network across Turkey, but no international business experience.
Conclusions	Both companies are worth further investigation and I have arranged further meetings in May.

2 Answer these questions.
   a Is the report for other managers, all staff or other distributors?
   b Is the purpose of the report to inform or to give recommendations?
   c What information does Charlie include about the companies he visited?

Writing Part 2

3 You work for a large soft drinks company in the United States. Write a report about a business trip you made to Indonesia. Look at the notes you made below. Write 120–140 words. Include a title and headings. Before you start, read the Task procedure Box on page 125 which contains instructions to help with the task.

Place visited: Indonesia (23-26 May)
Purpose of the trip: visit two companies with a view to their producing our soft drinks under licence
Had meetings with: Botol Jaya in Surabaya and Garuda Bottling in Bandung

Botol Jaya
Met with: Production Manager, Haris Sutopo
Facts and impressions: one of biggest, oldest plants in Indonesia; machinery outdated, slow; factory could be cleaner

Garuda Bottling
Met with: the owner, Adang Hartono
Facts and impressions: new company (four years old) - very well run; latest machinery; hygiene and quality control excellent

Conclusion: find out more about Garuda Bottling (have set up more meetings with them in July)

unit 10 sales

vocabulary

1 Have you ever attended a trade fair like the one above? What was it for? Who was there? What was it like?

2 Match the words (a–d) with the numbers on the photos.

a product b visitors c stand d exhibitors

3 Match the verbs (a–d) with the nouns (1–4).

a take   1 potential customers
b meet   2 products
c demonstrate   3 product literature
d hand out   4 a stand

4 Find the words in exercises 1 and 3 which have the same meaning as *exhibition/show* and *prospective*.

5 Complete the table using these words.

brochures business cards buyers catalogues competitors
customers enquiry cards suppliers samples

Things you hand out to customers	People who come to a trade fair
product literature	visitors
	exhibitors

6 Work with a partner and discuss these questions.

a Why might a company want to take a stand at an exhibition like this? Think of three reasons.

b Why might companies want to visit an exhibition like this? Think of three reasons.

7 Match the words (a–e) with the definitions (1–5) below.

a lead   1 the act of selling something
b sale   2 a document sent by a seller to a customer with details of the products provided, price and payment
c delivery   3 a piece of information that may help someone find new customers
d invoice   4 a reduction in the normal price of something
e discount   5 the process of getting the goods or products to the buyer

8 Work with a partner. Use these words to complete the guidelines for successful sales visits.

close   delivery   demonstration   discount   ~~leads~~   invoice   form
place   ~~present~~   replace   satisfied   set up

- Always follow up your (1) ..*leads*.............. with a visit as soon as possible.
- During the meeting, use your time to (2) ..*present*.......... the products. If possible organise a product (3) ....
- Be prepared to negotiate the final price and (4) .... dates.
- Always try to (5) .... the sale before the end of the visit.
- If all goes well, take the order and make sure you fill in the order (6) .... correctly.
- If the customer doesn't want to (7) .... an order, thank him for his time but try to (8) .... another appointment in a few weeks.
- After the visit, arrange the delivery details and send the customer the (9) ....
- Follow up your visit with a phone call to check the customer is (10) ....
- If the customer makes a complaint, always offer a solution, for example (11) .... damaged products or offer a (12) .... on the next order.

9 Look back at the guidelines in exercise 8 and complete the verb + noun combinations.

a follow up   ...*a lead*......... / ....
b set up   ....
c present   ....
d negotiate   .... / ....
e close   ....
f place   ....
g send   ....
h replace   ....
i offer   ....

10 Look at these noun + noun combinations. Circle the one that doesn't fit in each case.

a sales   lead / enquiry / hint
b delivery   date / period / delay / details
c order   list / form / number
d product   demonstration / presentation / show

11 You work for an office supplies and equipment company. Work in groups of three. Give a short talk for your graduate intake of sales people, explaining how to handle sales visits.

reading

1 Anyone can sell if they get the right training. Do you agree with this statement? Why / Why not?

REPORT ON SALES TEAM AT MK PRECISION, DENVER, CO

BACKGROUND

1 Following the concerns about the wide disparity in the efficiency of the Colorado–Kansas sales team, we were asked to evaluate the team and assess how far the behaviour of individual sellers was affecting their performance.

For the purposes of the investigation, each of the twelve people in the team was observed during a full day of customer visits.

FINDINGS

Discussion Focus 2 In successful visits, the sellers used most of the available time to talk about the products and the customer's order. Such sales-focused visits produced the largest orders. In other less focused visits, the customer used the time to voice complaints concerning prices, delivery, invoicing, or even the products themselves. Too much time was also spent discussing topics such as the customer's latest holiday, sport or political candidates. These unfocused visits nearly always produced small orders or no orders at all. A detailed breakdown of how time was spent in successful visits can be found in appendix A.

Time Management 3 All the sales team were reasonably efficient in keeping the time they spent travelling between customers to a minimum. Differences in time management began to appear, however, when the seller walked through the customer's door. Frequently the customer was not available immediately. Some sellers waited patiently for 20 to 30 minutes until the customer made time for them, but these visits seldom produced more than small orders. (See appendix B.) Once it became clear there would be a long delay, the more successful sellers tried to set up another appointment, at a more convenient time, and then left to follow up other sales opportunities.

Staying Power 4 For the less successful sellers in the team the early results of the day were a good indicator for the rest of the day. A few good early orders boosted their confidence and more sales followed. However, when initial visits were unsuccessful, sellers lost confidence, made mistakes, and consequently closed few sales. Naturally, strong sellers also experienced rejection, but appeared to deal with it better, and, in most cases, orders soon followed. The distinction between the strong and less successful sellers was not in their ability to conduct a successful sales visit, but in their ability to use their sales knowledge consistently, regardless of the setbacks they faced.

RECOMMENDATION

5 Our investigation confirms wide differences in the effectiveness of individuals within the team. Poor performance has occurred in all locations – sales staff covering downtown areas have produced very similar results to those operating in the suburbs or in rural districts. What is clear is that the sales staff have been left to get on with the job with little help or training. We recommend therefore that higher priority is given to on-the-job training, and that experienced sales managers spend time in the field, working with new sellers and those who are performing less well. This model has worked well in the Chicago office, where new training initiatives have resulted in a 20 per cent increase in total sales.

2 MK Precision, a US company which sells parts to car manufacturers and dealers, is concerned about the effectiveness of one of its sales teams. Read the report on page 80 by a team of consultants who have been called in to investigate the problem. Answer these questions.

a What's the purpose of the report?
b How did the consultants gather their information for the report?
c What three aspects of sales visits does the report look at?

3 Mark these statements about the report **True** or **False**. Correct any that are false.

a Management wanted the report done because the sales team was performing so badly.
b Staff who allowed plenty of time for small talk closed more sales.
c According to the report, not too much time was being wasted getting from meeting to meeting.
d Sales people who were prepared to wait a long time to see potential customers had the best chance of getting an order.
e For weaker sellers, lack of success in early visits usually resulted in poor sales for the rest of the day.
f According to the writer of the report, weaker members of the team don't know enough about selling.
g The writer believes that the performance of the weaker sales people can be improved by providing practical training.

4 Find words or phrases in the text which have these meanings.

a Paragraph 1 difference (noun)
b Paragraph 2 say what you think or feel (verb)
c Paragraph 4 the strength and mental energy to keep going until you reach the end of what you are doing (noun + noun)
d Paragraph 4 not being accepted by somebody (noun)
e Paragraph 4 direct or manage something (verb)
f Paragraph 4 always the same (adverb)
g Paragraph 4 something that delays somebody or makes things worse (noun)
h Paragraph 5 something that is more urgent or important than other things (noun)

5 Which of these nouns are used with the following verbs? Look back at the article to check your answers.

confidence   complaints   priority   rejection   sales visits

a voice (paragraph 2)
b boost (paragraph 4)
c experience (paragraph 4)
d conduct (paragraph 4)
e give (paragraph 5)

6 Work with a partner. Use the information in the report to prepare guidelines for the sales team at MK Precision. Do you think this advice would be suitable for a sales team in your country?

7 What qualities do you think a salesperson needs? Work in groups of three and brainstorm a list of five qualities. Rank the qualities you've chosen (1= most important), then explain your ranking to other groups.

language in use: the passive

1 The report on the sales team at MK Precision on page 80 contains examples of the passive. Look through the text and complete the sentences.

1 ... each of the twelve people in the team .... during a full day of customer visits. (paragraph 1)

2 Too much time .... also .... discussing topics such as the customer's latest holiday ... (paragraph 2)

3 ... the sales staff .... to get on with the job with little help or training. (paragraph 5)

2 Match each of the statements (a–c) below with one sentence in exercise 1.

The writer of the report doesn't say who performed the action because:

a he doesn't want to say, to avoid blaming anyone in particular.

b it's not important to readers of the report to know exactly who it was.

c it's already clear from the context.

3 How do you form the passive? Complete the explanation.

You use the verb .... in the appropriate tense and the .... of the main verb.

4 Use the passive form of these verbs in the positive or negative to complete some extracts from a report about a trade fair.

give   run   see

send   set up   translate

a Staff on the stand ....*were seen*..... talking to each other while visitors tried to catch their attention.

b On the last day of the fair customers .... last year's brochure because no up-to-date product literature was available.

c Follow-up letters .... to prospective customers, even though it is now over a month since the trade fair.

d A course in presentation techniques .... next month for all staff who deal with visitors at trade fairs.

e In the future, if we exhibit at trade fairs abroad, our product literature needs .... into different languages.

f For all trade fairs we recommend that a project team .... well in advance to handle all the arrangements.

See grammar reference pages 135 and 136

Reading Part 5

tip

There will never be more than one extra word in any line.

In most lines in these guidelines about exhibiting at trade fairs there is one extra word. If a line is correct, write CORRECT. If there is an extra word in the line, write it in CAPITAL LETTERS. Before you start, read the Task procedure box on page 123, which contains instructions to help with the task.

Exhibiting at trade fairs

0	Certain types of behaviour on the stand look unprofessional and give the	*CORRECT*
00	impression that you are not being interested in your customers. It looks	*BEING*
1	bad if you spend too much time talking to colleagues instead of focusing	....
2	on the people who visiting your stand. Remind staff they will only have	....
3	about 90 seconds to attract and interest a visitor, so the key to be success	....
4	is to be full prepared. The first thing you should do when you meet someone	....
5	new is find out who they are – for an instance, a buyer, competitor or decision-	....
6	maker – and where they are located. In this way you can avoid spending too	....
7	much time with a person who isn't in a position to make up decisions about	....
8	buying your product or service, or who is been based in a region which is not	....
9	served by your company. A good way to obtain this information is by asking	....
10	key questions or requesting for their business cards. It's also important to	....
11	keep records about prospective customers. Information can be recorded	....
12	on enquiry cards and followed up with a further contact when you return home.	....

listening

1 🎧 Rick Kent works in the Sales department of MK Precision. Listen to two phone calls he makes. Write one or two words or a number in the numbered spaces on the form or note below. Before you start, read the Task procedure box on page 126, which contains instructions to help with the task.

Conversation 1 You hear Rick call Visionone, a company which makes vehicle lighting.

ORDER FORM — VISIONONE

Customer Name:	Rick Kent	Order date:	Tues, 4.00 p.m.
Company:	MK Precision	Taken by:	Yolanda Anderson

Model and description	Product code	Quantity	Total price $
FL 75 (1).............................	019 0421	2	238
FL 100 Headlights	(2)...................................	4	340

Notes
- Organise delivery of fog-lights with Air Parcel Post. Must arrive by (3).......................... latest. Deliver rest of order in usual way.
- Delivery charge (4)...................................

Conversation 2 You hear Rick call Posnan Exhibition Services, a company which organises trade fairs and conferences.

Posnan Auto Show, July
Checklist
- Exhibitor numbers: Estimate for next show (5)..........................
- Visitor numbers: Last year 15,000
- Breakdown of visitors by nationality: 60% Poland, 40% other (6)........................... countries and the Middle East
- Cost of 40 sq. m: 16,400 Euros. Includes: basic furniture, lighting and electricity, inclusion in the (7)...........................
- Deadline for booking stand: (8)..........................

2 🎧 Listen to the calls again. Which of these strategies do the speakers use in each call to avoid mistakes and misunderstandings with the information during the calls? What phrases do the speakers use?

	Call 1	Call 2
a repeat key facts and figures to check they've been understood	✓	✗
b summarise what they think they've understood		
c correct mistakes immediately they occur		
d ask people to repeat information		

3 Work with a partner. Look at the extract from Visionone's brochure on page 120. Choose one or two items for an order. Take turns to phone the sales department to make your order. Use strategies from exercise 2 to avoid making mistakes with the information.

speaking

tip
- Listen carefully to the other candidate's talk and think of a question that relates back to something he/she said in the talk, e.g.
  I have a question about ...
  You said/mentioned ...
- If you can't think of a question directly related to a specific point in the talk, ask a general question on the topic, e.g.
  I have a general question about ...

1 🎧 In Part 2 of the Speaking test each candidate must ask a question about the other candidate's short talk.
Listen to a candidate giving a talk based on the topic card and complete the missing bullet points.

> **WHAT IS IMPORTANT WHEN ...?**
> Exhibiting at trade fairs
> - staff
> - stand size
> -
> -

2 When you ask your questions, it helps to use a short introductory phrase to relate the question back to the talk. Match each introductory phrase (a–d) with one of the questions (1–4) below.

Introductory phrases
a I have a general question about trade fairs.
b You talked about the importance of training.
c You said position was very important.
d I have a question about follow-up.

Questions
1 Can you say a little bit more about that?
2 What's the best way of getting back in contact with people?
3 Do you think they work equally well for all types of companies?
4 What type of training do you think would be most useful?

3 🎧 Listen to the talk again and prepare another general question on the topic, or a specific question which relates to one of the points in the talk. Use an introductory phrase like the ones in exercise 2.

4 Work in groups of three. Choose one of the topic cards below. Each student has a minute to plan a talk on the chosen topic. Take turns to give your talk. If you would like help with this task, read the Task procedure box on page 129.
Student A: Give your talk. Answer B's question.
Student B: Ask a question about A's talk.
Student C: Decide how appropriate B's question and A's answer were.

Topic card A

> **WHAT IS IMPORTANT WHEN ...?**
> Making sales calls
> - small talk
> - time-keeping
> -
> -

Topic card B

> **WHAT IS IMPORTANT WHEN ...?**
> Selecting people for a sales team
> - personal qualities
> - experience
> -
> -

Topic card C

> **WHAT IS IMPORTANT WHEN ...?**
> Working on a stand at a trade fair
> - appearance
> - body language
> -
> -

writing: a message summarising a phone conversation

1 Your company has received a complaint about some goods which arrived damaged. You don't know if the damage happened before they left your company or during transport. How would you deal with the problem? What solutions would you suggest to the customer?

2 Look at the message which Rick Kent left for his boss, summarising his phone call with Yolanda Anderson at Visionone. Add these words to complete the message.

promised to   wants us to   agreed to

> ## message
>
> to: *Sharon Silverman*
> from: *Rick Kent*
> *I contacted Yolanda Anderson at Visionone and ordered the two fog-lights for Mr Jackson. Delivery is normally six days, but she (1)..................... send them by Air Parcel Post. She (2)..................... get them here by Monday. She (3)..................... pay an extra $25 delivery charge.*

3 Look at the comments arising from a number of different complaints. Write a sentence reporting what was said, using the verb in brackets and these structures.

reporting verb + *to* + verb (e.g. *offer to pay*) or
reporting verb + object + *to* + verb (e.g. *wants us to pay*)

Example
If it would help, I'll fax you through a copy of the order form. (he / offer)
He offered to fax a copy of the order form.

a I'll give you an answer by the end of the day. (she / promise)
b Can you send me a replacement as soon as possible? (he / ask)
c OK, we'll give you a discount of 10%. (she / agree)
d Don't send me the rest of the order. (he / tell)
e I'd like you to take back all the faulty goods. (she / want)

4 You work for MK Precision. The order from Visionone for two fog-lights arrived damaged. Your boss, Sharon Silverman, asked you to contact Yolanda Anderson at Visionone to find out what happened.

Write a message of 40–50 words to your boss to summarise your conversation:

- giving Yolanda's explanation – damaged during transport.
- telling her Yolanda will contact delivery service, Air Parcel Post, for an explanation.
- informing her of Yolanda's solution – send replacement direct to Mr Jackson, the customer, by courier.

unit **11** motivation

vocabulary

1 Work with a partner. Look at the photos of people at work. How can you tell who is motivated and who is demotivated? What do you think are the main factors that create motivation or cause demotivation?

2 These words are often associated with motivation. Match each word (1–7) with its definition and add the words to the table below. Follow the examples.

1 pay package	a extra items offered by the company in addition to salary
2 job security	b holiday which can be taken while still receiving a salary
3 promotion	c the total money and benefits received by an employee
4 paid leave	d moving an employee to a higher level job
5 flexitime	e extra payment, e.g. for good results
6 fringe benefits	f a system where workers have to work a certain number of hours, but choose when they start and finish their work
7 bonus	g being able to rely on a steady job

PAY PACKAGE		THE JOB	
basic pay	*fringe benefits*	**working conditions**	**career prospects**
salary	company car	working hours	job responsibility
....	pension scheme	....	....
	health insurance	....	
	....	workplace layout	
		office equipment	

3 Match these words and phrases with ones from the table above which have the same meaning.

a compensation package   b flexible working hours   c perks

4 Look quickly through the extract on page 87 from a management book on motivation.

a Does it explain what motivation is exactly?
b Does it tell you how to get the best from people?
c Does it tell you how to deal with demotivated people?

Do not pay any attention at this stage to the numbered gaps in the text.

As you read through the text for the first time, you may recognise some of the missing words. Quickly make a note of any word you think you know. Then later when you look at the options for that gap, you can check to see if your word is in the list of options, or has a similar meaning to the word you noted down.

5 Choose the best word to fill each gap from A, B, C or D below. For each question 1–10, mark one letter (A, B, C or D). There is an example at the beginning (0). If you would like help with this task, reread the Task procedure box on page 123.

Motivation in the workplace

There are many (0) ..A..... you can offer to help motivate people and each has different (1) .... Some of the most commonly used are recognition, money, health and help with child care. If you are not in a (2) .... to offer financial incentives like pay rises and (3) .... , it is still possible to motivate staff by ensuring that the non-financial perks you offer are (4) .... to them. For example, you might offer a parking (5) .... to someone who drives to work.

To get the most from your staff, first (6) .... the individuals in the team. That will give you a better idea of the best (7) .... in which to motivate them to (8) .... their maximum potential. To get the best results from your team, it is important to (9) .... each individual's specific skills and talents and treat people on their own (10) .... Also remember that at different stages of their careers, people will be motivated by different things.

0	A incentives	B goals	C inspirations	D persuasions
1	A reasons	B effects	C influences	D conclusions
2	A site	B place	C position	D spot
3	A bonuses	B increases	C profits	D extras
4	A pleasant	B liked	C attractive	D suitable
5	A opening	B hole	C gap	D space
6	A estimate	B calculate	C assess	D value
7	A ways	B means	C methods	D processes
8	A complete	B achieve	C do	D win
9	A admit	B realise	C recognise	D award
10	A rewards	B merits	C rights	D goodness

6 These three people are at very different stages of their careers. Which of the motivational factors below do you think would most influence them, and why?

Name   Marie Besson
Age   24
Status single
Job   Ad Agency Assistant

Name   David Elms
Age   34
Status married with two children, five and eight
Job   Software Engineer

Name   Sheila Pickford
Age   54
Status married with one grown-up son
Job   International Marketing Manager

Motivational factors

- status within the company
- regular promotion opportunities
- plenty of time for a social life
- plenty of time for the family
- flexible working hours
- job security
- rewards in the form of annual bonuses
- high levels of responsibility
- lively office environment

1 Work with a partner. Look at the title of the article below. Discuss what you think it means. Then read the article quickly and check your ideas.

2 How quickly can you find the answers to these questions?

a Do many people find fulfilment at work?

b How do psychologists explain high levels of stress and dissatisfaction at work?

c How does the writer define skills?

d How does the writer define motivations?

What makes you tick?

Whether it's drinking a coffee with friends, or climbing mountains, finding out what you like doing and what you're good at is the key to having a job that satisfies you.

[1] We spend a lot of time doing it, often in the company of relative strangers. Sometimes we do it alone, and sometimes people don't even like doing it. (0)....*G*.... Ladies and gentlemen we are talking about work.

[2] A recent study showed that 90% of people are unhappy at work. We work hard to earn money, to maintain a certain standard of living, but too many of us rely on adding quality to our lives outside working hours, partly to compensate for the poor quality of our life at work. (1)..................... For example, one man in his thirties enjoys creating, working with his hands and being outdoors. His job, however, involves repetition, strict hours and deadlines, using a computer and working in an office. (2)................... Net result? Unhappiness at work.

[3] Psychologists talk about the importance of having a good or bad 'fit' between you and the job you have. A lot of people have a bad 'fit', but don't realise it; they just know they feel stressed and unhappy. One of the keys to finding the right job in the right career is to discover what your main skills and motivations are. (3)...................

[4] So what are these skills and motivations? Skills are the things you are good at doing, the result of your natural aptitudes and the experience you have gained in putting them to use in your career so far. If you are born with or acquire aptitudes through learning, then you strengthen them through practice. (4)..................... This is why choosing the right career is so important – because it makes life less stressful.

[5] Motivations are often a combination of factors that lead to the satisfaction of your desires and appetites. They are the things that inspire you and keep you interested. (5)..................... In short, motivations are the things you like doing, skills are the things you are good at. If you can find a job that uses both, you're on your way to a career you love.

tip When you have completed the task, read through the whole text with the missing sentences in place to check that it makes sense.

3 Read the article again and choose the best sentence from A–G to fill each of the gaps. Do not use any letter more than once. Before you start, read the Task procedure box on page 122, which contains instructions to help with the task.

A When you know that, you can confidently identify which jobs in which career will suit you best.

B Many people are unhappy in their careers and jobs because they are not doing the things they like, in the kind of contexts that they enjoy.

C Enjoying your work makes the learning experience seem easier, so you actually acquire a greater range of skills faster.

D They are the answers that you'll give to questions such as *What do I enjoy? What does success mean for me?*

E Once you know what it is, you increase your chance of finding the right job, in the perfect career.

F The things that really motivate him are not being used in the type of work that he does, and the job demands motivation and skills which he doesn't have.

G When we're not doing it, we're thinking about it, worrying because we haven't got it, or worrying because we have got it and hate it.

4 Which reference words in sentences A–G helped you to fit them in the gaps? Which words in the text do they refer to?

5 Find words in paragraphs 4 and 5 which have these meanings.

a the natural ability to learn something fast and do it well (plural noun)

b to learn or develop something, e.g. a skill (verb)

c make stronger (verb)

d give somebody new and creative ideas (verb)

6 When people become demotivated at work or during their studies, what do you think would help to improve the situation?

language in use: the -*ing* form

1 Look at these sentences about the article on page 88. Match each sentence with one of the uses of the -*ing* form (a–e).

1 90% of people are unhappy in their jobs because they are not <u>doing</u> the things they like.

2 His job involves <u>using</u> a computer and <u>working</u> in an office.

3 <u>Enjoying</u> your work makes it easier to learn.

4 One of the keys to <u>finding</u> the right job in the right career is to discover what your main skills and motivations are.

5 Skills are the things you are good at <u>doing</u>.

a after certain verbs
b as the participle in the continuous tense
c after a noun and a preposition
d after an adjective and preposition
e as the noun and subject of the sentence

2 Look through the article and sentences A–G. Complete the table.

verb (+ preposition) + -*ing* form	involve, rely on ....
noun + preposition + -*ing* form	the keys to ....
adjective + preposition + -*ing* form	....

3 Work with a partner. Student A: Look at the tip below for improving job satisfaction and complete it with the -*ing* form of these verbs. Student B: Look at page 120. When you're ready, exchange information about the tips.

be   enjoy   have   make   spend   take

Have more fun at work

All this emphasis on (1) .... successful at work could mean you are (2) .... life a little too seriously. If you are (3) .... most of your time at work, it's a good idea to find ways of (4) .... yourself while you are there. You need to create opportunities for (5) .... fun, but that doesn't mean (6) .... jokes every two seconds.

See grammar reference page 136

Reading Part 5

In most lines of the text there is one extra word. If a line is correct, write CORRECT. If there is an extra word in the line, write it in CAPITAL LETTERS. If you would like help with this task, reread the Task procedure box on page 123.

The right look for the job

0	How you look means a lot at work and experts agree that making a change	*CORRECT*
00	in your appearance can alter the way how your colleagues relate to you and	...*HOW*...
1	how you see yourself. Changing your appearance it doesn't necessarily	....
2	mean going to work in a formal business suit. One woman I know had been	....
3	dressed conservatively for six years and then started wearing more casual	....
4	clothes. However, if you don't intend to stay in your job for long time, avoid	....
5	spending a lot on a new image that could be totally wrong in your next job.	....
6	Often it is the people you work with who have influence how you feel	....
7	about your job. There will always be people who are difficult to deal with	....
8	them. Tactics for dealing with difficult colleagues include keeping your	....
9	relationship as professional as possible, concentrating on do the task	....
10	rather than the person, and being clear up about what you need from them.	....

listening

1 Read the complaints below that some employees have about their jobs. Match each complaint (1–8) with one of the causes of dissatisfaction (A–H) in exercise 2.

1 I'd like a job with more responsibility, but there are very few managerial posts available. *E*

2 I find the work rather boring.

3 They don't pay me enough.

4 All I do is work, work, work.

5 There are always rumours that jobs are going to be cut.

6 Nobody appreciates the amount of work I do.

7 I haven't got anything in common with my colleagues.

8 My office hasn't got any natural light.

Listening Part 2

tip

Remember! Each recording will contain some information designed to distract you. Sometimes this information will include words or phrases that are also used in an option. This is not necessarily the correct option.

2 🎧 You will hear five short recordings of people at Premier Solutions, a computer software company, talking about their lack of satisfaction with their jobs. For each recording, decide which is the main cause of dissatisfaction. Write one letter (A–H) next to the number of the recording. Do not use any letter more than once. If you would like help with this task, reread the Task procedure box on page 126.

1	A unsatisfactory working environment
2	B long working hours
3	C low salary
4	D lack of job interest
5	E lack of promotion opportunities
	F lack of job security
	G unsatisfactory relationships with colleagues
	H lack of recognition for work

3 🎧 Work in groups. Listen to two of the people again. What could you do to improve their job satisfaction?

1 Brainstorm some ideas.

2 Discuss each of your ideas.

3 Present your result to the other groups.

speaking

1 You are going to complete a questionnaire to discover the right job for you. Finish statements a and b with four different answers, each of which applies to you right now. Answer as honestly and quickly as you can.

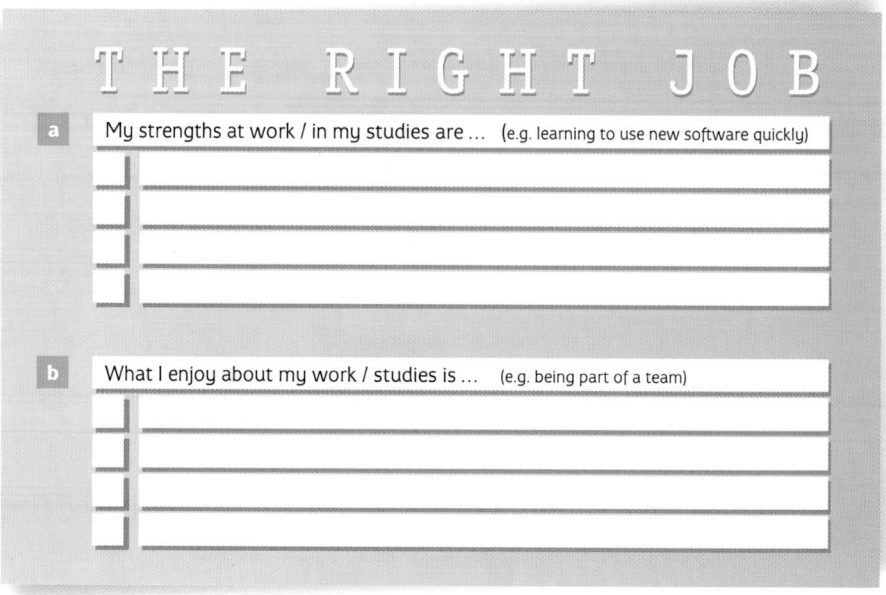

THE RIGHT JOB

a My strengths at work / in my studies are ... (e.g. learning to use new software quickly)

b What I enjoy about my work / studies is ... (e.g. being part of a team)

2 Rank your answers to a in exercise 1 in order (1 = most important). This will tell you what your skills are. Then do the same for b, which tells you about your motivations.

3 Work with a partner. Take turns to explain your ranking for each of the two points. Encourage each other to be as specific as possible by asking for more details and examples.

4 Interview each other to find out the four things you dislike about your work or studies and then fill in the card below. This will give you some ideas about the things you need to change or avoid.

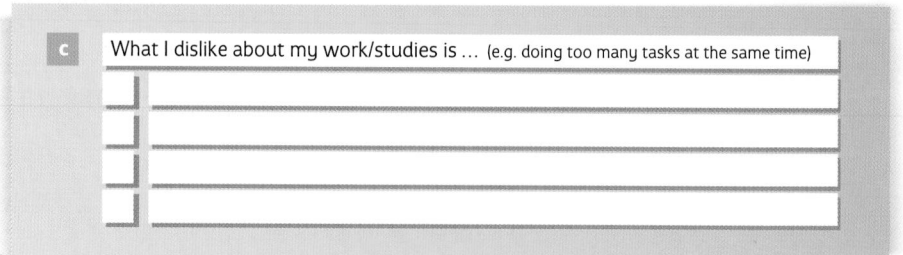

c What I dislike about my work/studies is ... (e.g. doing too many tasks at the same time)

5 Prepare a short presentation (one or two minutes). Include information about these points.
- what you've discovered about your skills and motivations
- any ideas about how you could change your job so that you enjoy it more, or the kind of job you should be looking for

Then find another partner and take turns in giving your presentation.

writing: a letter requesting information

1 Look at the brochure below from a company called Business Challenge. What type of training does it offer? Is training like this common in your country?

Writing Part 2

2 You work for Premier Solutions. They plan to run a series of team building events to improve staff morale. Your boss, David Reece, has asked you to write to Business Challenge.

Read Business Challenge's brochure and a message your boss left you, on which you have made some notes. Work with a partner. Put the notes in a logical order to make a plan for the letter. Then compare your plan with other students.

3 Using all your notes, write a letter to Business Challenge. Write 120–140 words. If you would like help with this task, reread the Task procedure box on page 125.

ask for proposal and costing - 28 April latest

Came across this company. Think it could be just what we need. Can you get an idea of what they can offer and likely costs for a two-day event for 30 people, in the next three months? I think we're talking groups of 8-10. I need info urgently for Departmental Managers' meeting on 1 May.

Thanks

David

explain requirements - NB end September deadline all training!

say how we heard about them

Business Challenge

TEAM BUILDING

Make your staff teams more effective

Send them on a residential Team Challenge. Co-operative activities include: hill walking, canoeing, bridge-building, whitewater rafting. They will be given objectives to reach, problems to solve, and all against the clock.

Contact us and we will work together to plan your ideal course.

express interest

say what we do and need

unit 12 customer service

vocabulary

1 Work with a partner. Discuss the questions below and decide which answer, a, b or c, you think is the most likely.

1 How much more do you think it costs to attract a new customer than to keep an existing one?
   a twice as much   b five times as much   c ten times as much

2 For every official complaint a company receives, how many other unhappy customers do you think there are who don't actually complain?
   a 1–10   b 10–20   c over 20

3 On average, how many friends, family members or colleagues do you think an unhappy customer tells about his or her problem with a company?
   a four or five   b nine or ten   c about twenty

4 Of the customers who do complain, how many do you think will do business with the same company again if their complaint is dealt with quickly and successfully?
   a over 90%   b 50–90%   c less than 50%

2 Check your ideas with your teacher. Are you surprised by any of the answers? If so, why? What conclusions can you draw about the importance of customer service from these statistics?

3 Look at the four comments (a–d) from customer service staff below. Which cartoon does each comment go with?

a 'I'll be with you in a moment.'
b 'I suppose you want the same as usual?'
c 'Yes, but not in *sea* water. Didn't you read what it says here?'
d 'I'm afraid the guarantee expired yesterday, so I'll have to charge you. Why didn't you take out one of our five-year guarantees?'

4 Match one of the titles (a–d) with each cartoon in exercise 3.

    a How not to deal with after-sales service
    b How not to deal with loyal customers
    c How not to deal with product returns
    d How not to deal with customers at the point of sale

5 Three of the titles above include typical adjective + noun or noun + noun combinations related to customer service. Rewrite them in the table below. Follow the example.

noun + noun		adjective + noun	
..after-sales..	service	....	customer
....	returns	....	products/goods
service	engineers		
service	....		
....	period		
customer	care/service		
customer	....		
customer	....		
....	policy		
....	business		

6 Match the words (a–g) with the definitions (1–7). Then use the words to complete the noun + noun and adjective + noun combinations in the table in exercise 5.

    a contract   c guarantee   e refund   g satisfaction
    b faulty   d loyalty   f repeat

    1 a written promise by a company to repair or replace a product free of charge, within a specific period of time
    2 a feeling of happiness or pleasure with what you've got
    3 money given back to somebody because they are not satisfied with the goods or services they have paid for
    4 the quality of maintaining support for something
    5 not working properly
    6 a formal written agreement between two or more groups which says what each must do
    7 happening again

7 Use some of the combinations from the table in exercise 5 to complete the two extracts on customer care. Follow the examples.

Extract 1

> **New** (1)......refund policy........
>
> It has come to our attention that customers are not happy with the way we deal with (2)............................... . Accordingly, from next month, all customers will be offered an automatic refund on (3)...................................... , provided they are returned to the shop within 30 days of purchase. We believe this will encourage (4)...................................... and increase the amount of (5)...................................... we get.

Extract 2

> To improve our (6).customer satisfaction. we are extending the (7)...................................... on all our equipment to two years. All customers will receive free (8)...................................... during this period. Thereafter, they may take out a (9)...................................... with us. This will provide 24-hour telephone support and advice through our call centre, and free maintenance and repairs by our team of (10)...................................... .

1 Have you ever had difficulties contacting a big company at a call centre? Discuss your experiences with a partner.

2 🎧 You will hear three telephone conversations. Write one or two words or a number in the numbered spaces on the notes or forms below. If you would like help with this task, reread the Task procedure box on page 126.

Conversation 1 (Questions 1–4)

Look at the note below. You will hear someone phoning an airline office.

> Tom
> Tried three times to get through to Swiftjet to book
> flights to Geneva at Christmas, but all I got was
> recorded messages! I still don't know the (1)...........................
> times, as it seems the (2)........................... has not come
> into operation yet. Could you have a look on their
> (3)........................... this evening? It could be quicker, and
> they'll give us (4)........................... off if we book on-line.
> Thanks,
> Jenny

Conversation 2 (Questions 5–8)

Look at the form below. You will hear a man phoning the call centre of an Internet Service Provider.

CUSTOMER SERVICE ACTION FORM		
Customer Douglas Johnson	**Time and Date**	3.10 p.m., 28 Sep
	Originator	Sharon
User name douglasj	**Department**	General Enquiries

Situation requiring action

The customer waited (5)........................... before his call was answered.
His enquiry was about accessing his e-mail from (6)........................... .
He felt it was unclear which (7)........................... would handle this enquiry
and so he was unable to choose which of the (8)........................... on the
recorded menu was the most appropriate.

Suggested action

Conversation 3 (Questions 9–12)

Look at the form below. You will hear a man phoning a Technical Support Centre.

ACE TECHNICAL SUPPORT LOG	
ACE Technical Support Call Log	
Date	10 August
Time	08.17
Call taken by	Jason
Customer reference number	Not given
Customer contact name	Rod Weaver
Position	(9)...........................
Company name	(10)...........................
Problem	(11)........................... in factory not functioning
Diagnostic self-test performed?	not working
Results of diagnostic self-test	none
Action taken	referred to (12)........................... Manager for immediate action

language in use: third conditional and past modals

1 🎧 You will hear an extract from Conversation 2 on page 98 again. As you listen, fill in the missing words.

Customer I'm going abroad for a couple of months and I want to know if I can still use my usual e-mail address while I'm away.

Sharon I see. You .... button two. That's Accounts and Billing.

Customer Yes, well if .... that was the department I needed, I ....

2 Answer these questions about the extract.
   a Did the customer press button two?
   b Did he know which department he needed?

3 Look at the example of the third conditional in exercise 1. What verb forms do you use? Complete the table.

function	verb form	
	if clause	result clause
links an impossible situation to its result		

4 Match the phrases (a and b) below with the idea they express (1 and 2).
   a He should have pressed button 2.
   b He could have made an official complaint, but he decided not to.
   1 He had the opportunity to do this, but he didn't take it.
   2 This was the right thing to do, but he didn't do it.

5 Look back at the four cartoons on page 94 and complete the sentences using the third conditional. Follow the example.

   Example
   Cartoon 1 If the customer had read the instructions, *she would have taken the watch off before going in the sea.*

   She wouldn't have bought the watch if she had known it wasn't completely waterproof.

Cartoon 2 If the guarantee hadn't expired, the woman …
Perhaps she would have taken out a five-year guarantee if …

Cartoon 3 The customer would not have felt angry if …
If I had been in the customer's position, …

Cartoon 4 The waiter would probably have been more polite if the customer …
If the head waiter had not been so excited about his new customer, …

6 Work with a partner. Talk about how the customer service could have been better in each cartoon. Follow the example.

   Example
   Cartoon 1

   A *I think the assistant **should have told** her not to use the watch in the sea.*

   B *Or at least she **could have suggested** that she read the instructions first.*

7 🎧 Listen again to the three conversations you heard in the Listening section of this unit. How would you rate the customer service in each call? Complete the table.

Company	Standard of customer service			
	very good	good	fair	poor
Swiftjet				
Interserve				
ACE				

8 Compare your ratings with a partner and discuss the reasons for your choices. Use third conditional sentences and past modal forms where appropriate.

   Example
   A *I've only rated them fair because I think the customer should have got through to a person faster.*

   B *But she didn't wait that long. She could have hung on a bit longer. She had the right line, so if she'd done so, she'd have been able to book her flights.*

See grammar reference pages 136 and 137

speaking

During the exam, don't worry if the interviewer interrupts you when you are giving your short talk. This means that you have already spoken for a minute, not that you have done something wrong.

1 Work in groups of three. Student A look at Topic card A, Student B Topic card B and Student C Topic card C. You have a minute to write down some ideas about the topic.

Topic card A

> **WHAT IS IMPORTANT WHEN ...?**
>
> Setting up a customer satisfaction programme
>
> • feedback from customers
> • rewards for loyal customers
> •
> •

Topic card B

> **WHAT IS IMPORTANT WHEN ...?**
>
> Training customer service staff
>
> • telephone techniques
> • face to face communication
> •
> •

Topic card C

> **WHAT IS IMPORTANT WHEN ...?**
>
> Dealing with customers at the point of sale
>
> • attitude of staff
> • refund policy
> •
> •

2 You are going to practise Speaking Part 2. Student C plays the role of Interviewer.

Interviewer   Invite A to speak for a minute on his/her chosen topic. (Stop him/her after a minute). Then invite B to ask A a question about the talk. When A and B have finished, give A some feedback. Remember to say some positive things, not just to criticise errors! Tell him/her:
  • if the talk was relevant and well organised.
  • what grammar and vocabulary he/she used correctly and appropriately.
  • if there were any points of grammar or vocabulary that could be improved.
  • if there were any serious problems caused by his/her pronunciation.

Student A   Speak for a minute. Answer B's question.
Student B   Ask a question when A has finished speaking.

3 Change roles and repeat the steps until each person has played every role.

writing: a memo reporting on a problem

1 Do you know what a *mystery shopper* is? How do you think staff would react if they knew their company was using a mystery shopper?

Writing Part 1

tip

For the writing tasks in the exam, try to divide the time so that there is time to plan, draft, edit and finally check your writing.

2 You are the Customer Service Director of a chain of department stores. Sales in your Birmingham store have been going down for several months. You sent a mystery shopper to find out what was going on.

Write a memo of 40–50 words to the Personnel Director and the Training Manager:

- reminding them of the problem.
- explaining the mystery shopper's findings – staff not interested in helping customers and unhappy in their jobs.
- suggesting that you meet to talk about possible solutions.

If you would like help with this task, reread the Task procedure box on page 124.

3 Work in groups of three. When you've written your memo, pass it on to the next person. Following the checklist below, write suggestions in the margin of each memo.

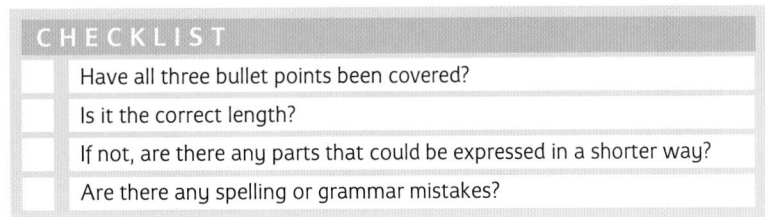

CHECKLIST	
	Have all three bullet points been covered?
	Is it the correct length?
	If not, are there any parts that could be expressed in a shorter way?
	Are there any spelling or grammar mistakes?

4 When you have received all the comments from your group, revise your memo.

unit 13 business ethics

vocabulary

1 The photos (1–5) below illustrate a company's relationships with different organisations and groups of people. Match one of the titles (a–e) with the photos.

a Suppliers   d Banks and other providers of money
b Customers   e The environment and the wider public
c Employees

a company

2 When dealing with these groups of people, companies must think about both *ethics* and *legislation*. Match each of these words with its definition (a or b).

a The things that a country has decided must or must not be done. When doing business internationally, a company must consider both its own laws and those of the other countries it operates in.

b The things that a group of people has decided should or should not be done. When doing business internationally, a company must remember that different countries may have different ideas about what behaviour and business practices are acceptable.

3 Complete the quotes (1–8) below with one of the words or phrases (a–h).

a bribery   c child labour   e made redundant   g shareholders
b charities   d equal opportunities   f pollution   h sweatshops

1 'When I went out to visit our factory there, I discovered they were using .... : some of the workers were as young as ten years old!'

2 'We really wanted that government building contract, so my boss told me to take the politician and his wife on a free weekend trip to Paris. I said that was .... , but he told me to keep quiet and do what he said.'

3 'The company believes in .... , and I think it's done well in that area – when I joined ten years ago only two of the managers were women, and now we have eight female managers.'

4 'I work for a construction company. Most of our work involves building houses, so I think it's appropriate that we give some of our profits to .... for homeless people.'

5 'My boss persuaded a lot of her friends to invest their money in her company when she set it up, so I don't think she should spend so much on entertaining potential customers. After all, they're the .... , so they should be consulted about the money that she's spending.'

6 'The company was hoping to win a big contract in Saudi Arabia, but they didn't get it, so that was it – all of the factory workers were .... , even the ones who'd worked there for twenty years or more.'

7 'I used to swim in this river when I was a child, but the .... from that new factory means I wouldn't let my own children do that now.'

8 'Our sports clothes were really fashionable until the public discovered that most of them were made in .... in the Far East. When the news came out about the terrible working conditions and bad pay in these factories, our sales declined dramatically.'

4 Which groups of people listed in exercise 1 are affected by the ethical situations in each quote (1–8)?

5 In what ways could the opinions of the groups in exercise 1 affect the ethical decisions of an international fast-food retailer?

6 Complete the text below using the words and phrases below. Use each word or phrase once only.

animal welfare   food retailers   packaging materials
customer demand   issues   policy
employees   labour practices
environmental damage   local cultures

McDONALD'S AND SOCIAL RESPONSIBILITY

The international fast-food chain McDonald's has been attacked for everything from the quality of its food and its treatment of (1).............................. to its impact on (2).............................. and the environment. Now the company has published a 46-page social responsibility report which addresses many of these (3).............................. ,

summarising its activities and goals under four headings: community, environment, people, and the wider marketplace. The last heading includes (4)..............................
at McDonald's suppliers.

In the past few years, the company has been working closely with pressure groups and independent scientists to try to minimise (5).............................. . In this latest report, the company points out that it has a long-standing (6).............................. not to buy

beef from rainforest lands. It also says it is investigating buying paper from sustainable forests and is testing new (7)..............................
other than paper or plastic.

The company has also been working on improving (8).............................. .
In response to (9)..............................
and pressure from animal rights activists, McDonald's has set new US standards, for example on the way chickens are housed, that other leading (10)..............................
are following.

1 Work with a partner. What do you think a company might include in its code of ethics? Then read the first paragraph of the article below and compare the writer's answers with your suggestions.

Reading Part 3

2 Read the full article and the questions on page 105. For each question 1–6, mark one letter (A, B, C or D) for the answer you choose. If you would like help with this task, reread the Task procedure box on page 123.

Ethics count

Ali King on secondment in Madurai, Southern India.

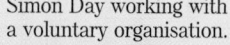

Simon Day working with a voluntary organisation.

[1] Bored with lining your boss's pockets? Want to work for a company you feel is doing some good in the world? Join the club. Research shows that nowadays employers' ethics are often the deciding factor when someone opts for a particular post. Increasingly, companies in Britain are responding to this situation by drawing up codes of ethics so that current and prospective staff can see how seriously they take their moral responsibilities. A typical code will address corporate policy towards its various stakeholders: employees, shareholders, customers, suppliers and the wider public. Standards relating to suppliers frequently include a commitment to ensuring that there is no child labour at any stage of the supply chain, and that wages and working hours are reasonable.

[2] As part of their code, some companies, including chain store Marks & Spencer, have joined the Ethical Trading Initiative (ETI), 'a membership body that exists to set standards for labour within supply chains,' explains David Steele, its Information Officer. Other employers send inspectors on regular visits to check the ethical standards and practices of all their suppliers of goods and services – whether in east London or the Far East.

[3] 'Recently there have been a lot of documentaries highlighting conditions in factories overseas, as well as on issues like child labour in this country. As a result, workers are now taking a broader interest in the companies for which they work,' claims David Steele. 'The fact that the Internet has created a global economy is also significant. We no longer think of a sweatshop in Korea as being so far away.'

[4] Nevertheless, research also shows that some employers write a code of ethics simply to enhance their image. Upon closer inspection, there may be little real commitment. 'That's why candidates who care about ethical issues should ask at the interview stage not only whether there is a code, but whether they can see it,' advises Rachel Ormond, an academic researcher in ethics and employment. 'It should exist in document form, and in many cases it is now included on the company website.'

[5] 'You might also want to ask whether your prospective employer encourages staff to get involved in giving something back to society,' she adds. Employees sometimes do voluntary work, for example, either wholly or partly in company time, and usually on projects initiated by the company. The financial services provider Zurich sends staff on one-month secondments to help with projects in India. Marks & Spencer sets up 100-hour part-time secondments for staff who want to get involved with local community projects.

[6] However, it is not only in order to present themselves as caring employers that companies are becoming increasingly concerned about ethical issues. Professor Malcolm McIntosh of Warwick University Corporate Citizenship Unit explains that in our rapidly changing world, organisations need to have values. Now, he says, businesses have to take responsibility for such matters as human rights, environmental impact and social responsibility. 'Business does not operate in a vacuum. The rules of the game are such that we have to be aware of all stakeholders, customers, staff and the communities in which companies operate. You can't make money unless you understand people's values.'

1 In paragraph 1, why does the writer say some companies are introducing codes of ethics?
   A to help attract new employees
   B to encourage their staff to behave ethically
   C to prove to suppliers that they treat their staff well
   D to help improve their employees' working conditions

2 The Ethical Trading Initiative's objective is to
   A advise companies about ethical issues and check on ethical standards.
   B ensure acceptable pay and working conditions for everyone involved in producing goods.
   C improve the quality of goods sold by its members.
   D make sure suppliers behave ethically.

3 David Steele believes people are more aware of ethical issues nowadays
   A because of the efforts of the organisation he works for.
   B because of media coverage of these issues.
   C because some well-known companies have drawn up codes of ethics.
   D because they buy goods from foreign suppliers over the Internet.

4 Job candidates should ask to see a company's code of ethics because
   A some companies haven't yet written one.
   B the company may be pretending to have one.
   C it may not be posted on the company's website.
   D the company may not really care about ethical issues.

5 Some companies now encourage their employees
   A to do charity work in their spare time.
   B to go abroad in order to get job experience.
   C to help people during their working hours.
   D to work for one month in the local community.

6 According to Professor McIntosh, paying attention to ethical issues will
   A help companies adapt to a changing world.
   B teach companies social responsibility.
   C improve companies' public image.
   D help companies stay profitable.

3 Find words or phrases in the text which have these meanings.
   a Paragraph 1 chooses (verb + preposition)
   b Paragraph 1 people who have an interest, but not necessarily a financial one, in a company (plural noun)
   c Paragraph 2 a network of companies which provide goods or services to other companies which sell to the public (noun + noun combination)
   d Paragraph 4 improve (verb)
   e Paragraph 6 beliefs about what practices and types of behaviour are right (plural noun)

4 Work with a partner. Discuss the benefits of doing voluntary work in the company's time for these three groups.
   - for the company itself
   - for the employees who volunteer
   - for the community

language in use: articles

1 The sentences (1–4) below are from the reading text on page 104. Focus on the underlined words in the sentences and match them with their meanings (a or b).

a a specific firm or firms
b firms in general or an unspecified firm

1 Want to work for <u>a company</u> you feel is doing some good in the world?
2 Workers are now taking a broader interest in <u>the companies</u> for which they work.
3 Employees sometimes do voluntary work ... usually on projects initiated by <u>the company</u>.
4 Increasingly, <u>companies</u> in Britain are ... drawing up codes of ethics ...

2 There are two articles in English: the indefinite article (*a/an*) and the definite article (*the*). Sometimes no article is used (*0*). Look again at sentences 1–4 in exercise 1 and complete the table with *a/an*, *the* or *0*. Follow the example.

	general reference	specific reference
countable nouns in the singular		the
countable nouns in the plural		

3 Which form (*a/an* or *0*) is used for general reference with uncountable nouns, e.g. *research* and with plural nouns, e.g. *goods*?

4 In this internal memo some articles are used incorrectly. Decide which are correct and change any that are wrong. The nouns have been underlined to help you.

Memo

<u>Team</u> of <u>consultants</u> is conducting a <u>survey</u> for us about ethical issues at the <u>work</u>. <u>Questionnaires</u> will be sent to everyone in a <u>company</u> next week. Please complete and return <u>questionnaire</u> to <u>head</u> of your department by Friday 20 March. <u>Results</u> of <u>survey</u> will be published in a <u>company newsletter</u> in May.

5 Look at paragraphs 2, 3 and 5 of the text on page 104. Find the items below and note which form of the article is used with each.
a company names   c an organisation / official body's name
b names of countries

See grammar reference page 137

6 The text below is about Richer Sounds, a retailer which gives a lot of help to charities. Add articles where needed in the gaps, or write *0* if no article is needed.

Giving something back

Until some years ago, each month (1)................... directors of (2)................... Richer Sounds would look at every request for donations that had been sent in and would send off (3)................... cheques to any causes they felt deserved (4)................... help. Then (5)................... company decided it should take (6)................... more active role and set up (7)................... foundation to support (8)................... charities. All their staff are actively encouraged to suggest new causes which are close to their own hearts. For example, two employees knew (9)................... people who had suffered serious injuries to their spines. (10)................... employees suggested (11)................... foundation should contact (12)................... Spinal Injuries Association to see how it could help. Thanks to (13)................... money which (14)................... foundation gave them, (15)................... charity was able to set up (16)................... telephone helpline for (17)................... people with (18)................... spinal injuries.

listening

Listening Part 2

tip
Remember that Listening Part 2 contains *two* sections of multiple matching questions.

1 🎧 You will hear five short recordings in which people are talking about ethical issues. For each recording, decide which issue the speaker is talking about. Write one letter (A–H) next to the number of the recording. Do not use any letter more than once. If you would like help with this task, reread the Task procedure box on page 126.

1 ....
2 ....
3 ....
4 ....
5 ....

A equal opportunities
B ethical trading
C offering bribes
D accepting bribes
E employee misusing company property
F child labour
G environmental pollution
H employees' working conditions

2 🎧 Sometimes, by trying to act ethically, companies create other problems for themselves. You will hear three of the recordings again. This time, listen and complete each of the following sentences with a word or words you hear in the recordings.

a We don't want to employ children, but without their .... , many families would not be able to survive.

b We don't agree with bribery, but we don't want our suppliers to feel .... if we refuse their gifts.

c We want our suppliers to be paid a fair wage. However, this means that our shareholders make smaller .... and our .... pay a little more for our products.

3 Read the headlines (a–c) about three ethical initiatives and match them with the three photos (1–3) which represent the potential negative impact of such initiatives. Can you think of any other situations in which trying to behave ethically may create other problems?

b **Unsafe chemical plant closed down at last**

a **HYDRO-ELECTRIC POWER STATION brings cheap, clean energy to the area**

c **Survey shows huge rise in public demand for organically-grown food**

speaking

Speaking Part 3

1 Work in groups of four. Students A and B: see below. Students C and D: Look at page 121. If you would like help with this task, reread the Task procedure box on page 129.

Student A: You are going to play the role of the examiner. Students C and D are going to discuss the problem below. Your teacher will give you copies of the task sheet to give to them. Ask them to speak for three minutes and give them 30 seconds to prepare. When three minutes have passed, stop them. Ask one or two follow-up questions from the list below.

tip It makes it easier to communicate with your partner if you look at him/her during your discussion, not at the examiner.

An ethical problem

Your company recently received a letter from a member of the public saying that one of your foreign suppliers employs child labour. Your company has worked with this supplier for a long time, has always had a good relationship with them and thought they knew you don't approve of child labour.

Discuss the situation together and decide:

- how you could find out if the story is true or not.
- what you should do if it turns out to be true.

Follow-up questions

- What ethical situations in business concern you most?
- Would you buy goods if you knew children had helped to make them?
- Are there any products you never buy for ethical reasons?

Student B: You are going to assess Student C and D's interactive communication. Use the checklist below to help you. When C and D have finished the discussion and answered one or two extra questions, give them feedback, politely, about what they did well, and any areas which could be improved.

CHECKLIST		
Did each of them:	C	D
take an active part in the discussion?		
take turns to speak?		
listen to each other's ideas and opinions?		
ask the other person to explain or clarify his/her ideas if necessary?		
express agreement or disagreement politely and appropriately?		

2 Swap roles. Students A and B are the candidates. Students C and D interview them.

writing: a report on progress

1   You are the assistant to the Press and Information Officer of a large company. You and she have been involved in drawing up the company's first code of ethics and now have to report on progress to the department heads.

Read the memo and the 'To do' list below, on which your boss has made some notes. Then, using all the notes, write your report. Write 120–140 words.

MEMO

From	Vanessa Currie, Press and Information Officer
To	You
Re	The company's code of ethics

Have to go to an urgent press conference! Can you write the report for the department heads, please? Let them know what we've done so far and what we're going to do next, and include my suggestion for the sales staff and buyers. I attach some quick notes I've made for you on my checklist.

TO DO

Circulation
Send the code to all employees in the form of booklets.   *done*

Annual Report
Reproduce a copy of the code in the report to let the   *will go in next report*
shareholders know we care about and act on ethical matters.

Spanish and Italian done – French next
Translation
See that the code is translated for use in our Spanish, Italian and French sales subsidiaries.

Distribution
Distribute copies of the code to business partners (suppliers, customers, etc.) so they know how we feel about bribery, child labour, etc.   *extra copies given to purchasing and sales staff – suggest they distribute them*

---

2   Use the checklist below to help you check your report after you've written it.

CHECKLIST	
	Does the report have a title?
	Is it divided into sections with headings?
	Is the length correct?
	Are articles (a/an, the, 0) correctly used?
	Are the verb tenses correct? e.g. The code has been translated into Spanish (not ~~The code is translated into Spanish~~)
	Do verbs agree with their subjects? e.g. Booklets have been circulated to all staff (not ~~Booklets has been circulated to all staff~~)
	Is the spelling correct?

unit 14 new directions

vocabulary

1 Combine the words below to make three terms for different systems of working. Match each term with a definition, then with one of the three photos.

home-   desking
hot-   conferencing
video-   working

a people work in an office, but don't have their own desk
b a system which allows people in different locations to communicate using images
c people work at home, often at a computer, and communicate by telephone and via a modem

2 Match these words with A–D on the photos.

1 workstation   2 mobile phone   3 storage   4 desktop computer

3 Which of the systems of working shown in the photos have these benefits? Some go with more than one photo.

a reduces travel costs for the company
b leads to a more economical use of office space
c reduces the time spent commuting for employees
d allows companies to reduce costs for premises
e makes it possible for employees to work remotely
f improves team work and co-operation in an office
g makes it easier for people in different countries to communicate

4 Words to describe flexible working often begin with the prefix *tele-* which means *at or over a long distance*. It can be attached to many nouns or verbs. Work with a partner to complete these definitions. What other *tele-* words do you know?

a Tele.............................. : A general term describing any way of working at a distance using a combination of computers and telecommunications.

b Tele.............................. : Another term, common in the US, describing a way of working at a distance using a combination of computers and telecommunications. The emphasis is on doing away with the journey to work.

c Tele.............................. : Holding a 'virtual' meeting with participants in different locations, either via telephone or video.

d Tele.............................. : A building, usually in the country, equipped with computers so that people can work without travelling to an ordinary office in a town.

Reading Part 4

5 Read the text below about hot-desking. Choose the best word to fill each gap from A, B, C or D below. For each question 1–14, mark one letter (A, B, C, or D). There is an example at the beginning (0). If you would like help with this task, reread the Task procedure box on page 123.

No place to call your own

With rental costs for offices increasing, the (0) ....*B*.......... use of space is an issue for every firm. Estimates suggest that the (1) .... office worker spends more than six weeks away from their desk each year, so there are good (2) .... for giving up the traditional idea of a personal desk and a filing (3) .... for each employee. Thanks to the recent advances in ICT (Information and Communication Technology), many companies are now (4) .... the idea of 'hot-desking'. Workers can sit at any (5) .... desk and work by (6) .... the company's computer network through the desktop computer at that (7) .... , or by (8) .... in their personal laptop computer. As messages and other documents are available at a keystroke, paper is either eliminated, or (9) .... to only what is needed immediately and can be carried. Group work sessions and meetings are (10) .... in specially designed rooms or in comfortably furnished open areas. In (11) .... to the financial benefits, some companies say hot-desking has improved their staff's productivity by fifty per cent or more. Employees generally (12) .... well to the flexibility and informality. Many say that hot-desking means they (13) .... more with their colleagues and that teamwork becomes easier when they are not (14) .... in separate offices.

0 A sensible	B efficient	C capable	D professional
1 A usual	B standard	C regular	D average
2 A reasons	B results	C ideas	D chances
3 A box	B cabinet	C folder	D shelf
4 A adopting	B choosing	C agreeing	D preferring
5 A open	B abandoned	C absent	D vacant
6 A entering	B accessing	C opening	D admitting
7 A workstation	B workplace	C worktop	D workshop
8 A filling	B putting	C plugging	D switching
9 A limited	B controlled	C defined	D reserved
10 A done	B held	C given	D made
11 A keeping	B contrast	C comparison	D addition
12 A answer	B reply	C respond	D report
13 A contact	B transact	C react	D interact
14 A lonely	B isolated	C distant	D remote

6 Work in groups. Would you like to work in the type of office described in exercise 5? Why / Why not?

Flexible working

1 Yesterday's buildings and yesterday's office environments are increasingly difficult to use efficiently. (0)...*G*.... Staff work where they happen to be, not where the work is best done. Time and productivity are wasted through unnecessary travelling.

2 Although many management 'gurus' would have us believe otherwise, the office is not dead. Instead, information age technology is altering our concept of what 'the office' actually is. (1)........... With the right information and communication technology solution, the office can be anywhere. In particular, with the arrival of desktop video-conferencing, the notion of the 'virtual' or 'follow me' office will certainly become even more powerful.

3 In the search to support more productive working methods and lower costs for premises, companies are using a number of options. One example is enabling mobile workers such as sales people or travelling professionals to work effectively from any location using their homes or local offices as bases. (2)........... Instead staff are more likely to have 'touch-down' space or meeting rooms – tailored to suit individual work tasks.

4 The conflicting demands of work and home result in tensions and stresses affecting both work performance and family life. How we organise work, and where and when it takes place, is central to these conflicts. Commuting to work simply to use a computer and telephone is pointless and expensive if the same tasks can be performed at or nearer to home. (3).......... Clearly, digital technologies enable work to take place at more friendly times and locations.

5 To take full advantage of flexible working, staff must be trained to use the new technology and to deal with managing or being managed at a distance. Flexible working schemes fail when technology is thrown at staff and they are left to just get on with it. (4).......... In most cases, flexible working does not mean never seeing your colleagues! It means being in the best place for a particular task to be carried out. In the future, we may visit the office only when we need to be there.

6 Work in principle can take place any time and anywhere. To make this happen, however, the right technologies and systems have to be in place. Quality equipment is a key consideration in particular desktops and laptop PCs with high-speed access, using fixed or mobile telephony. (5).......... They need to be able to access their e-mail, corporate intranet and other systems at any point.

- Cross out sentences you have already chosen from the selection A–G to make it easier to see which choices are left for the more difficult gaps.
- When you transfer your answers to the answer sheet, check that you have not used any of the letters A–G more than once.

2 Read the article on page 112 about flexible working in the information age. Choose the best sentence from below to fill each of the gaps. For each gap 1–5, mark one letter (A–G). Do not use any letter more than once. If you would like help with this task, reread the Task procedure box on page 122.

A And travelling in the rush-hour or just at the time when the children have to go to school adds to the strain.

B It is changing the physical nature of offices and giving them flexible boundaries.

C In addition, the right policies must be in place to ensure good communication and to avoid feelings of isolation.

D This change means companies will have to invest in advanced communication technology.

E This move to more flexible, location-independent working makes a dedicated office space for each person hard to justify.

F Equally important, people need to be able to get into the same corporate networks whether they are in or away from the office.

G Not only are they expensive to run, they also lead to inefficient working practices.

3 These verbs are all from the article. Look quickly through the complete article and find verbs which have a similar meaning.

1 Paragraph 1   lead to
  Paragraph 4   ......*result in*..............

2 Paragraph 2   altering
  Paragraph 2   ....

3 Paragraph 4   performed
  Paragraph 5   ....

4 Paragraph 6   get into
  Paragraph 6   ....

Which of the verbs are used with these nouns?

.... a task

.... a computer network / e-mail

4 Complete this sentence from paragraph 4.

Clearly digital technologies enable .... *at more friendly times and locations.*

Make sentences using *enable(s)* + object + *to* + verb to explain the benefits of these technologies.

- mobile phones
- video-conferencing
- the Internet

language in use: degrees of future certainty

1 Look back through the article on page 113 and underline the three predictions the writer makes about work in paragraphs 2, 3 and 5. Say if the prediction is something the writer expects (E), thinks is a possibility (P) or is certain about (C).

2 Look at the predictions (1–5) below and answer these questions.

a Which sentence contains an adverb? Where does it go?

b Which two structures are used with *certain* and *likely*?

1 The office of the future will certainly look different.
2 The office of the future is certain to look very different.
3 It's certain that the office of the future will look very different.
4 People are likely to spend less time in the office.
5 It's likely that people will spend less time in the office.

3 Find different ways to express the predictions (a–e) on the right without changing their meaning. Use some of these words.

definitely   certainly   probably   certain
probable   likely   possible   unlikely

Example

More people are likely to work from home.
It's probable that more people will work from home.

a Managers will definitely need very different skills to manage remote teams.
b With an ageing population, more people will probably work until their mid-70s.
c It's clear that ICT will have a dramatic effect on the way we work.
d I don't think the new communication technologies will make our lives easier.
e I think these changes may occur much more slowly than predicted.

4 Read the predictions below. Discuss how probable you think these changes are in the short term and in the long term. Include expressions from exercises 2 and 3.

> Automated language translation software will enable most of the world's people to communicate directly with one another. This will mean people will no longer need to learn languages and human translators will disappear. As language barriers fall there will be an explosion in travel.

See grammar reference page 138

Reading Part 5

tip When you've finished, don't forget to read through the text one more time to check it all makes sense.

In most lines of the text about video-conferencing there is one extra word. If a line is correct, write CORRECT. If there is an extra word in the line, write it in CAPITAL LETTERS. If you would like help with this task, reread the Task procedure box on page 123.

The value of video-conferencing

0	Video-conferencing technology allows two or more people can	*CAN*
00	at different locations to see and hear each other at the same	*CORRECT*
1	time. In addition, it is often possible to share with computer	....
2	applications such as the Internet pages, company literature, or	....
3	software. This rich communications technology offers both new	....
4	possibilities for businesses in activities such as meetings and	....
5	interviews. The visual made connection and interaction among	....
6	participants improves understanding and helps to participants	....
7	feel closely involved than with each other. This helps to build	....
8	relationships in a way that through e-mail, phone, or online	....
9	chat systems cannot so, by supporting collaboration among	....
10	traditionally isolated locations. At a practical level, it also saves huge sums in travel costs.	....

listening

1 Would home-working appeal to you? Why / Why not?

2 🎧 Sam Jeffrey is doing some consultancy work for the UK subsidiary of a German pharmaceutical company. You will hear a discussion in which Dagmar Brun, the company's Personnel Officer, asks Sam some questions about the practicalities of introducing home-working.

For each question 1–6, mark one letter (A, B or C) for the correct answer.
If you would like help with this task, reread the Task procedure box on page 127

1 In Sam's experience, isolation is a problem for
   A staff who work from home but don't have families.
   B anyone who spends time working from home.
   C staff who work mostly from home.

2 According to Sam, there's more potential for distractions for staff who
   A are office-based.   B have children.   C work from home.

3 Sam says working long hours is more of a problem for
   A employees who work from home.
   B staff in managerial positions.
   C people who are office-based.

4 According to Sam, the best way to prevent home-workers from feeling out of touch with the office is through
   A team building activities.
   B the company intranet.
   C face to face meetings.

5 According to Sam, the costs for the employee of setting up a home office are
   A often met by the employer.
   B in the region of £2,000.
   C minimal.

6 Who does Sam think could be included in Dagmar's home-working scheme?
   A those who score high in psychological assessments
   B everybody
   C those who are very organised and disciplined

3 🎧 Listen again. What solutions does Sam offer to counter these objections to home-working schemes?

objections	solutions
a feelings of isolation	
b distractions	
c extra costs of setting up and running an office at home	

4 Do you agree that home-working would work for everyone? Why / Why not?

speaking

1 Work with a partner. You are going to ask and answer questions. Student A: Look below for your questions. Student B: Look at page 121 to see your questions. Take turns to be the examiner.

Student A
Choose some of these questions and interview B. This should last for about one and a half minutes.
- What kind of job do you have? / What are you studying?
- What attracted you to this course/job?
- What do you find most challenging about the job/course?
- If there was one aspect of your work you could change, what would it be? Why?
- What do you see yourself doing in the next five years?
- Do you think it's better for your career to stay with one company for a long time or move from company to company?

2 Work in groups of three. Choose one of these three topic cards for your talk. You have one minute to note down some ideas for the talk on your chosen topic. Follow the instructions below and then swap roles until each person has given their talk.

Student A: Give your talk. Answer B's question.

Student B: Listen to the talk and ask a question at the end of A's talk.

Student C: Act as timekeeper. Be prepared to stop A when the minute is finished.

Topic card A

WHAT IS IMPORTANT WHEN ...?

Setting up flexible working arrangements for staff
- equipment
- training and technical support
-
-

Topic card B

WHAT IS IMPORTANT WHEN ...?

Redesigning an office
- ventilation and heating
- storage
-
-

Topic card C

WHAT IS IMPORTANT WHEN ...?

Choosing ICT equipment for staff working from home
- access to the company networks
- space
-
-

3 Read the task sheet below. Work with a partner and discuss the situation together. Remember you have 30 seconds to prepare and you should talk for three minutes.

> ### Home-working
>
> Your company has decided to try out a home-working scheme for the twenty people in sales and customer support teams. You have been asked to plan the introduction of the trial which is scheduled for two months' time.
>
> Discuss the situation and decide:
> - how to convince the sales and customer support teams it is a good idea.
> - what you need to do before the trial begins.

writing: an informal report making proposals

1 What do you think staff working in this office would be unhappy about?

Writing Part 2

2 As part of a project to redesign the office space at your company's head office, you have carried out a survey of staff attitudes to the current workspace. You now have to write a report summarising the main findings and recommending changes that need to be incorporated in the new design.

Look at the results of the survey below, on which you have already made some handwritten notes. Write your report using the notes in 120–140 words.

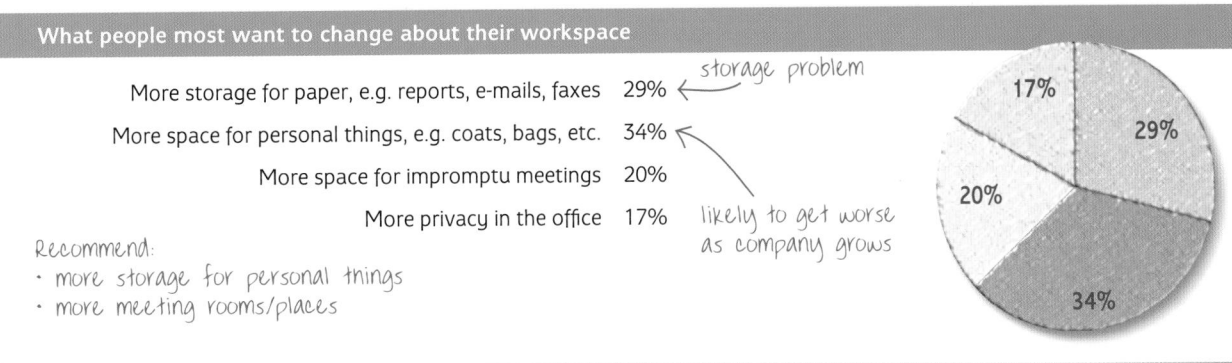

What people most want to change about their workspace

More storage for paper, e.g. reports, e-mails, faxes	29%
More space for personal things, e.g. coats, bags, etc.	34%
More space for impromptu meetings	20%
More privacy in the office	17%

storage problem

likely to get worse as company grows

Recommend:
· more storage for personal things
· more meeting rooms/places

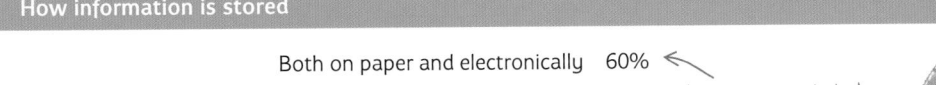

How information is stored

Both on paper and electronically	60%
Only in electronic formats	30%
Only on paper	10%

too much printed out so mention figure – will probably get worse

Recommend training course in electronic data storage

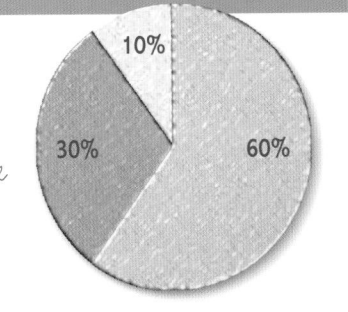

SOURCE: STEELCASE WORKPLACE SURVEYS

1 Plan your report. Decide on your headings and sub-points.
2 Draft your report.
3 Go back through your report and check you've included all the points in the notes and are within the word limit of 120–140 words. Make any necessary edits.
4 Read your report once more to double-check for any mistakes.

pairwork pages

unit 2

Speaking page 20, exercise 5

Student A: Your task is to initiate and maintain a conversation with Student B about his/her work or studies. Ask about:

- where he/she works or studies.
- what usual activities he/she carries out there.
- what current projects he/she is involved in.
- what he/she likes and dislikes about the type of work he/she does.

Student B: Respond to Student A's questions using these strategies:

- Answer questions by giving a little more information than you've been asked for.
- Express enthusiasm by using words and phrases such as: *fulfilling, satisfying, challenging, dynamic*; *It's good to … , It's fun to … , It's interesting to … .*
- Soften negative comments by adding the words *rather* or *a bit*, for example: *a bit dull, a bit hard, a bit difficult, rather hectic, rather stressful.*

Student C: Listen to the conversation and complete this feedback form.

Did Student B:	Yes/No	Any comments?
• answer Student A's questions fully?		
• succeed in sounding interested and enthusiastic about the course/job?		
• use the present tenses correctly?		

unit 4

Speaking page 36, exercise 1

2 With the other students in your group, complete sentences a–d below to make useful questions related to graphs A and B.

a *How many* … stores did Mariposa have in *the US/Europe* in *2001/2002/2003* ?

b How many people ………………… in …………………?

c ………………… this number change the year after that?

d Sorry, I didn't catch that. Could you …………………?

3 Form a pair with one student from group A. Ask your questions about graphs A and B and complete the missing information. Then answer their questions about graphs C and D.

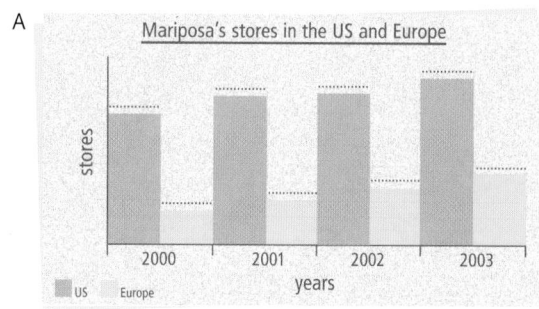

A Mariposa's stores in the US and Europe

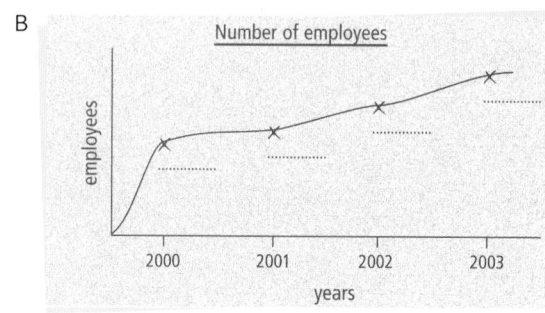

B Number of employees

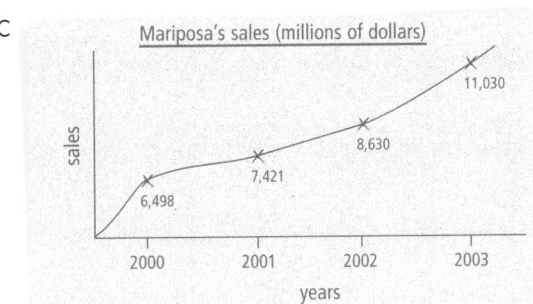

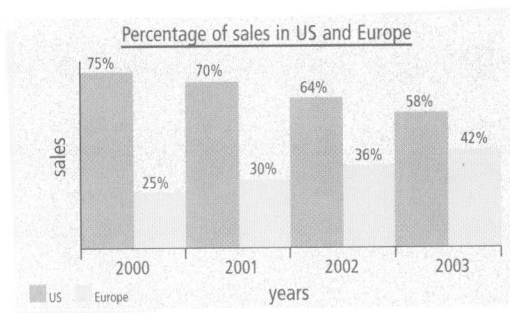

unit 6

Speaking page 52, exercise 2

Topic card B

WHAT IS IMPORTANT WHEN ...?

Working regularly with computers

- equipment
- breaks
-
-

unit 7

Speaking page 60, exercise 1

Extract 1

A So, ... the communication problems first?

B OK. Well, I think it's very important that customers get a good impression of the company, and the first contact is often by phone. .... telephone skills training .... help our staff to sound more friendly and interested in our customers.

A Yes, ... And what's more ...

Extract 2

A You know, it occurs to me that the problem could be that our sales staff have too much work to do and that's why they seem unhelpful and don't answer letters and e-mails.

B .... I hadn't thought of that. .... recruit more staff, then?

A Well, ... Or .... give the existing staff training in time management skills.

B .... And that would be cheaper than hiring more people.

A OK, ... three .... Any other ideas?

B Not at the moment.

A .... the delivery problems, then.

Rewrite the phrases and sentences from the tapescripts under the following headings.

managing the interaction	making suggestions	agreeing
Shall we talk about ...?		

unit 7

Speaking page 60, exercise 3

Graduate job fair

Your company is finding it difficult to attract well-qualified graduates, especially for its legal and financial departments. For this reason, the management have decided that, for the first time ever, the company should exhibit at a graduate job fair. You have been asked to help with planning this event.

Discuss the situation together and decide:

- which staff from the company should attend the fair, and why.
- what arrangements you will need to make before they exhibit there.

unit 8

Speaking page 68, exercise 5

Managers of The Rite Bite: Listen carefully to the presentation and, at the end, ask questions about any part of the campaign which you would like to hear more details about. Give marks to each group for the points below to choose the best campaign.

> **Rank each group's presentation (1–5) for each of these points:**
>
> Does the campaign have a clear message? ....
> Does it emphasise the special features of the service? ....
> Would it persuade the target customers to use the service? ....
> Would it catch the target customers' attention? ....

unit 10

Listening page 83, exercise 3

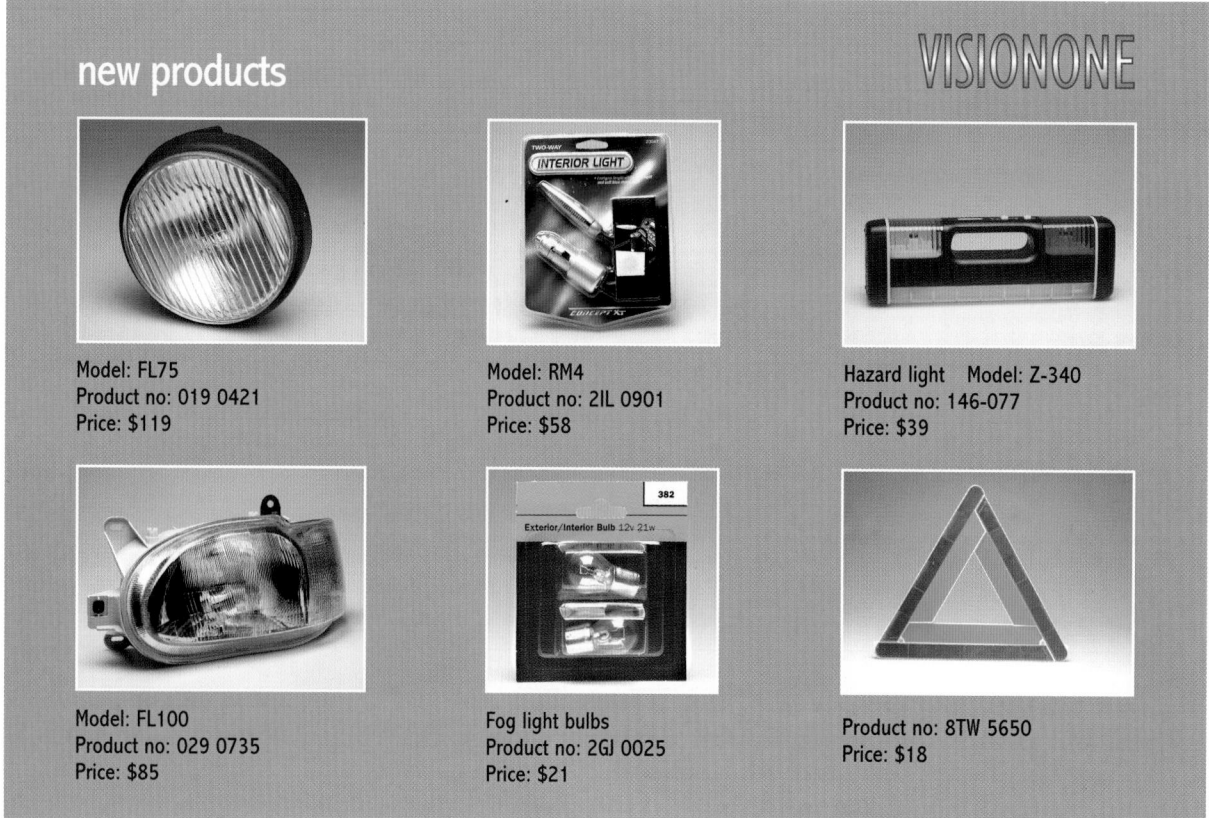

new products

VISIONONE

Model: FL75
Product no: 019 0421
Price: $119

Model: RM4
Product no: 2IL 0901
Price: $58

Hazard light   Model: Z-340
Product no: 146-077
Price: $39

Model: FL100
Product no: 029 0735
Price: $85

Fog light bulbs
Product no: 2GJ 0025
Price: $21

Product no: 8TW 5650
Price: $18

unit 11

Language in use page 90, exercise 3

Student B: Look at the tip below for improving your time management and complete it with the *-ing* form of these verbs. When you're ready, exchange information about the tips.

come   deal   do   make   prioritise

> **Learn to manage your time**
>
> Good time management involves (1) .... decisions about what's important. It doesn't mean (2) .... everything in your in-tray. Concentrate on (3) .... with the things that are really important first. One well-known psychologist suggests (4) .... in early to look at everything in your in-tray, all your e-mails, and then (5) .... everything you have to do this week, next week and so on.

1 Students C and D: You are going to play the role of the candidates. Students A and B will interview you. Student A will give you a task sheet to discuss. You will speak for three minutes and have 30 seconds to prepare.

2 Now you are going to play the role of the examiners.

Student C: You are going to play the role of the examiner. Students A and B are going to discuss the problem below. Your teacher will give you copies of the task sheet to give to them. Ask them to speak for three minutes and give them 30 seconds to prepare. When three minutes have passed, stop them. Ask one or two follow-up questions from the list below.

tip It makes it easier to communicate with your partner if you look at him/her during your discussion, not at the examiner.

Ethics in business

Your company is concerned about doing business ethically, but has discovered that the public and many of the employees are not aware of this fact.

Discuss the situation together and decide what the company should do:

- to raise the staff's awareness about business ethics.
- to improve its public image.

Follow-up questions

- Do you think trying to behave ethically is important in business nowadays?
- Would you accept a very well-paid job with a company that didn't have a good ethical image?
- Is it more important to treat customers well or employees well?

Student D: You are going to assess Student A and B's interactive communication. Use the checklist below to help you. When Students A and B have finished the discussion and answered one or two extra questions, give them feedback, politely, about what they did well, and any areas which could be improved.

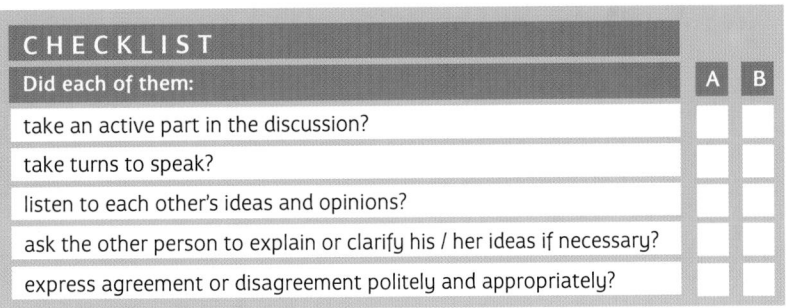

CHECKLIST		
Did each of them:	**A**	**B**
take an active part in the discussion?		
take turns to speak?		
listen to each other's ideas and opinions?		
ask the other person to explain or clarify his / her ideas if necessary?		
express agreement or disagreement politely and appropriately?		

Student B: Choose some of these questions and interview Student A. This should last for about one and a half minutes.

- Where do you work/study?
- What do you do? / What are you studying?
- What aspect of your job/studies do you most enjoy? Why?
- What were you doing before you got this job / started this course?
- How do you see your career developing over the next few years?
- Which do you think is more satisfying: working in a big company or a small company?

exam information

Test of Reading

1 If it helps you to identify the correct answers, you may underline sections of the texts on your question paper.

2 Don't spend too long trying to answer a question which you find very difficult. Leave it blank and come back to it if you have time left over after completing all of the Reading paper.

3 Don't leave any questions unanswered. Even if you just guess, you have a chance of getting the correct answer!

4 Never write two alternative answers to one question. Even if one answer is correct, they will both be marked as wrong.

5 You must transfer all your answers to the answer sheet at the end of this paper, but remember no extra time is allowed for this.

6 The Reading paper is marked by computer, so follow the instructions for completing the answer sheet carefully.

Reading Part 1

Matching sentences to texts or paragraphs

Format	Four short texts (A–D) on a related topic, or a longer text divided into four paragraphs, and seven statements about the texts (1–7).
Objective	You must match each statement (1–7) with the text or paragraph (A–D) that it relates to. This task tests your ability to understand points of detail and specific information in a text.

Task procedure
1 Read each text/paragraph quickly to get an idea of the general meaning.
2 Read each statement 1–7.
3 Read statement 1 again and scan the text(s) to find which short text or paragraph it relates to.
4 Follow the same procedure for statements 2–7.

You will find examples of this task in Unit 2, page 16; Unit 6, page 49; Unit 8, page 64 and Unit 12, page 96.

Reading Part 2

Gapped text and sentences

Format	One long text which has had six sentences removed from it and seven sentences (A–G).
Objective	You must match each gap in the text with the sentence which best fits. The first gap will always have been completed as an example, leaving you a choice from six sentences to fit in five gaps. This task tests your ability to understand the meaning and structure of a text.

Task procedure
1 Read the whole text to get an idea of the general meaning.
2 Read the sentences (A–G) to be fitted into the gaps.
3 Read the two sentences in the text before and after the first gap carefully.
4 Read sentences A–G again, looking for clues to where they might fit in. These could be similar words in both the text and a sentence, reference words (this, that, these, etc.) or linking words and phrases.
5 Repeat steps 3 and 4 for each gap.

You will find examples of this task in Unit 4, page 33; Unit 7, page 57; Unit 11, page 89 and Unit 14, page 113.

Reading Part 3   Multiple choice

Format   One long text and six four-option multiple-choice questions.

Objective You must choose the best option (A–D) to answer a question or
complete a sentence. This task tests your ability to understand
opinions and infer meanings expressed in a longer text.

Task procedure
1 Read the whole text quickly to get an idea of the general meaning.
2 Read the questions or statements you have to complete.
3 Read the text again, highlighting or underlining any sentences or phrases you
think contain the answers to the questions.
4 Look at question 1 and the options, then reread the part of the text you have
highlighted very carefully and select the best option.
5 Do the same for the remaining questions.

You will find examples of this task in Unit 3, page 25; Unit 5, page 41;
Unit 9, page 73 and Unit 13, page 104.

Reading Part 4   Cloze

Format   One short text with sixteen gaps and four options to complete
each gap.

Objective You must choose the best option (A–D) to fill each gap in the text.
The first gap will always have been completed as an example. This
task tests your knowledge of vocabulary.

Task procedure
1 Read the text quickly to get an idea of the general meaning. Don't worry
about the missing words at this stage.
2 Look quickly though the text again and try to guess the missing words.
3 Read the sentence which contains the first gap and the sentence that follows
it carefully.
4 Look at the four options A–D and choose the best one to complete the
sentence.
5 Do the same for the remaining gaps.

You will find examples of this task in Unit 5, page 39; Unit 9, page 71;
Unit 11, page 87 and Unit 14, page 111.

Reading Part 5   Error correction

Format   One short text with fourteen numbered lines.

Objective You must decide if each numbered line of the text is correct or if
it contains an unnecessary word. The first two lines will always
have been completed as examples. This task tests your knowledge
of grammar.

Task procedure
1 Read the text quickly to get an idea of the general meaning.
2 Read the text again, line by line. Mark any lines you think are correct with a
tick (✔) and any you think contain an unnecessary word with a question
mark (?).
3 Read the lines you've marked with a question mark again in detail. Identify
which word is unnecessary.
4 Finally, read through the full text again to check it still makes sense without
the words you've marked.

You will find examples of this task in Unit 5, page 42; Unit 7, page 58;
Unit 10, page 82; Unit 11, page 90 and Unit 14, page 114.

Test of Writing

1 You have 45 minutes to write two texts, one short and one long. Part 1 is worth one third of the total marks for the Writing paper, and Part 2 is worth two thirds of the marks. Divide your time between the two tasks accordingly. As a rough guide, allow:

- five minutes for planning your answer to Part 1
- five minutes to write your answer to Part 1
- five minutes to check, correct and (if necessary) rewrite a clean copy of your answer to Part 1
- ten minutes for planning your answer to Part 2
- ten minutes to write your answer to Part 2
- ten minutes to check, correct and (if necessary) rewrite a clean copy of your answer to Part 2

2 You may make notes on the question sheet if you want to, but your final answer to the tasks must be written on the paper provided for you during the exam. Allow time to transfer your final answers to this answer sheet if you have written a draft version.

3 Try to write clearly. If your handwriting is totally illegible, you will not get any marks at all.

4 Keep within the word limit for each task. If you write less than 25 per cent of the words asked for, you will get no marks at all. You will also lose marks if you write more than the number of words asked for.

5 The following points will be considered when your writing is marked:
- Have you included the correct content points?
- Are there grammar or vocabulary mistakes in the text which make it difficult to understand?
- Have you used a good range of vocabulary and grammatical structures?
- Is the text well-organised, with appropriate phrases linking the ideas together?
- Is the style appropriate to this type of communication?
- What effect will the text have on the person who reads it?

Writing Part 1

About the task

This task checks your ability to write very concise and clear English. You write a short note, memo, fax or email of just 40–50 words. The instructions for the exercise give you the context for the writing, and who you are writing to. Three bullet points tell you what information you must include, but you may also need to invent some other facts.

Task procedure

1 Read the instruction and the prompt with the bullet points carefully.
2 Draft your piece of writing, keeping your sentences short and simple. Normally, you will need to write only one sentence for each bullet point.
3 Go through your draft and check carefully that you have included all the information in the bullet points.
4 Check the length. If it's too long, edit out any words which are not absolutely necessary.
5 Write a clean copy of your text on the answer sheet.

You will find examples of this task in Unit 2, page 21; Unit 3, page 29; Unit 5, page 45; Unit 6, page 53; Unit 10, page 85 and Unit 12, page 101.

About the task

This task checks your ability to organise and write a longer text. You write a short report, proposal or piece of business correspondence which should be between 120 and 140 words long. The instructions for the exercise give you the context for the writing, and who you are writing to. You will also be given other information which you should include in the text you write – this may be in the form of tables, graphs, memos or handwritten notes.

Task procedure

1 Read the instructions for the task carefully.
2 Read all the other input material (e.g. tables, graphs, memos, etc.).
3 Underline or highlight all the points in the input material which you think should be included in the text you write.
4 Write a first draft of your text, making sure you include all the points you have identified.
5 Check the length. If it's too short, check that you have not left out any essential information. If it's too long, rephrase parts of your draft to say the same thing in fewer words.
6 Write a clean copy of your text on the answer sheet.

You will find examples of this task in Unit 4, page 37; Unit 7, page 61; Unit 8, page 69; Unit 9, page 77; Unit 11, page 93; Unit 13, page 109 and Unit 14, page 117.

Test of Listening

1 If you miss the answer to a question on the first listening, don't worry about it. Listen for the answers to the following questions. When you hear the recording the second time, you can concentrate on catching any answers you missed the first time.

2 During the Listening paper you write your answers on the question paper. Once you have heard all the recordings twice, you have ten minutes to transfer your answers to the answer sheet.

3 Don't leave any questions unanswered. Even if you just guess, you have a chance of getting the correct answer!

4 Never write two alternative answers to one question. Even if one answer is correct, they will both be marked as wrong.

5 The Listening paper is marked by computer, so follow the instructions for completing the answer sheet carefully.

Listening Part 1

Note-taking

Format   Three short recordings of conversations or answerphone messages and three texts each of which has four gaps.

Objective You must write one or two words or a number in each gap. You will hear each conversation or message twice. This task tests your ability to understand facts in a spoken text.

Task procedure

1 Read the instructions and look carefully through each text to see what type of information you are looking for, e.g. a name, a time, a date or a place.

2 As you listen to the recordings, make a note of the answers. Don't worry if you don't catch all the information the first time.

3 As you listen again, check your answers and complete any items of information you missed the first time.

You will find examples of this task in Unit 3, page 27; Unit 5, page 43; Unit 10, page 83 and Unit 12, page 98.

Listening part 2

Multiple matching

Format   This part has two sections. Each section has five short monologues and a set of eight words, phrases or statements (A–H).

Objective You must match each monologue to one of the items (A–H). In each section there will be three items which you do not need to use. You will hear each monologue twice. This task tests your ability to understand the gist or main ideas of a short monologue and to recognise contexts, topics, opinions, etc.

Task procedure

1 Read the instructions and list of options (A–H) carefully. For each option, try to predict some phrases or vocabulary you might hear.

2 As you listen the first time, note down any answers you are sure of, and any you think may be possible.

3 As you listen again, focus on trying to answer the items you were not sure of or found more difficult.

4 Complete your answers and check that you have not used any of the letters more than once.

You will find examples of this task in Unit 2, page 18; Unit 6, page 51; Unit 11, page 91 and Unit 13, page 107.

Format   One long recording of a conversation (e.g. an interview or discussion) or a monologue (e.g. a presentation), and eight three-option multiple-choice questions.

Objective   You must choose the best option (A, B or C) to answer a short question or complete a short statement about the spoken text. You will hear the recording twice. This task tests your ability to understand details and main ideas.

Task procedure
1 The instructions and questions for the task contain useful clues about the context for the listening, so read them carefully in the time allocated before you hear the recording the first time.
2 As you listen the first time, try to get a general understanding of the meaning. Note down any answers you are sure about. If you are not sure, move quickly on to the next question.
3 In the pause before the second listening, reread the questions where you missed the answers or were not sure about them.
4 As you listen again, complete the missing answers and check the choices you have already made.

You will find examples of this task in Unit 4, page 34; Unit 7, page 59 and Unit 14, page 115.

Test of Speaking

At each Speaking test there will be two examiners and two (or occasionally three) candidates. One examiner (the interlocutor) conducts the test and asks all the questions. The other (the assessor) listens and evaluates the candidates' performance, but does not interact with the candidates.

General tips

1 Try to take an active role in the test. The only times when it is not appropriate for you to speak are during the other candidate's short presentation (Part 2) and if he/she is answering a question which has been asked specifically to him/her, rather than both of you.

2 Always ask for clarification if you have not understood the instructions for a task. This will not lose you marks, but doing the wrong thing may do so.

3 Before you go to the Speaking test, make sure you know appropriate phrases for asking for repetition, asking for clarification, and checking your understanding of what the interlocutor or the other candidate says.

4 Be ready to answer questions about your current job or future career and your interests. However, do not prepare speeches on these topics in advance. The examiners will realise if you have memorised a speech and you will lose marks for this.

5 Listen to what your partner says during Part 2 and Part 3 so that you can ask an appropriate question and react to their ideas.

6 Do not dominate your partner and refuse to let them speak – you will lose marks if you show that you are unaware of the need to take turns during a conversation.

7 You will be marked on your ability to speak English, not on your business knowledge, so none of the questions will need specialist knowledge in order to be able to answer them.

The following points will be considered when you are assessed on your Speaking skills:

• Are you able to use a good range of vocabulary and grammatical structures both accurately and appropriately?

• Are you able to organise your ideas, keep them relevant to a topic and speak about them for an appropriate length of time?

• Is your pronunciation of individual sounds, words and sentences clear enough that the listener can understand what you say?

• Are you able to take an active part in a discussion and to respond appropriately to what others say?

Speaking Part 1

Personal questions

Format	This part of the test lasts about three minutes. The interlocutor will ask each candidate alternately some general questions about topics such as their job or studies, their home and their interests.
Objective	To test your ability to give information about yourself, and to express preferences and opinions.

Task procedure
1 Listen carefully to the examiner's questions.
2 When you are answering questions, don't just say *Yes* or *No*; be pepared to give extra information.
3 You will be asked questions individually, so don't interrupt the other candidate or try to answer their questions.

You will find examples of this task in Unit 1, page 12 and Unit 14, page 116.

Short presentation

Format   This part of the test lasts about six minutes. Each candidate in turn gives a one-minute presentation on a topic chosen from three alternatives. Each topic has four bullet points: two with ideas already included, and two blank. You have one minute to prepare a short talk based on the topic card you have chosen. At the end of each candidate's talk, the other candidate must ask him/her one question about the topic.

Objective   To test your ability to give an extended speech on a subject, and to express and link ideas.

Task procedure
1 Read the topic card you have chosen carefully.
2 Think up two extra points and make a note of them. (You will be given a pencil and paper to help you prepare your talk.)
3 Think of two or three things to say to support each main point.
4 Quickly plan your talk. Include main and supporting ideas, but just write down key words to help you remember what you want to say.
5 Give your talk, trying to cover each of your points.
6 Answer your partner's question.

You will find examples of this task in Unit 3, page 28; Unit 6, page 52; Unit 10, page 84; Unit 12, page 100 and Unit 14, page 116.

Two-way conversation

Format   This part of the test lasts about five minutes. The interlocutor will give each of you the same card and ask you to discuss the points on it. You have thirty seconds to prepare some ideas about this topic. You will then be asked to discuss it together for about three minutes. During this time the interlocutor will not generally speak. At the end of the three minutes, you will be asked some further, more general, questions related to the topic.

Objective   To test your ability to take part in a discussion, interact with another person, agree, disagree, and take turns appropriately.

Task procedure
1 Read the topic card carefully so that you are clear about the situation and the points for the discussion.
2 Use the 30 second preparation time to think of some ideas for both bullet points.
3 If necessary, with your partner decide on any extra details for the context, e.g. what the company produces or where it is based.
4 Discuss the first point together, making sure you support your ideas with reasons or examples.
5 Summarise any decisions you've reached.
6 Move on to the second point and discuss it.
9 Summarise any decisions on this point.

You will find examples of this task in Unit 5, page 44; Unit 7, page 60; Unit 13, page 108 and Unit 14, page 116.

grammar reference

unit 1 question forms

1 Primary auxiliaries

Most questions contain one of the three primary auxiliaries (*be, have, do*).

Are you here for the meeting?
Have you seen my pen?
Do you know how to use the printer?

a If a statement contains the auxiliary *be* or *have*, we simply put the auxiliary in front of the subject.

   She is Italian. > Is she Italian?
   He has applied for the job. > Has he applied for the job?

b If a statement does not contain the auxiliary *be* or *have*, we put *do*, *does*, or *did* in front of the subject, followed by a bare infinitive.

   They fly first class. > Do they fly first class?
   They bought a new computer. > Did they buy a new computer?

2 Modal auxiliaries

To form a question with a modal auxiliary (*can, could, will, should, would*), the word order is modal + noun + bare infinitive.

Could you phone me tomorrow?
Will you send me a copy of the invoice?
Would you like a coffee?

3 Closed, open and indirect questions

a Closed questions

   Questions beginning with a primary or a modal auxiliary are known as 'closed questions' because they can only be answered by *yes* or *no* (or phrases with similar meanings).

   Are you married? Yes, I am. / No, I'm not.
   Can you answer my phone while I'm out? Yes, certainly.

b Open questions

   Questions which begin with words like *Who, What, When, Where, How* are known as 'open' questions, and require fuller answers than 'closed' questions.

   What's your company like to work for?
   How does the photocopier work?

c Indirect questions

   We can make questions more polite or open up a discussion by starting with a short introductory phrase such as *Do you mind if …? Could you tell me …?*

After these phrases, the word order is the same as in a normal statement.

Do you mind if we start the meeting later?
Could you tell me why you want to work for us?

unit 2 present simple and present continuous

1 We use the present simple

a for usual activities and routines.

   I walk to work three times a week.
   They review my salary once a year.

b with adverbs of frequency that tell you how often something happens.

   They never pay on time.
   I usually leave for work at eight.

c for facts, information and statistics.

   IBM sells computers.
   Over 50 per cent of business people fly economy class.

d for things which are timetabled, scheduled or fixed.

   The train leaves Hamburg at 6.08 and gets to Frankfurt at 8.23.
   The UK tax year runs from 6 April to 5 April.

e for proverbs, sayings and general truths.

   Time is money.
   Money makes the world go round.

2 We use the present continuous

a to describe something that is temporary.

   We're staying in a little hotel near the conference centre.

b to describe something that is happening now or is ongoing.

   I'm working on my report.

c to talk about future plans and arrangements.

   We're launching three new products next month.
   They're restructuring the company early next year.

d to talk about a trend that started some time ago and will probably continue for some time in the future.

   Businesses are moving out of town centres.
   Our sales are growing year on year.

e with *always* to express annoyance that something happens far too often.

   This photocopier is always breaking down just when I need it.

3 Stative verbs

Be careful how you use a small group of common verbs (e.g. *believe, belong to, hate, know, like/dislike, love, mean, need, prefer, seem, surprise, want* and *wish*) which are known as 'stative verbs'.

Stative verbs are divided into two groups:

a Verbs in the first group (e.g. *believe* or *belong to*) are never used in the present continuous.

I **believe** in the importance of good customer care. (not *am believing*)
Netcare **belongs** to the RGF group of companies. (not *is belonging*)

b Verbs in the smaller second group (e.g. *see*) change their meaning when they are used in the present continuous as compared with the present simple.

Compare the following pairs of sentences:

What do you **think** of the new Sales Manager? (= what is your opinion?)
We **are thinking** of building a new factory in Malaysia. (= considering)

You must **see** her CV. It's excellent. (= have a look at)
There are four people on the short list. We**'re seeing** them all tomorrow. (= meeting / interviewing)

unit 3 comparatives and superlatives

1 Comparatives

a For short adjectives with one syllable, we add *-er*.

This report is taking **longer than** I expected.
Our sales are always **stronger** in autumn.

b For adjectives with two syllables, we use *-ier* for adjectives ending in *-y*. Otherwise *more* or *less* is used.

It's **easier** to e-mail the report than post it out to everybody.
Please be **more careful** in future.

c For adjectives with three or more syllables, we use *more* or *less*.

She always flies economy class. Although the seats are **less comfortable** than in first class, she finds the people **more interesting**.

d We use *as ... as* for similarity and *not as ... as* for difference.

I've got a new mobile phone. It's **as** small **as** my old one, but it's **not as** reliable **as** I'd hoped.

e We can modify or qualify a comparative by using phrases such as *a little, a lot, much more, much less, far more, far less*.

Business is **a little** better these days.
The retail sector is **much more** competitive in the South East.
Business rates are **far more** reasonable in this part of town.

Further points about comparatives:

f A double comparative is often used.
The **more** I earn, the **more** tax I pay.

g *More and more* and *less and less* are used to express a strong increase or reduction.
The market is getting **more and more** competitive.
As a result, we're making **less and less** profit.

2 Superlatives

a For adjectives with one syllable, we use *the + -est*.
Costmart is **the biggest** retail outlet in the area.

b For adjectives with two syllables, we use *-iest* for adjectives ending in *-y*. Otherwise we use *the most* or *the least*.
Frankfurt is **the busiest** airport in Germany.
It is **the most useful** report we've received.

c For adjectives with three or more syllables, we use *the most* or *the least*.
This is **the most interesting** job I've ever had.
We're going to sell off **the least profitable parts** of the business.

d A superlative is often used with:

- a possessive pronoun (*my, your, his*).
  China is **our biggest** market.
  Is that **your lowest** price?

- cardinal numbers (*two, five*) and ordinal numbers (*second, fifth*).
  The **three most important** shareholders own 64% of the company.
  Tourism is **our biggest** industry. Electronics is the **second biggest**.

3 Irregular forms

a Irregular adjectives and adverbs use different words to form the comparative and superlative:

good	better	the best
bad	worse	the worst
well	better	(the) best
badly	worse	(the) worst
little	less	least
much	more	most

b Some comparatives and superlatives have irregular endings.

Adjectives with one syllable that end in *-e* form the comparative by adding *-r* and the superlative by adding *-st*:

| large | larger | the largest |
| wide | wider | widest |

Adjectives with one syllable that end in a vowel plus consonant often form the comparative and superlative by doubling the consonant:

| hot | hotter | the hottest |
| fat | fatter | the fattest |

unit 4 past simple and present perfect

a We use the present perfect to describe 'what' happened without saying 'when' it happened. If you want to say when an event took place, you must use the past simple.

Compare the following pairs of sentences:

*I **have been** to Cairo.*
*I **went** to Cairo **in 2001**.*

***Have** you **been** to Cairo?*
***When did** you **go** to Cairo?*

Although we don't use specific days, dates or times with the present perfect, we can use adverbs such as *just, already, ever, yet, recently* and *still*.

Compare the following pairs of sentences:

*I **have just spoken** to the Managing Director.*
*I **spoke** to the Managing Director **five minutes ago**.*

*They**'ve already had** the meeting.*
*They **had** the meeting at midday.*

b The present perfect is used for a state or situation that began in the past, continues into the present and (probably) will continue into the future.

*I**'ve lived** in this village all my life.*

The past simple describes a different world where the present is different from the past.

*I **lived** in a tiny flat while I was at university.*

Compare the following sentences:

*I**'ve worked** for BP for ten years.* (= so far, up until now)
*I **worked** for BP for ten years.* (= but now I do something else)

unit 5 countable and uncountable nouns

1 Countable nouns

a Most nouns are countable. You can refer to them as a single, individual thing (e.g. *a book, an orange*), or in the plural as two or more things (e.g. *a couple of books, a dozen oranges*).

b In the singular, these nouns can be used with *a, an, the, each* and *every*.

*Can you send me **a catalogue**?*
*He's writing **an article** about corporation tax.*
*Could you pass me **the calculator**?*
*We test **every battery** before it leaves the factory.*

c In the plural, these nouns can be used with *several, various, all sorts of, all kinds of, hundreds of, thousands of*, etc.

***Several companies** have tendered for the contract.*
*We've had **all kinds of problems** with the new software.*
*There have been **hundreds of complaints**.*

2 Uncountable nouns

a There are fewer uncountable nouns. They can only be referred to in the singular form, and for this reason they always take a singular verb.

***Money doesn't** always make people happy.*
*I'm sorry we're late. The **traffic was** terrible.*

b The following nouns are uncountable:

accommodation, advice, behaviour, bread, equipment, evidence, furniture, information, jewellery, justice, knowledge, luggage, money, news, peace, progress, research, traffic, truth, weather

c There are no fixed rules to say whether a noun is countable or uncountable, but uncountable nouns are often abstract, philosophical concepts (e.g. *truth, justice, progress*), or 'umbrella' words that describe a category of things (e.g. *accommodation, equipment, furniture*).

d When we add phrases like *a bit of, a piece of, a slice of, a kind of, a type of* or *a sort of*, uncountable nouns behave like countable nouns.

Compare the following sentences:

*Where's your **luggage**?*
*There **were** a thousand **pieces of luggage** in the hold of the plane.*

3 Nouns that can be both countable and uncountable

a There is a small group of nouns which can be used both in a countable and uncountable sense, but with a change of meaning.

Compare the following pairs of sentences:

*We did presentations in five European **capitals** last week.*
*Most of our **capital** is provided by a merchant bank.*

*She wrote a thesis about the early **works** of Shakespeare.*
***Work** is the most important thing in her life.*

b Many common materials (e.g. *glass, wood, paper, iron, coffee, tea*) change in the same way.

Compare the following sentences:

***Iron** is used to make steel.*
*I need to press these trousers. Can I borrow **an iron**?*

4 Combinations

a We use *a lot of* (or *lots of*) with both countable and uncountable nouns, but notice how the verb form changes.

There **are a lot of** foreign **words** in English. (*word* is countable)
There's **a lot of** information in Danny's report. (*information* is uncountable)

b We use *much, little, a little* with uncountable nouns; *many, few, a few* with countable nouns.

How **much market research** have you done?
How **many copies** do we need?
Can I make **a few suggestions**?

c *Some, any,* and *all* can be used with any kind of noun (countable or uncountable).

I need **some advice**. Would you like **some biscuits**?
Do you need **any help**? Have you got **any questions**?
All the equipment is brand new. **All** our **rooms** have air-conditioning.

unit 6 modals

1 Modal auxiliaries

a Don't add *-s* for the third person singular.

He can meet you tomorrow. (not *He cans*)

b Don't need *do, does, did* to make questions or negatives.

Shall we start the meeting?
You **mustn't** park your car in the Director's space.

c Modal auxiliaries are followed by a bare infinitive.

Could you **explain** your proposal in more detail?
We **should consider** the impact of these plans.

2 Uses

a Ability

We use *can* and *can't* for general and present ability.

Shares **can go** up as well as down
I **can't speak** Portuguese.

b Possibility

• We use *may, might* and *could* to talk about something that is possibly true, but we don't know for sure.

We **may / might** be late for the meeting.
This **could** be the best opportunity for the company.

• We use *can* for a stronger possibility.

Working too much overtime **can** make you tired.

c Advice

We use *should* and *shouldn't* to give advice or to make a recommendation.
You don't look very well. You **should** see a doctor.
They **shouldn't** drink so much coffee.

d Obligation

We use *must, mustn't* and *have to*:

• to talk about legal obligations.

Drivers and passengers **must** wear seatbelts.

• to explain what is absolutely necessary.

You **must / have to** check in now. The flight is about to close.

• to explain what is required.

I often **have to** spend nights away from home when I'm travelling on business.

• when giving strong advice.

You **mustn't** eat so much sugar. It's bad for you.

e Lack of obligation

We use *don't have to, needn't* or *don't need to* when there is no legal requirement or necessity to do something.

I **don't have to** pay tax on the first £4,000 I earn.
You **needn't** send me a hard copy. I've got the e-mail on file.

f Permission

We use *can, can't, mustn't, may* or *may not* to explain what is or isn't allowed.

Smokers **can** use the designated areas for cigarette breaks.
Staff **can't / mustn't** smoke in their own offices.
Visitors **may not** use this car park.

unit 7 connectors of contrast and addition

1 Linking two similar aspects of the same subject

We use *also, not only ... but also, what's more, in addition* and *moreover* when we want to add further information.

a We can put *also* at the beginning of a sentence or in front of a main verb.

The candidate wasn't qualified for the job. **Also,** she didn't show much enthusiasm.

The local authority found us a site near a motorway. They **also** helped us to apply for three government grants.

b We use *not only* to introduce the first point, and *but also* to introduce the second point. These two points must either both be positive or both be negative.

The Japanese Bullet train is **not only** fast, **but also** incredibly comfortable.
When you set up in a different country, there are **not only** problems of language, **but also** of culture.

c The phrases *what's more* (informal) and *in addition* (formal) are often used when you have already made several points.

They gave us a 30% discount, half-price insurance, a two-year warranty and free delivery. **What's more,** *the manager gave me a couple of tickets for the opera.*

To get a mortgage, you will probably need to have a regular job, good credit references and some savings. **In addition,** *the bank will ask you to provide at least two reference letters.*

d *Moreover* is the most formal of all these terms, and is usually seen in more formal articles or correspondence.

Countries wishing to join the Eurozone must have low inflation, a stable exchange rate and diminishing levels of debt. **Moreover,** *they must adhere to strict fiscal and monetary controls.*

2 Contrasting two aspects of the same subject

We use *while, although* and *however* to show different aspects of the same subject.

a *While* can be found at the beginning or in the middle of a sentence.

While *home-working saves people the frustrations of commuting, it can also lead to feelings of isolation and loneliness.*
The Chairman sets out the general strategy **while** *the CEO has a more hands-on role.*

b *Although* indicates a surprising or clear contrast. You can find it at the beginning of a sentence (where it sounds more emphatic) or between clauses.

Although *she had the flu, she still came into work.*
She wasn't wearing a coat **although** *it was freezing cold.*

c *However* emphasises the fact that the second point contrasts with the first. It can be placed at the beginning of a sentence (followed by a comma), or at the end (between a comma and a full stop).

Market conditions are really tough. **However,** *we're still making a profit. (We're still making a profit,* **however.***)*

3 Contrasting two different subjects

In contrast indicates a clear, fundamental difference between two subjects.

The last company I worked for expected the staff to dress formally at all times. **In contrast,** *the company I now work for doesn't mind if we come to work in casual clothes.*

unit 8 future forms

We can talk about the future in a number of different ways.

1 *Will* + the bare infinitive

a for things we predict, expect or promise.

We'll **break even** *next year.*
She'll **be** *an excellent manager.*
I'll **put** *the cheque in the post tonight.*

b when we make a spontaneous decision or offer.

I'll **have** *a steak, medium rare, a side salad and a mineral water, please.* (I didn't make this decision until I got the menu)

You've dropped your napkin. Don't worry. I'll **get** *it for you.* (the thought, the offer and the act all happen at the same time)

2 Present continuous / *going to*

It often sounds more *natural* to talk about planned or arranged events with the present continuous or *going to* + bare infinitive.

I'm **showing** *the clients around the factory tomorrow.*
(this is already arranged)
We're **going to switch** *production to the Philippines.*
(this is our intention)
We're **not going to renew** *your contract.* (this is our intention)

3 Present simple

We use the present simple

• for things that are timetabled, scheduled, or fixed.

Our financial year **starts** *on 1 January.*
What time **is** *the meeting tomorrow?*

• after time clauses with *when, while, after, before, as soon as, until,* etc.

Could you wait here **while** *I* **go** *and* **get** *the file?*
We can't make a decision **until** *we* **get** *your answer.*
I'll phone you **as soon as** *I* **get** *to the hotel.*

4 Future perfect

We use the future perfect (*will* + *have* + past participle) to describe something that will be finished by a particular time in the future.

We'll make a decision at 6. We'll **have seen** *all the applicants by then.*
Scientists **will have found** *a cure for cancer* **by the end of the century.**

5 Future continuous

We use the future continuous (*will + be + -ing*) to describe something that will be in progress at a particular time in the future.

> **This time next week I will be sitting** on a beach in the Caribbean.
> Don't ring me **between 7.30 and 9.30**. I'll be **watching** the football.

unit 9 conditionals 0, 1 and 2

We use a conditional form to suggest a connection between an action or situation and its result.

> *If the CEO resigns, our share price will fall.*
> *If we increased our market share, we'd make more profit.*

1 The zero conditional

We use *if + present simple + present simple* to describe a situation that always has the same result. It usually refers to something that is obvious, easy to do, a general truth or a scientific fact.

> *If you **stand** in the rain, you **get** wet.* (obvious)
> *If you **push** this button, the TV **comes** on.* (easy to do)
> *If you **look after** your staff, they **stay** longer.* (a fact of business life)

2 The first conditional

We use *if + present simple + will/won't + bare infinitive* to refer to something in the future which is likely or possible.

> *If they **improve** quality, there'll be fewer complaints.*
> *If business **increases**, we'll **move** to a bigger office*
> *If you **buy** 2000, you'll **get** a discount.*

3 The second conditional

a We use *if + past simple + modal + bare infinitive* to refer to an unlikely or hypothetical situation.

> *If I **won** the lottery, I'd **retire**.* (but that's easier said than done)
> *If we **raised** interest rates, inflation **would come down**.* (but there would also be less growth)
> *If we **opened** the shop on Sundays, we'd **increase** our turnover.* (but on the other hand we'd have to pay the staff more)

b The second conditional is often used when negotiating, bargaining or trying to resolve a dispute.

> *If we **paid** you in cash, **would** you **give** us a discount?*
> ***Would** you **increase** our hourly rate if we **called off** the strike?*

4 Further information on conditionals

The subjunctive form (*I were*) is sometimes used, especially when giving advice.

> *If **I was/were** you, I would change the suppliers. They're not reliable.*
> *If **I was/were** promoted, I would earn more money.*

unit 10 the passive

Compare the active and passive sentences below.

> a *The Managing Director **opened** the sales conference.*
> b *The sales conference **was opened** by the Managing Director.*

Although the information in these two sentences is the same, the emphasis is different. The active sentence a emphasises 'who' and the passive sentence b emphasises 'what'. The passive puts less emphasis on people and more on things, so it is often seen as being more impersonal and neutral than the active voice.

1 We use the passive

a when it's the action which is important, not the person doing it.

> ***Are** you **being served**?*
> *Why **haven't** these invoices **been paid**?*

b when we don't need to explain who did something because it's obvious from the context.

> *Three of my colleagues **have been made redundant**.* (by the company)
> *When **was** the new tax **introduced**?* (by the government)

c when the speaker is trying to be impartial or objective, giving information without blaming anybody.

> *Fred and his boss had an argument. Shouts **were heard** and a window **was broken**.*

d when we don't know or we don't explain who did something.

> *My car's **been stolen**.*
> *The new headquarters **were built** last year.*

e for a formal or legal notice. The effect is impersonal but clear.

> *Smoking **is forbidden**.*
> *Goods **will** only **be exchanged** on presentation of a valid receipt.*

f to describe a process.

> *Details of orders **are sent** to Accounts and an invoice **is** then **sent** to the customer. Two days later the goods **are dispatched**.*

g with modals.

*All passes **must be shown**.*
*Only one piece of hand luggage **can be taken** on board.*
*All electrical equipment **should be turned off** at the end of the day.*

2 Further information on the passive

a Only transitive verbs (e.g. *raise*) can be put into the passive. Intransitive verbs (e.g. *rise*) have no passive form.

*We **raised** £1,000,000 for charity last year.* (active)
*£1,000,000 **has been raised** for the new hospital.* (passive)

Inflation has risen again. (not ~~Inflation has been risen~~)

b An active sentence with two objects will often have two passive forms.

*The advertising agency showed **us three short films**.*
***We** were shown three short films (by the advertising agency).*
***Three short films** were shown to us (by the advertising agency).*

c The passive is found in all the main tenses.

*Dinner **will be served** at eight.*
*By the time we got to the theatre all the tickets **had been sold**.*
*I couldn't get hold of him. His mobile phone **may have been switched off**.*

unit 11 the *-ing* form

1 We use the *-ing* form

a after the verb *be* in all the continuous tense forms.

***I'm studying** for an MBA.*
*When **are** they **going** to set up the company?*
*It **was snowing** when the train arrived.*
*Next January, she will have **been working** here for 25 years.*

b after certain verbs, such as *admit, avoid, deny, enjoy, feel like, finish, involve, mind, miss, risk* and *suggest*.

*How can I **avoid paying** so much tax?*
*I really **enjoyed working** in Milan.*
*I don't **feel like working** today.*
*Do you **mind having** to do shift work?*

c after all prepositions, with these three different structures:

* verb + preposition + *-ing*

  *She **learned** Spanish **by watching** Mexican soap operas.*
  *She **paused before answering** the question.*

* adjective + preposition + *-ing*

  *I was **tired of listening** to her complaints.*
  *He's not very **good at making** speeches.*

* noun + preposition + *-ing*

  *What was the **cost of hiring** the room?*
  *Someone told the media about the accident, but there's no **way of knowing** who did it.*

d after certain phrases such as *it's no use, it's no good, there's no point* and *can't stand*.

***There's no point staying** in a job if you're unhappy.*
***It's no good shouting** at me. It won't change anything.*
*He **can't stand losing**. He's very competitive.*

e as a noun or as part of a noun phrase, often as the subject of a sentence.

***Smoking** is forbidden.*
***Shoplifting** adds about four per cent to our costs.*
***Getting to know what your customers want** can take years.*

Note: we often replace the *-ing* form with a pronoun when we speak about something for a second time.

***Working** in an open-plan office is quite difficult.*
*Don't worry. You'll soon get used to **it**.*

2 Infinitive or *-ing* form?

A few verbs (e.g. *like, mean, stop*) can be followed by either the *-ing* form or an infinitive.

a Sometimes there is no real change of meaning.

*I **like to eat** in expensive restaurants.*
*I **like eating** in expensive restaurants.*

b With certain verbs, the two structures carry different meanings.

Compare the following pairs of sentences:

*I **meant to send** you an e-mail, but I just forgot. Sorry.* (*mean* + *to* + infinitive = intend)
*If you take the job, it'll **mean working** one weekend in four.* (*mean* + *-ing* = involve/require)

*We all **stopped talking** when the boss walked in.* (we were talking, we stopped)
*I **stopped to buy** a sandwich on the way to work.* (I stopped in order to buy it)

unit 12 third conditional and past modals

1 The third conditional

a We use *if* + past perfect + modal + present perfect to link an impossible situation in the past to its result.

*If the plane **hadn't been** delayed, we **would have caught** our connecting flight.* (but it was, and we had to change our plans)

*If you **had opened** that e-mail, the virus **would have wiped out** your hard disk.* (but you didn't, thankfully)

2 Past modals

a We use *should* + *have* + past participle to criticise past actions.

*Why are you so late? You **should have been** here at six. They **shouldn't have closed down** the factory. It was still making a profit.*

b We use *could* + *have* + past participle to talk about things that were possible, but didn't happen.

*I **could have left** this company years ago, but I decided to stay.*

c We use *would* + *have* + past participle to talk about things that didn't happen or were impossible.

*Our last MD **would have done** things very differently. (but he is no longer with the company)*

unit 13 articles

1 *A* or *an*?

We use *a* before:

a the 21 consonants.

*Is there **a fax** machine at the hotel?
Let's have **a break**.*

b *eu-* and *u-* when they are pronounced /juː/.

*How much is **a euro** worth?
She's **a university** professor.*

We use *an* before:

a the five vowels; *a, e, i, o, u.*

*Do you have **an e-mail** address?
We've asked the bank for **an overdraft**.*

b a silent *h.*

*It's **an honour** to be asked to give the opening speech.
It took us **an hour** to get through customs.*

2 We use *a* and *an*

a to refer to a single countable noun.

*She works for **an insurance company**.
They installed **a new phone** in the office.*

b for jobs.

*I'm **an** engineer.*

c in certain expressions with numbers, where the indefinite article means *each* or *every*.

*The minimum wage is **$10 an hour**.
Our main call centre handles about **400,000** enquiries **a year**.*

3 We use *the*

a when we refer to a specific, understood thing.

*Why don't we have lunch in **the staff canteen**?
Can you distribute **the minutes** of **the meeting**?*

b for things which are unique.

***The earth** goes round **the sun**.
What effect has **the Internet** had on your business?*

c with an adjective, to describe a social group or the people who come from a particular country.

*According to the report, **the rich** are getting richer and **the poor** are getting poorer.
When inflation rises, it's **the elderly** who suffer most.
The French are famous for their love of good food.*

d for various international organizations.

*China joined **The World Trade Organisation** in 2002.
The President is giving a speech at **The United Nations** tomorrow.*

e for rivers, seas, oceans, groups of islands, chains of mountains and deserts.

***The Amazon** is the longest river in South America.
The best caviar comes from **the Caspian Sea**.
The Azores are in **the Atlantic**.
This part of **the Sahara** has an annual rainfall of 23 mm.*

4 We use no article with

a plural and uncountable nouns, to refer to things in general.

*Most of the countries that export **oil** belong to OPEC.*

But in a more specific sense:

***The oil** we use for heating is different from **the oil** we use in cars.*

b cities, continents, islands, mountains, sports and countries (but there are a few exceptions such as *The UK* and *The Philippines*).

*Mozart was born in **Vienna**.
Australia is the biggest island in the world.
Mount Fuji is approximately 100 kilometres from **Tokyo**.
I watched a lot of **cricket** when I worked in **India**.*

5 Further information on articles

We often use the indefinite article (*a* or *an*) the first time we refer to something, and the definite article (*the*) when we refer to it a second time.

*We have vacancies for **a** Market Research Assistant and **an** Accounts Clerk. **The** Market Research Assistant will work in the Marketing department and **the** Accounts Clerk will be responsible for salary payments.*

unit 14 degrees of future certainty

a When we talk about the future, we can make our comments more emphatic or precise by adding an adverb like *certainly*, *definitely*, *possibly*, or *probably*.

*I'll **probably take** the overnight train.*
*We'll **certainly need** to borrow more money.*
*We're **probably** going to eat out tonight.*

b The construction *it is + certain/clear/possible/ likely/probable + that + noun + will* is more formal and objective.

***It's clear that** higher interest rates will slow growth.*
***It's probable that** more people will work at home in the future.*

c *certain* and *likely / unlikely* can also be placed after a noun, with this construction: noun + *am/are/is + certainly/likely/unlikely* + full infinitive.

*Managers **are certain to** object to the new measures.*
*The bank **is unlikely to** increase our overdraft.*

d When we want to express a more personal, softer, and less certain view, we often use a modal.

*I think we **may see** a strong recovery in the second quarter.*
*We **might open** a branch in Cairo.*
*There **could be** some interesting changes next year.*

tapescripts

unit 1

Listening 2

Journalist So, Ms Malvini, I'll make some notes during our interview. Do you mind if I record our conversation as well?

Maria Of course not, but ... um ... my surname is actually Maldini, not Malvini. But please just call me Maria.

Journalist I'm sorry, I must have misheard that when we spoke on the phone. How do you spell your family name?

Maria M-A-L-D-I-N-I. It's an Italian name.

Journalist OK. I've got it now. Sorry about that.

Maria No problem.

Journalist So Maria, you organise fitness training and beauty treatments for working women.

Maria That's right.

Journalist Could you tell me how you first got the idea for the business?

Maria Certainly. I suppose it all started about five years after I came to live in England. I was on holiday back home in Italy and I had a very bad skiing accident. I found that the only thing that helped the pain was massage and gentle exercise, like yoga or stretching exercises, so I used to go to therapists and classes after work.

Journalist Where did you work at that time?

Maria In the training department of a media company.

Journalist I see.

Maria But then I got a promotion to Training Manager. That meant I worked longer hours and it was difficult to get to classes. I asked some of my teachers if they would come to my house instead and, to my surprise, most of them agreed. It was more expensive, of course, but I thought it was worth it. Lots of my friends liked the idea too, so I recommended people to them. That's when I began to realise that maybe I could make a business out of this.

Journalist Did you give up your job then?

Maria No, not immediately, the idea was too scary. I had a good job, which I liked, with a good salary, and starting my own business seemed a bit risky. So I just did it as a hobby, really.

Journalist So what was your reason for becoming self-employed?

Maria Well, the decision was made for me, really. My company decided to relocate to a different town. They offered me the choice of relocating with them, or quite a large sum of money if I preferred to leave. I know an opportunity when I see it, so I took the money!

Journalist Good for you! How long have you been in business?

Maria I started the company just over a year ago.

Journalist Are you pleased with the way things are going?

Maria Very! I already have about 50 beauty therapists and fitness trainers on my books, and 300 regular customers in this area.

Journalist Does the treatment or training always take place in the customer's home?

Maria Yes. That's what makes my service different. It's particularly popular with busy career women because it's very easy for them – they can visit my website to see the range of services I offer. Then, if they want to try a treatment, they call me or send me an e-mail, I contact the therapist or trainer and arrange the appointment, and she goes to the customer's home.

Journalist What do you like most about working for yourself?

Maria I enjoy the freedom. I can make my own decisions without having to ask anyone else. And of course, I'm doing something I enjoy and believe in. I've tried every treatment myself that I offer to my customers, so I know that they work and help people to relax or just feel better in themselves.

Journalist Is there anything you miss about working for a company?

Maria Only the friends I had there. But I still see some of them socially and I have a lot of contact with people over the phone in this job, so it's not a big problem. But basically, I have no regrets!

Journalist That's marvellous. So things seem to be going very well now. What about the future ...?

unit 2

Listening 2

Most of the components for the medical equipment we produce are made at our own production facilities both here and abroad, but some of the sub-components such as electrical microchips come from external suppliers. My team has responsibility for sourcing them and negotiating prices and delivery dates. It's very important that these sub-components conform to the same standards which we set for our own materials and components. This means we have to work very closely with Quality Control.

Listening 4

1 In my team we usually spend about 25% of our time here and the rest of the time on the road visiting customers. Our customers are mainly doctors and other health professionals. Apart from selling the products, a big part of our work is to educate customers about the products. We work closely with Marketing to produce product information and specifications. Currently, we're working on specifications for the new Byron range. I'm co-ordinating the project. We're launching the Byron range in Asia next month, so tomorrow I'm seeing the Product Manager to discuss product training for the sales team in Asia.

2 Ours is primarily a service function, as our main role is to ensure that the business systems within the entire company run effectively. These range from e-mail and office systems to the complex computer systems which run our automated production lines. At the moment, I'm working with the Software Development team. We're developing a new order processing system for Sales. Whatever the project, one of our main priorities is to ensure that all our systems are accessible and easy to use.

3 One of my team's main tasks is to develop packages to provide the necessary information for sales teams in the company's thirteen subsidiaries. These packages include product specifications for the various products and different types of advertising material. Currently, we're developing brochures and leaflets for the launch of the Byron range in the Asian market. I'm co-ordinating activities with the advertising agency who are doing the design work. It's interesting to work for a truly international company, dealing with people from all over the world. They all have different views on things, different cultures, and so on.

4 I originally joined the company in Production as an engineer. Now my main responsibility is making sure every product leaves the factories in perfect condition. My team also works with Marketing to produce technical documentation for all our subsidiaries. This ensures that the same standards are maintained throughout the company. At the moment, we're working on a joint project to prepare a set of guidelines for operators in our new factory in Malaysia. In fact, I'm going there next month to train personnel in the new procedures.

Language in use 1

Extract 1
In my team we usually spend about 25% of our time here and the rest of the time on the road visiting customers.

Extract 2
Our customers are mainly doctors and other health professionals. Apart from selling the products, a big part of our work is to educate customers about the products. We work closely with Marketing to produce product information and specifications.

Extract 3
Currently, we're working on specifications for the new Byron range. I'm co-ordinating the project.

Extract 4
We're launching the Byron range in Asia next month, so tomorrow I'm seeing the Product Manager to discuss product training for the sales team in Asia.

Speaking 1

Extract 1
Woman   Where do you work?
Marco   At Sonic Laboratories.
Woman   Oh, really? I don't know the company, I'm afraid. What do they do?
Marco   We produce medical equipment.
Woman   That must be very rewarding. And what do you do yourself?
Marco   I work in Quality Assurance.
Woman   I see. So what are you working on at present?
Marco   A project in Malaysia. We're opening a new factory there.
Woman   Malaysia. That sounds very interesting.
Marco   Well, yes and no. I'm doing a lot of travelling at the moment and my family don't like that.

Extract 2
Woman   Where do you work?
Marco   I work in the Quality Assurance department at Sonic Laboratories. I don't know if you know the company. We produce very specialist medical equipment for hospitals. That might sound a bit dull to a non-engineer, but actually I find the job fulfilling. It's good to know that you're helping people to overcome difficulties.

Woman   Yes, I can imagine that must be very satisfying. So what are you working on at the moment?
Marco   A big project in Malaysia. We're opening a new factory there and I'm responsible for setting up quality procedures.
Woman   That sounds very interesting.
Marco   It is, and challenging too. It's rather hectic at the moment as I'm doing a lot of travelling and that's a bit hard on my family, but otherwise I really enjoy the work.

unit 3

Listening 3

Conversation 1
Enrica   Is that Alicia Gomez?
Alicia   Yes, speaking.
Enrica   Hello, It's Enrica Grasi from Geneva.
Alicia   Hello, Enrica. How can I help you?
Enrica   I'm fixing up the next project team meeting and I just wanted to check some possible dates with you.
Alicia   Fine. Let me just get my diary. OK. Which dates are you thinking of?
Enrica   I've spoken to the others and they prefer either the third week of October or the first week of November.
Alicia   Yes, both those weeks are pretty clear at the moment, except for the twenty-third.
Enrica   Right, I've got that.
Alicia   So, where's the meeting taking place this time?
Enrica   It was going to be in Geneva, but I spoke to Carlos Rivas in Mexico City and he suggested New York. He thinks it'll be more convenient for most of the team.
Alicia   He's probably right. It would certainly be much easier for me. And I'm sure you could find a meeting room somewhere near the airport.
Enrica   That's a good idea. I'll check out some hotels in that area and get back to you towards the end of the week …
Alicia   Fine, but I'm not in the office on Friday.
Enrica   OK. I'll call you later in the afternoon on Thursday.
Alicia   No problem. By the way, Enrica, who's going?

Listening 5

Conversation 2
Patricia   Could I speak to Enrica Grasi, please?
Karl   I'm afraid she's not in the office right now. Can I take a message?
Patricia   Yes. My name is Patricia Callahan from the Crowne Hotel.
Karl   Sorry. Can you spell your last name?
Patricia   Yes, it's C-A-double L-A-H-A-N.
Karl   OK, got it. And what's the message?
Patricia   Ms Grasi rang me yesterday about a meeting she's organising.
Karl   Ah yes, the meeting in New York.
Patricia   That's right. And I'm getting back to her with some prices.
Karl   OK.
Patricia   Prices for the rooms first. For five people for two nights, it's a total of $2,180. That's our group rate.
Karl   OK.
Patricia   And for a meeting room for two days, it's $150 per day. That includes a buffet lunch, soft drinks and coffee.
Karl   OK. Fine. While you're on the phone, there is one other thing …

Conversation 3

Hello, Martyn, this is Enrica Grasi from Geneva. I'm calling about the team meeting in New York. I'm really sorry, but you're the only one who preferred November. Everyone else has gone for October, so the final dates are now the twenty-fifth and the twenty-sixth. I hope you can manage to reschedule your other commitments. I'm proposing a ten o'clock start so people can fly into New York on the first morning of the meeting if they want to. The hotel is the Park Avenue and it's very near the airport at La Guardia.

My assistant Karl Davidson is booking rooms at the same hotel. Could you let him know which nights you want to stay? Thanks. Oh, one other thing, I'm putting together the agenda for the meeting. If you have any points that you want to add …

Speaking 2

In my opinion, the most important thing when choosing a hotel for an international meeting is the meeting room or rooms. For example, you may need a large room where everyone can be together for presentations, and smaller meeting rooms for informal group discussions.

Then, if people are coming from different countries, you need to find out about rooms for them to stay in. These should be spacious and comfortable, and have facilities for using e-mail and laptops, as people have to keep in touch with their offices even when they're away.

My next point is amenities for hotel guests – things like a bar, a good quality restaurant and fitness and sports facilities. These are important because delegates need to be able to relax after a long day of meetings and get to know each other in informal situations.

Finally, for an international meeting where delegates are coming from different countries, it can be very useful to choose a hotel which has good transport connections with the nearest airport. This can save everybody a lot of time.

unit 4

Listening 2

Interviewer	Today in our series on dotcom businesses we'll be talking about the infamous collapse of boo.com, the high profile on-line clothing retailer which was set up in November 1999 and went out of business a mere six months later. I have Marlene Preiss and Frank Tam, retail analysts, in the studio with me. Marlene, would you say that it was inevitable that boo.com got into trouble?
Marlene	Absolutely. Even by Christmas '99 it was becoming clear that the company had big financial problems. Sales were much lower than anticipated at that stage.
Interviewer	How did they get into that situation?
Marlene	I'd say it was down to poor management decisions. They were over-ambitious and I think they made a big mistake when they decided to launch the site in eighteen countries – all at the same time, and in five different languages. It increased their start-up costs enormously. Another factor was the high level of spending on technology and marketing, for example, in the first three months they spent £25 million on advertising – ads on TV, on the radio and in expensive fashion magazines like *Elle*.

Interviewer	The directors of boo.com had a reputation for extravagance. Do you think they deserved it?
Marlene	There were certainly lots of stories about Concorde flights and lavish parties all around the world. Basically, they were spending too much for the amount of business they were bringing in.
Interviewer	Would you agree with that, Frank?
Frank	Yes, but I don't think you can put all their difficulties down to excessive spending, there were a lot of technical problems. In fact, the site was five months late launching because it took so long to develop the order processing system. And then, even after the site was launched, it got a lot of bad press as it was so slow and complicated to use. The design looked great, but it was too technically advanced for most computers and getting around was frustratingly slow.
Interviewer	How did they deal with these problems?
Frank	Well, after Christmas the site was totally redesigned to make it easier to use. They also reduced prices by as much as 40 per cent on some products. The strategy seemed to work and sales began to recover in the spring.
Interviewer	So how come everything went wrong in May?
Marlene	They ran out of money. By then they'd used up all the initial £80 million funding and were looking for an additional £20 million to survive. They didn't get it. The original investors – the banks, JP Morgan and Goldman Sachs, and Benetton, the Italian design company – lost confidence in the company and refused to put in the extra money.
Interviewer	And that was the end of boo.com?
Marlene	Pretty much. They tried in vain to find a buyer, so everyone was made redundant in London and at boo's other offices abroad.
Interviewer	Do you think a company like boo would attract that level of investment in today's business climate?
Frank	I doubt it. The collapse of boo made investors very nervous. At that time, people were prepared to put money into almost any on-line business. I think that's changed and today's investors are only interested in high quality businesses with experienced people, and a really good business plan. boo had a great idea and some very talented people, but they really hadn't thought it through.

unit 5

Listening 3

Message 1

Katie	Hi, James. It's Katie here. One of my children is ill, so I won't be in the office today. There are a couple of things I need you to do for me. First, can you call Martin Jarvis at CFI Training? He sent me a brochure about their skills development courses a few days ago and I'm interested in a course on time management. There's one at the end of June. If it's not full, can you book me on it? Second, I need to follow up on last week's department meeting, so can you e-mail me the minutes? Oh, James, sorry to give you so much extra work. I'll call you after two to see how everything's going. Bye for now.

Message 2

Jacques Hello, this is Jacques Barbier from Packaging Solutions in Brussels. It's eight a.m. on Monday. I'm afraid I have a problem with our meeting at two-thirty on Wednesday afternoon. I have to go to head office in New York, unexpectedly. I'm leaving later today and I won't be back until Thursday morning. I know it's very short notice, but could we change the meeting to Friday? I can be at your offices by ten. Can you ... can you let me know if that's OK? I'll be here in the office until three this afternoon. After that you can contact me at the Plaza Hotel in New York on 212 993 5050.

Listening 5

James Can I speak to Martin Jarvis, please?

Martin Yes, speaking. How can I help you?

James My name's James Riley from Caramia. You sent a colleague of mine a brochure a couple of days ago and I'd like to register her for one of your courses.

Martin Excellent. Just a minute while I get a registration form. Right. I just need to take down some details. So what course is it for?

James Time Management. I've got the code in front of me. It's TM 15.

Martin OK. Which dates are you thinking of?

James Sometime towards the end of June.

Martin OK. Let me see. It's a two-day course. We've got one starting on the 22nd and another the following week, beginning on the 29th.

James The second date would be better.

Martin OK. I just need the name now?

James It's Katie Whiteley. That's W-H-I-T-E-L-E-Y. Katie's one of our product managers.

Martin OK. Great. And who should I send the invoice to?

James Can you mark it for the attention of Mary Fraser? She's the PA for the marketing team.

Martin No problem. Let me make a note of that. OK. I've got all the information I need. Is there anything else you want to ask me?

unit 6

Listening 3

1 You're really meant to wear gloves when you're adding the toner, but if you don't, you should at least always wash your hands immediately afterwards. Apparently, people quite often lick their finger to lift a sheet of paper just after putting in the toner and it seems this can cause an infection, and we certainly don't want that.

2 My main concern is the question of access to fire exits and extinguishers. On my tour of the building I noticed several of these were obstructed by boxes and cartons which could cause fatal delays in the event of an accident. You should arrange for immediate clearance of these areas and train your staff to keep them clear.

3 Well, it seems that the cleaner was called away in the middle of cleaning the entrance hall to answer an urgent personal phone call – her mother is seriously ill in hospital, I believe – so she didn't mop the tiles dry as usual. She was back a minute later, but the client had already slipped on the wet surface and fractured his hip.

4 That's a good question. Yes, the law also applies to any members of the public injured on your premises. You don't need to inform us if they suffer a minor injury, but if they

are taken to hospital you must let us know immediately by phone and follow this up with a completed accident report form within ten days.

5 I told him that my eyes were dry and sore, but he just prescribed eye-drops and told me to use the computer less often – as if I could in my job! Then I read this leaflet that says photocopiers make the air dry, and I've got one just next to my desk. So really the company should do something about it.

Listening 5

1 Yes, well, I do think some of our practices here are far from satisfactory, and that's not good news. It's really a question of information. You can't be aware of what you don't know, or don't remember. There should be signs up everywhere, not just in the HR office, listing all the dos and don'ts of what we should and shouldn't do. That way we'd see them more often, not just when we went in with a pay query or shift changes.

2 There's not much space in here anyway. We really want bigger offices to accommodate the flow of people we get through here, and all the stuff that we have to store. In the meantime, we ought to have more and better lamps installed, which would make the place seem airier and reduce the shadows over some of the desks that can cause eyestrain from peering at screens all the time, especially on the evening shift.

3 In my training when I first joined the company, they explained the necessity of working in shifts. But the way they organise them means we get tired. And given that we're operating heavy machinery, it's a dangerous situation, because we're much more likely to make mistakes and cause injury. They should replace the current set-up of making people work such long hours at different times with something better. It's putting money before safety, and that can't be right.

4 Sure, there are quite a few signs up around the place about safety, though I don't know how many people actually read them. And there are just as many about turning off lights to save electricity, anyway. We should have more direct training, and it should be at times when people doing different shifts can make it, too, so we all get regular reminders of what to do and not to do to avoid danger.

5 Well, I'm frankly surprised we haven't had more accidents. This place is so badly laid out – it's claustrophobic. Papers and files are piled up on desks and chairs, even against fire exits, getting all dusty, and in people's way. We need proper storage units put in to accommodate it all, and then we could have enough space to move around in here, instead of people bumping into things all the time.

unit 7

Listening 3

Mark So, you've been in the Human Resources department at Romtech for three years. And I see from your CV that you joined them straight after university.

Margot That's right.

Mark So can you tell me a bit about the job?

Margot Well, my first job was Human Resources Assistant. I was part of a team of eight which looks after general human resources for the company – everything from recruitment, compensation and benefits packages, right through to giving help and advice to the employees. But my main task was recruitment administration.

Mark   So, what did that involve?

Margot I had to liaise with the managers and the candidates, for example, make sure that all the CVs were circulated to the right people, set up interviews and then deal with follow-up correspondence, check references. All that kind of thing.

Mark   And what did you like most about the job?

Margot I suppose the contact with people. You get to know a lot of people in the company very quickly and a lot of people know you.

Mark   And was there anything you didn't like?

Margot Oh, yes, having to tell candidates that their application had been turned down. I found that quite difficult, especially if I'd had a lot of contact with them on the phone.

Mark   I can understand that. I find that difficult myself. But at that stage you didn't do any actual interviewing?

Margot No, but as part of my general training I did some courses in interviewing techniques and presentation skills.

Mark   And did they help you in your job?

Margot Well, at the time I didn't find them that useful in my day-to-day work, but when I moved into graduate recruitment in January last year, I had to do a lot of interviewing and give presentations about the company, so I was able to put the skills I'd learnt into practice. It gave me a lot of confidence to do the job.

Mark   Right. OK. Can I now ask you a few questions about your work in graduate recruitment? How different is it from your first job?

Margot I have two people working for me, so nowadays I can spend more time interviewing candidates and making contacts with university careers staff, and less time on day-to-day administration.

Mark   And what do you find difficult about the job?

Margot One problem is I don't have a background in IT and sometimes I get asked difficult technical questions during interviews which I just can't answer. That can be a bit embarrassing.

Mark   So how do you deal with it?

Margot I find honesty's the best policy. I just tell them it's not my area, and promise to contact one of our people from that field and e-mail them back.

Mark   And they're happy with that?

Margot Yes, it usually works.

Mark   OK. I see you have some experience of job fairs. How useful do you think they are?

Margot Yes, attending job fairs at universities is an important part of my job. I think they're really useful for making contact with careers development staff and prospective candidates. It can be pretty tiring though, and it means you're out of the office a lot in the autumn and the spring, so we try to share the work between the three of us.

Mark   That's fine. OK. Can you think of any task where you've had to work independently?

Margot Yes, I have sole responsibility for the UK side of the job swap programme for our graduate trainees.

Mark   A job swap programme? How does that work?

Margot Well, Romtech wants its graduates to get as much international experience as possible, so about eighteen months ago they set up a programme which allows graduates from the different subsidiaries to swap jobs for three months. For example, a graduate in the Belgian subsidiary can exchange jobs with someone on the UK graduate programme.

Mark   That's interesting. Has it been successful?

Margot Yes, I think so. In the first year I arranged exchanges with two graduates from Spain, and three from France. And this year there are even more people interested.

Mark   What did you find particularly challenging about the project?

Margot Mmm ... I think for me the most difficult thing was setting the project up and fitting it in with my normal work. I was really busy at the time.

Mark   How did you manage it?

Margot Well, in the end I had to do a lot of extra hours at the weekends, but it was a great learning experience, and I've made some useful contacts in the other Romtech companies.

Mark   So why do you want to leave this wonderful job ...?

Speaking 1

Extract 1

A   So, shall we talk about the communication problems first?

B   OK. Well, I think it's very important that customers get a good impression of the company, and the first contact is often by phone. Perhaps telephone skills training would help our staff to sound more friendly and interested in our customers.

A   Yes, that's a good idea. And what's more ...

Extract 2

A   You know, it occurs to me that the problem could be that our sales staff have too much work to do and that's why they seem unhelpful and don't answer letters and e-mails.

B   You could be right. I hadn't thought of that. So you think we should recruit more staff, then?

A   Well, that's one possibility. Or another idea would be to give the existing staff training in time management skills.

B   That's true. And that would be cheaper than hiring more people.

A   OK, so we've got three possible solutions. Any other ideas?

B   Not at the moment.

A   Let's move on to the delivery problems, then.

unit 8

Listening 1

Extract 1

PD   Maybe you could start by telling me a little more about your business and your customer base. I'm actually an occasional customer of yours myself, so I know something about what you do ...

SC   That explains it – I thought I recognised you from somewhere. I wish I'd known who you were before! I approached a couple of other agencies before I came to you, but I wasn't really impressed with their work, and it was my friend Janet Parker at the Small Business Association who told me about you.

PD   What a coincidence! Now we're both clients of each other!

SC   So, you know then that we specialise in take-out salads and low calorie hot lunches. We started out five years ago with just sandwiches and the business evolved into what it is now, more or less by chance. I introduced the salads first, and soon they were selling better than the sandwiches. Then my partner, Maggie, joined me. She's a nutritionist and runs evening weight-loss classes and she said lots of working women in her groups found it hard to stick to their diets at lunch-time, because there were so few places to eat healthily in the time available. That's when I introduced the low calorie hot meals, and they've been a big success.

PD So am I right in thinking that most of your customers are office workers?

SC The majority, yes, though I also get shoppers who want to take something home for lunch with them.

PD I see. And you say you're going to start a delivery service?

SC That's right. A lot of our regular customers say they know plenty of other people who'd love our products, but they work too far away to get to us, so we're going to take our products to them.

PD And that's why you've come to me.

SC Exactly. We think the delivery service will be popular, but we're making a big investment in delivery staff and motorcycles, so we want to be sure it pays off. That means we need to reach people who don't know about us yet.

PD What kinds of advertising have worked for you so far?

SC To tell the truth, we haven't done much of anything up to now. Most of our business has come through word-of-mouth, or people just passing by and seeing that we're doing something different. Every so often we distribute sample menus to offices in the area, but that's about it.

Extract 2

PD I see. So we've identified your main customers as office workers, both male and female. What about your USP?

SC My what? Oh, right ... the unique selling proposition – you know, I'm never quite sure what it means.

PD Well, it's basically just the features and benefits that make your product different from the competition. In other words, what does a customer get by buying your product or service instead of someone else's?

SC Right – well, a ready lunch that's healthy, low in calories, tasty and made with fresh ingredients. And once the delivery service starts, the big point is convenience, because it'll be delivered straight to their desk.

PD OK, good. Well, since it's the new delivery service that you want to promote, we'll certainly emphasise the aspect of convenience. What else? I mean, of all the other things you mentioned – healthy food, low-calorie meals, tasty, fresh ingredients – what do you think is the main one that keeps your target buyers coming back to you?

SC Well, it's hard to narrow it down to one thing – I think the fact that it's healthy food is very important, and the low-calorie meals are just one aspect of that, because the salads are healthy too. But I think the real point is that people find our food tasty – you might eat something once or twice because it's good for you, but you probably won't come back again if it doesn't taste good.

PD That's very true. OK, then, so the ads we create for you need to emphasise the health aspect, the taste and the convenience of having the food delivered.

SC Yes, definitely.

PD OK. Tell me, when exactly are you launching the delivery service?

SC On 1 October.

PD Right, that gives us about five weeks. Now, from what you said on the phone about your advertising budget, I think your most cost-effective option would be to combine advertising on local radio for two or three weeks before your launch, with advertisements in the local newspaper in the week leading up to the launch. You may want to consider some kind of promotional

offer too like coupons in the paper giving discounts to the first customers of the delivery service.

SC Maggie and I actually talked about that before, and I still think it's a good idea.

PD OK, so we'll put together a proposal for you along the lines we've discussed, including a script for a radio commercial, copy for the print ads and a couple of different options for an introductory promotion. I'll get back to you in the middle of next week and we can arrange another meeting at which we will present our ideas.

SC Oh, I meant to ask – it is you who's responsible for arranging the radio air time and newspaper ads, isn't it?

PD That's right. We'll arrange all the media buying for you – that's included in the fee I quoted to you on the phone.

SC Great!

Language in use 1

Extract 1
SC ... they work too far away to get to us, so we're going to take our products to them.

Extract 2
SC We think the delivery service will be popular, but ...

Extract 3
PD Tell me, when exactly are you launching the delivery service?

Extract 4
PD I'll get back to you in the middle of next week and ...

Extract 5
PD ... we can arrange another meeting at which we will present our ideas.

unit 9

Listening 1

Duncan Patrick, I'd like to ask you about how FDC gets into new markets. When the company is expanding into different countries, how do you manage it?

Patrick Well, ideally we like to buy up a distribution company or set up our own sales office, which means we can then control the product all the way from our warehouse to the eventual customer. It also means, of course, that we keep all the profits ourselves, instead of paying someone else for doing part of the job. That isn't always possible though, and especially in a new market we often work with a local distributor.

Duncan So how do you set about finding a distributor?

Patrick We need to do a lot of research. But, if we have any difficulties one of the best ways of arriving at a short list is to go through the British Embassy. We tell them exactly what we want, and they check whether any local companies have contacted them about distributing goods from the UK. That worked very well for us last year when we wanted to change our distributor in Spain.

Duncan I see. So when you've got your short list – what do you do then?

Patrick First, we contact the likely companies on the short list and brief them about our business and what we're looking for.

Duncan	Do you do that by phone?
Patrick	Not initially, no. We start off with some sort of formal letter, and then, if they're interested, we discuss things over the phone. After that, we set up meetings and I go out and visit them personally – check out exactly how they operate, the size of their operations, what sort of contacts they have, things like that. This is absolutely vital. Unless you go out and meet these people personally and look around their offices you won't find out how good they are at doing their job.
Duncan	Of course. And if you like what you see …?
Patrick	If any of them look particularly promising, I'll visit them again to discuss the financial and marketing details.
Duncan	If it was a company you didn't know much about, would you go about it in a different way?
Patrick	We'd be extremely cautious! Before we got into detailed discussions, I'd try to find out the names of other companies this distributor was working for, and if there were any British companies, I'd contact them to check the distributor's reliability. If their reports weren't good, we wouldn't go ahead.
Duncan	So, it seems it can be quite a long process before you're finally in a position to sign the final contract?
Patrick	That's right. But it's time well spent. We need to be absolutely sure before we sign, because mistakes can be very costly.

Language in use 1

Extract 1

Patrick	We need to do a lot of research. But, if we have any difficulties, one of the best ways of arriving at a short list is to go through the British Embassy.

Extract 2

Duncan	Do you do that by phone?
Patrick	Not initially, no. We start off with some sort of formal letter, and then, if they're interested, we discuss things over the phone. After that, we set up meetings and I go out and visit them personally – check out exactly how they operate, the size of their operations, what sorts of contacts they have, things like that. This is absolutely vital. Unless you go out and meet these people personally and look around their offices, you won't find out how good they are at doing their job.
Duncan	Of course. And if you like what you see …?
Patrick	If any of them look particularly promising, I'll visit them again to discuss the financial and marketing details.

Extract 3

Duncan	If it was a company you didn't know much about, would you go about it in a different way?
Patrick	We'd be extremely cautious! Before we got into detailed discussions, I'd try to find out the names of other companies this distributor was working for, and if there were any British companies, I'd contact them to check the distributor's reliability. If their reports weren't good, we wouldn't go ahead.

Speaking 1

Jenny Burns	OK. So we need to decide what gifts to take. Alex, have you got any ideas?
Alex McKinsey	Well, I know Mr Wada plays golf, so we could give him a set of golf clubs.
Patrick O'Connor	Golf clubs? I don't think that would be right. It's too personal. I think it needs to be something more representative of Scotland. What about some top quality malt whisky?
Jenny Burns	Alcohol. No, that might not be appropriate, but I do like the idea of something that's representative of Glasgow and the company.
Alex McKinsey	I agree, but if we do that I think it should be something that represents us as a modern progressive country, not just the traditional image of Scotland.
Patrick O'Connor	I've got another idea. How about an original piece of art? Glasgow's got an international reputation for modern art, so we could commission a painting with images of the city from history and today.
Jenny Burns	I really like that idea, Patrick. Alex, what do you think?
Alex McKinsey	It's certainly unusual, but do you think we could get it done in time?
Patrick O'Connor	I don't see why not. In fact, I know just the person and I think her work would be right. If you like, I could ask her to bring in some examples of her work.
Jenny Burns	Great, but you'll need to get it moving pretty quickly. If her work's not suitable, we'll need to think of something else.

unit 10

Listening 1

Conversation 1

Rick	Hello, this is Rick Kent from MK Precision in Denver. I'd like to make an order.
Yolanda	Just a moment while I get an order form. OK. So what's the order for?
Rick	Car lights. I need two FL75s.
Yolanda	FL75s. Ah, yes – fog lights.
Rick	Yeah, I have the catalogue in front of me. Do you want the product number?
Yolanda	That'd be great.
Rick	It's 0-1-9 0-4-2-1.
Yolanda	OK. The FL75s are $119. That comes to $238. Anything else?
Rick	Yes, I also need four sets of headlights. I'll just give you the number: 0-2-9 0-7-3-5.
Yolanda	0-7-3-5. So, four FL100s. The unit price for those is $85. That's $340 for the four.
Rick	Fine. When will you be able to deliver?
Yolanda	We guarantee a six-day delivery anywhere in the States.
Rick	Good. So I'll have them by Monday.
Yolanda	No, by Wednesday. We only count full working days, but you'll definitely have them next Wednesday.
Rick	That's a bit late. Is there any way you can get the order to me quicker? My customer needs them for Monday.
Yolanda	So you want everything on Monday?
Rick	No, just the fog lights. Wednesday's fine for the rest.

Yolanda	OK. I'll send them by Air Parcel Post. You should get them on Friday, but I'm afraid I'll have to make a $25 charge for the delivery.
Rick	That's no problem.
Yolanda	OK. I just need a few delivery details …

Conversation 2

Ania	Good morning, Posnan Exhibition Services. How can I help?
Rick	Oh, hello. I'd like some information about exhibiting at the next Posnan Auto Show.
Ania	The Auto Show. Let me just get the pack. So what would you like to know?
Rick	First, can you give me an idea of how big the fair is?
Ania	Well, 250 companies had stands last year, and that figure should be up to 280 next time.
Rick	Sorry, how many?
Ania	280.
Rick	OK. What about visitor numbers?
Ania	Over the two days we had 15,000 visitors, so with more stands we'd hope for more people this time.
Rick	And where did they typically come from?
Ania	About 60% were from Poland and the remainder from other European countries, and the Middle East.
Rick	That's interesting. Now a couple of practical questions. We're thinking of taking a stand of about 40 square metres. How much will that cost us?
Ania	410 euros per square metre.
Rick	Sorry, can you give me the cost again?
Ania	Yes, it's 410 euros. So, if you're looking at 40 square metres it would be – let me see – 16,400 euros. But that's just the cost for a basic stand.
Rick	What does the price include?
Ania	You get a listing in the catalogue in Polish, German and English, some basic furniture – a desk and four chairs – and electricity and lighting.
Rick	OK. So anything else would be extra?
Ania	That's right.
Rick	OK. One final thing. When would we need to book by?
Ania	The closing date is 21 December, but if you want your choice of location, you'd need to do it soon. A lot of companies who were here last year have already booked the space they want. I could take your booking if you like.
Rick	No. I need to talk to my colleagues, but I'll get back to you early next week …

Speaking 1

The first point is to have well-trained staff on the stand. Remember that attention spans are short and most visitors will leave in about 60 seconds if they don't receive help. So it's important to train staff to be welcoming. Even if staff are dealing with someone else, they should make eye contact with a new visitor and tell them someone will be with them in a few minutes.

Obviously your stand has to look attractive and be the right size, so you can show your products to their best advantage. The amount of space you need will depend on things like whether you want to demonstrate your products or whether you just want to hand out literature.

Position is also important. If your stand is hidden away, it will be more difficult to attract visitors, and existing customers who want to visit you may have trouble finding you.

Finally, you need to keep records of the people who visit your stand so that you can follow up your leads when you get back to the office. You can get visitors' contact details from their business cards, but you also need to keep notes about what they're interested in – a card system is good for that.

unit 11

Listening 2

1 I took a drop in salary when I first joined Premier two years ago, but I didn't mind because I thought I'd be getting a lot of good experience, but it hasn't worked out like that. I've been doing the same administrative job for two years. It's not that the job's boring, but I don't find it challenging any more. They've said they'll increase my money, but unless they can come up with a better job at a higher level, I don't think I'll stay.

2 Since I joined last year I haven't had much time for a social life. Everyone puts in very long hours and we often work at weekends too. It's not a problem because I really like the people I work with. We have a lot of fun. The pay's a problem though. All my friends who left university at the same time as me earn a lot more than I do. I suppose that's the one thing that would make me think of changing my job.

3 Premier's doing really well, which is great because I've got a young family and having a secure job is really important. The problem is I'm always in the office, and when I'm not in the office, I'm away on business. Some weeks I hardly see my children from one day to the next. They've offered me a higher salary, but that's not the point. I don't see how I can let the situation go on much longer; it's putting too much strain on my family.

4 I used to get up in the morning and think my job's so boring I don't want to go to work. Not any more. I've got the job I've always wanted. There's only one thing I'd like to change and that's my boss. It's not that he's a difficult person, but he never says thank you, even when I know I've done something well. I don't think he really appreciates the amount of effort and time I put into the job.

5 Everything was going fine until I got a promotion to the New Products section. It's a really interesting job, but I don't think my face fits. There's a culture of working late and then going out drinking, but I've got a family, so I need to get home. I don't feel they accept me as part of the team. I spoke to my boss about it and he was surprisingly understanding. He thinks I need to give it time, but I'm not sure.

Listening 3

Presenter	Lucia works as a marketing assistant She's been in her job for six months.
Lucia	I used to get up in the morning and think my job's so boring I don't want to go to work. Not any more. I've got the job I've always wanted. There's only thing I'd like to change and that's my boss. It's not that he's a difficult person, but he never says thank you, even when I know I've done something well. I don't think he really appreciates the amount of effort and time I put into the job.
Presenter	Brad's recently been promoted as a Systems Engineer and is spending a lot of time visiting customers.
Brad	Premier's doing really well, which is great because I've got a young family and having a secure job is really important. The problem is I'm always in the office, and when I'm not in the office, I'm away on business. Some weeks I hardly see my children from one day to the next. They've offered me a higher salary, but that's not the point. I don't see how I can let the situation go on much longer; it's putting too much strain on my family.

unit 12

Listening 2

Conversation 1

Recording Thank you for calling the Swiftjet customer service line. Your call is being held in a queue and will be answered as soon as one of our Customer Service Representatives is available. In order to speed up your enquiry, please press one of the following buttons on your telephone. If you have an enquiry about current flight times, please press 'one'. Our winter timetable comes into operation two weeks from now. If you have a query about this timetable, please press 'two'. If you want to make a reservation, please press 'three'. For all other enquiries, please press 'four'. Thank you. Please hold the line. Thank you for holding. You are connected to the Swiftjet reservations line. Your call will be answered as soon as one of our Customer Service Representatives is available. Alternatively, you may visit our website at Swiftjet.com. Here you will find details of our current and winter flight times and can make reservations. Please note that customers booking on-line receive a £10 discount on all return flights.

Woman Oh, I give up!

Conversation 2

Sharon Interserve Customer Service, General Enquiries. Sharon speaking. How can I help you?

Douglas Ah, at last!

Sharon I'm sorry?

Douglas At last, a person! I've been trying to get through for twenty minutes and either the line's been engaged or I've got a recorded message asking me to push a choice of buttons.

Sharon What exactly is your enquiry?

Douglas I'm going abroad for a couple of months and I want to know if I can still use my usual e-mail address while I'm away.

Sharon I see. You should have chosen button two. That's Accounts and Billing.

Douglas Yes, well if I had known that was the department I needed, I would have done. But it was far from clear which of the options was suitable for me, so I hung on for General Enquiries.

Sharon I'm sorry you've waited so long. Do you wish to make an official complaint?

Douglas No, it's OK. But I think you ought to make your menu of options a bit clearer.

Sharon I'll make a note of that, sir. Now, about your query. Can I have your user name, please?

Douglas Yes, it's douglasj.

Sharon One second, please. Right, Mr Johnson, I have your details on the screen now. Which country ...

Conversation 3

Jason Ace Cooling and Ventilation Technical Support line. Jason speaking. How can I help you?

Rod Good morning. This is Rod Weaver, the Production Manager at Southside Electronics.

Jason May I have your customer reference number please, Mr Weaver?

Rod I don't know what it is. My secretary has the details and she's not in yet. Listen this is really serious ...

Jason Sorry, what was the company name?

Rod Southside Electronics.

Jason OK, I'm searching for your details now. They may take a while to come up on the screen.

Rod Right.

Jason What exactly is the problem?

Rod The cooling system in the factory's not working. Completely dead.

Jason Have you tried the diagnostic self-test function on the central processing unit?

Rod Yes, that's dead too.

Jason Mmm. I see. Well, the earliest I can get a service engineer out to you would be around lunch-time today.

Rod Look, I've got half a million pounds worth of highly sensitive production equipment here which is going to have to be shut down if something's not done soon.

Jason Ah, I've got the details now, Mr Weaver. OK, I'll tell you what I can do. I'll call our Site Support Manager on his emergency number, Mr Weaver, and get him to ring you back within ten minutes.

Rod Thank you.

Language in use 1

Douglas I'm going abroad for a couple of months and I want to know if I can still use my usual e-mail address while I'm away.

Sharon I see. You should have chosen button two. That's Accounts and Billing.

Douglas Yes, well if I had known that was the department I needed, I would have done.

unit 13

Listening 1

1 I don't see why she got so excited about it. After all it was just a packet of photocopy paper. But she went on and on about it and when I pointed out she'd never mentioned it before, she said that was because I used to work from home sometimes, but because I don't any more it was unacceptable!

2 Well, of course I believe that people in developing countries should earn a living wage, but the problem is that the adults don't always do so. For this reason, a youngster's earnings are often essential to their family, which means that all our well-intentioned efforts to prevent them from working may actually be making things worse.

3 And when I saw the look on his face, so proud and pleased, and waiting to see if I liked what he'd brought, I just couldn't say 'no' in case I offended him. But I see now that I've put us in a compromising position and I deeply regret that. And I assure you that nothing like this will ever happen again.

4 We'd always prided ourselves on our ethics, so it came as a shock when we discovered the workers were paid in tokens which they could only use in the plantation shop. So now we've helped them to set up their own co-operative. As a result, our profits are a bit lower, and our produce is slightly more expensive than our competitors', but the majority of our customers appreciate what we've done and have stayed loyal to us.

5 Quite frankly, I think all the fuss is about the wrong things. OK, I agree it's not right that the shoes they sell are made in some sweatshop in the Far East where the workers are paid a pittance. But what about the young girls who work in their shops here? They're desperate for a job – any job

– so they'll work all the hours they're asked to do for the minimum rate of pay. We should be looking at the situation for workers here at home where we can actually influence things.

Listening 2

2 Well, of course I believe that people in developing countries should earn a living wage, but the problem is that the adults don't always do so. For this reason, a youngster's earnings are often essential to their family, which means that all our well-intentioned efforts to prevent them from working may actually be making things worse.

3 And when I saw the look on his face, so proud and pleased, and waiting to see if I liked what he'd brought, I just couldn't say 'no' in case I offended him. But I see now that I've put us in a compromising position and I deeply regret that. And I assure you that nothing like this will ever happen again.

4 We'd always prided ourselves on our ethics, so it came as a shock when we discovered the workers were paid in tokens which they could only use in the plantation shop. So now we've helped them to set up their own co-operative. As a result, our profits are a bit lower, and our produce is slightly more expensive than our competitors', but the majority of our customers appreciate what we've done and have stayed loyal to us.

unit 14

Listening 2 ·

Dagmar We're planning to set up home-working for our Sales and Marketing team, but I'm worried that they might start to feel rather isolated.

Sam Well, that can be a problem, especially where people are primarily based at home which, in our experience, is never a good idea. But that's not what we're suggesting for your team. They won't be at home every day; they'll be out meeting clients, having meetings, so they'll have plenty of opportunities for professional contact. And as a bonus, they'll have more time to spend with their families and their communities.

Dagmar Don't people find there are too many distractions at home?

Sam And there aren't at the office? You must know lots of managers who take work home in the evenings so that they can concentrate in peace and quiet. In fact, many companies find home-based workers get through a lot more work. Of course, there can be a lot of interruptions at home, for example, if there are children around, but I don't think they're any worse than in a busy office. But it's really important for staff to have somewhere quiet to work.

Dagmar Isn't there a danger staff will find themselves working late into the evening and not be able to stop?

Sam Well, many professionals, especially managers, tend to do that anyway; being properly set up at home is a lot nicer than working away in an empty office when most of the other people have gone home. It's not as though long hours only happen at home. And on the plus side, at least you can be more flexible, for example, you can take a break when the kids get home from school and then finish later if that suits you.

Dagmar That makes sense, but I can imagine that it's very easy for people to feel out of touch with the office. How do you deal with that?

Sam It's up to management to make sure that home-workers are kept up to date with what's going on. Much of this can be done electronically, for example, via the company intranet, but I think it's even more important to have regular meetings where everyone can discuss problems and air new ideas. Team-building events can also help to create a good team spirit.

Dagmar I've heard a lot of complaints that setting up and running an office at home actually costs the worker money. Do you find that's true?

Sam Well, there can be some tricky negotiations over the cost of setting up at home. Start-up costs can be high, but, in my experience, most companies cover those initial costs. And remember, commuting to work costs most people much more than a bit of extra money for the additional electricity used at home. A lot of people commuting to London, for example, pay more than £2,000 a year for their journeys.

Dagmar We have about fifty people in Sales and Marketing – how can we tell which of them will work well from home?

Sam That's a difficult question. Some companies go to great lengths with psychological assessments. Others leave out any staff they … they feel aren't disciplined enough to work alone. But personally, I think all that's irrelevant. Basically, you have to ask yourself what's best for your company. The way we work is changing and staff need to be able to adapt. As long as you provide the right type of support, I don't see any reason why it couldn't work for all your staff.

glossary

unit 1

automotive *adj* connected with motor vehicles *the automotive industry*

aviation *n* the designing, building and flying of aircraft

beverages *n* drinks of any type, except water *laws governing the sale of alcoholic beverages*

brochure *n* a small magazine or book containing pictures and information about sth or advertising sth *Send for a free colour brochure today!*

burglary *n* the crime of entering a building illegally and stealing things from it

career *n* the series of jobs that a person has in a particular area of work, usually involving more responsibility as time passes *What made you decide on a career as an engineer?*

career ladder / company ladder *n* a series of stages by which you can make progress in a career or an organisation

confirm *v* to state or show that sth is definitely true or correct, especially by providing evidence *Has everyone confirmed in writing (that) they're coming?*

critical *adj* extremely important because a future situation will be affected by it *Your decision is critical to our future.*

customised *adj* made or changed to suit the needs of the buyer or owner *a customised car*

detergent *n* a liquid or powder that helps remove dirt, for example from clothes or dishes

dominate (be dominated by) *v* to be the most important or noticeable feature of sth

enrol *v* to arrange for yourself or for sb else to officially join a course, school, etc. *You need to enrol before the end of August.*

entrepreneur *n* a person who makes money by starting or running businesses, especially when this involves taking financial risks

entry code *n* a combination of letters, numbers, or both, which allows you to open a gate or door

entry system *n* an electronic system, or device, which opens a door or gate to a building, or part of a building

family business/firm *n* a company owned and run by members of the same family

firm *n* a business or company *an engineering firm*

fitness *n* the state of being physically healthy and strong *a fitness trainer/class/test*

freelance *adj, adv* earning money by selling your work or services to several different organisations rather than being employed by one particular organisation
(*adj*) *a freelance journalist*
(*adv*) *I work freelance from home.*

fulfilment *n* feelings of happiness and satisfaction with what you are doing or have done
to find emotional/personal fulfilment

income *n* the money that a person, a region, a country, etc. earns from work, from investing money from business, etc.
a rise in national income

information technology *n* the study or use of electronic equipment, especially computers, for storing, analysing and sending out information
Recent advances in information technology have led to important changes in the operation of offices.

install (be installed) *v* to fix equipment or furniture into position so that it can be used *He's getting a phone installed tomorrow.*

job security *n* the guarantee that you will keep your job

lifetime employment *n* a job with the same company for the whole period of your working life

logo *n* a printed design or symbol that a company or an organisation uses as its special sign
All over the world there are red and white paper cups bearing the company logo.

media *n* the main ways that large numbers of people receive information and entertainment, that is television, radio and the newspapers
the news/broadcasting/national media

multinational *adj, n*
(*adj*) existing in or involving many countries *multinational companies/corporations*
(*n*) a company that operates in several different countries, especially a large and powerful company *The country's industry is largely controlled by the multinationals.*

on my/the books *exp* to have an official list or record of people who are able to provide a specific service or do a certain job

personal care *n* business sector producing soap, toothpaste, shampoo, cosmetics and other goods used for the face and body

petroleum *n* mineral oil that is found under the ground or the sea and is used to produce petrol

pharmaceuticals *n* drugs or medicines

profile *n* description of sb/sth that gives useful information
We first build up a detailed profile of our customers and their requirements.

profitable *adj* that makes or is likely to make money *a highly profitable business*

project *n* a planned piece of work that is designed to find information about sth, to produce sth new, or to improve sth
a research project/a building project

promotion *n* a move to a more important job or rank in a company or an organisation *Her promotion to Sales Manager took everyone by surprise.*

relocate *v* make a person or company move from one place to another

retail *n* the selling of goods to the public, usually through shops/stores
the retail trade/sector

sector *n* a part of an area of activity, especially of a country's economy
the manufacturing sector

select *v* to choose sb/sth, usually carefully, from a group of people or things

self-employed *adj* working for yourself and not employed by a company, etc.
I decided to become self-employed.

spreadsheet *n* a computer program that is used, for example, when doing financial or project planning

standardised *adj* being of the same type or having the same features or qualities
a standardised contract/design/test

state-owned *adj* belonging to the state or country

survivor *n* a company which has managed to stay in business despite difficult economic conditions

talent *n* a natural ability to do sth well

telecommunications *n* the technology of sending signals, images and messages over long distances by radio, telephone, television

therapist *n* a specialist who treats a particular type of illness or problem, or who uses a particular type of treatment
a speech/beauty therapist

toiletries *n* things such as soap or toothpaste that you use for washing, cleaning your teeth, etc.

transform (be transformed) *v* to completely change the appearance or character of sth, especially so that it is better *The company has been transformed from a family business to a multi-million-pound operation.*

work patterns / working practices *n* methods of working

unit 2

administrator *n* a person whose job is to manage and organise the public or business affairs of a company

analyse *v* to examine the nature or structure of sth, especially by separating it into its parts, in order to understand or explain it *The job involves gathering and analysing data.*

analysis *n* the detailed study or examination of sth in order to understand more about it; the result of the study

analyst *n* a person whose job involves examining facts or materials in order to give an opinion on them

automated production line *n* section of a production process which is carried out by machines or robots

brand *n* a type of product made by a particular company
Which brand of toothpaste do you use?

breakdown *n* detailed information that you get by studying a set of figures *First, let's look at a breakdown of the costs.*

brochure – see unit 1

budget *n* the money that is available to a person or an organization and a plan of how it will be spent over a period of time
an advertising budget of $2 million

challenging *adj* difficult in an interesting way that tests your ability

complaint *n* a reason for not being satisfied; a statement that sb makes saying that they are not satisfied
The most common complaint is about poor service.

component *n* one of several parts of which sth is made
the components of a machine

conform (to or with) *v + prep* obey a rule, law, quality standard, etc.
The building does not conform to/with safety regulations.

contract *n* an official written agreement or a specific piece of work done on the basis of a written agreement *to win/be awarded a contract to build a new school*

distribution *n* the system of transporting and delivering goods
distribution costs/network

faulty *adj* not perfect; not working or made correctly
Ask for a refund if the goods are faulty.

finance *n*
1 money used to run a business, an activity or a project
2 the activity of managing money
the finance department

findings *n pl* information that is discovered as the result of research into sth
The findings of the commission will be published today.

guidelines *n* rules or instructions that are given by an official organisation telling you how to do sth, especially sth difficult

hectic *adj* very busy; full of activity
a hectic schedule

hospitality *n* food, drink or services that are provided by an organisation for guests, customers, etc.

human resources *n* the department in a company that deals with employing and training people

information technology – see unit 1

interpret *v* to decide that sth has a particular meaning and to understand it in this way *The data can be interpreted in many different ways.*

invoice *n* a list of goods that have been sold, work that has been done, etc., showing what you must pay

journal *n* a newspaper or magazine that deals with a particular subject or profession

laboratory *n* a room or building used for scientific research, experiments, testing, etc.

leaflet *n* a printed sheet of paper to advertise or give information about sth

market research *n* the work of collecting information about what people buy and why

marketing *n* the activity of presenting, advertising and selling a company's products in the best possible way

microchip *n* a very small piece of a material that is used to carry a complicated electronic circuit

negotiate *v* to arrange or agree sth by formal discussion
to negotiate a deal/contract

on schedule *exp* at the planned time
They finished the project on schedule.

on the road *exp* travelling, especially for long distances or periods of time

order *n* a request to make or supply goods

packaging *n* materials used to wrap or protect goods

personnel – see **human resources**

presentation *n* a talk in which someone explains a new product or idea, or shows something to people

priority *n* something that you think is more important than other things and should be dealt with first
Our main priority is to improve quality.

product launch *n* an event, or series of events, which make a product available to the public for the first time

product manager *n* a person who is in control of the design and quality of goods made by a company

production *n* the department in a company that is responsible for making goods
a production manager/process

production facility *n* factory

promote *v* to help sell a product, service, etc. or make it more popular by advertising it or offering it at a special price

promotion *n* activities done in order to increase the sales of a product or service; a set of advertisements for a particular product or service

purchasing *n* the department in a company that is responsible for buying everything the company needs to make its products

quality assurance *n* the practice of managing the way goods are produced or services are provided to make sure they are kept at a high standard

quality control *n* the practice of checking goods as they are being produced, to make sure that they are of a high standard
Practical measures such as quality control and testing are very important in the manufacturing process.

raise (money) *v* to manage to get or borrow money *to raise funds /a loan*

range *n* a collection of similar items
We stock a wide range of video cameras.

recruit *v* to find new people to join a company
He's responsible for recruiting at all levels.

rewarding *adj* (of an activity, etc.) worth doing; that makes you happy because you think it is useful or important
a rewarding experience/job

sales conference *n* an event at which all the sales staff of a company meet to have discussions or learn about new products and ideas

service function *n* department or section of a company which helps the other departments to do their job, but does not directly earn money for the company

source *v* to get materials, components, etc. from a particular place

specification(s) *n* a detailed description of how sth is, or should be, designed or made *the technical specifications of the new model*

standards *n* officially agreed levels of quality for products, or services

sub-component *n* a smaller part of a component (see **component**)

subsidiary *n* a company that is owned or controlled by another larger company
She's working for an overseas subsidiary of the company.

support *v* to give or be ready to give help to sb if they need it

support staff *v* employees whose job is to help other members of staff perform their work

trade fair *n* an event at which many different companies show and sell their products

warehouse *n* a building where large quantities of goods are stored, especially before they are sent to shops/stores to be sold

unit 3

access *n* a way of entering or reaching a place *There is easy access by road.*

agenda *n* a list of items to be discussed at a meeting *The next item on the agenda is the publicity budget.*

amenities *n pl* features that make a place pleasant, comfortable or easy to live in

availability *n* the state of being able to be bought or found
the availability of cheap flights

cabin *n* one of the areas for passengers to sit in a plane

check in *v* to go to a desk in a hotel, an airport, etc. and tell an official there that you have arrived *Please check in at least one hour before departure.*

check-in *n* the place where you go first when you arrive at an airport, to show your ticket, etc.

convenience *n* the quality of being useful, easy or suitable for sb

convenient *adj*
1 useful, easy or quick to do; not causing problems *I'll call back at a more convenient time.*
2 near to a particular place; easy to get to *The house is very convenient for several schools.*

cost-effective *adj* giving the best possible profit or benefits in comparison with the money that is spent

cramped *adj* not having enough space for the people in it
working in cramped conditions

delegate *n* a person who is chosen to represent a group of people at a meeting, conference, etc. *The conference was attended by delegates from 56 countries.*

efficiently *adv* done well and thoroughly with no waste of time, money, or energy

facilities *n pl* buildings, services, equipment, etc. that are provided for a particular purpose *sports/leisure facilities*

fix up *v* arrange (a meeting)

go for *v* choose

headache *n* a person or thing that causes worry or trouble *The real headache will be getting the bank to lend you the money.*

ignorance *n* a lack of knowledge or information about sth

jet lag *n* the feeling of being tired and slightly confused after a long plane journey, especially when there is a big difference in the time at the place you leave and that at the place you arrive in

junior *n* a person who has a job at a low level within an organisation

laptop *n* a small computer that can work with a battery and be easily carried

luxurious *adj* very comfortable; containing expensive and enjoyable things *a luxurious hotel*

out of touch (with) *exp* unable to contact / be contacted by

perk *n* something you receive as well as your wages for doing a particular job *Perks offered by the firm include a car and free health insurance.*

queue *n* a line of people, cars, etc. waiting for sth or to do sth

reception *n* a formal social occasion to welcome sb or celebrate sth *They hosted a reception for 75 guests.*

recover (from) *v* to get well again after being ill/sick, hurt, very tired, etc. *He's still recovering from his operation.*

recycled *adj* treated so that it may be used again *This envelope is made from recycled paper.*

reservation *n* an arrangement for a seat on a plane or train, a room in a hotel, etc. to be kept for you

routine *adj, n*
(*adj*) done or happening as a normal part of a particular job, situation or process *The fault was discovered during a routine check.*
(*n*) the normal order and way in which you regularly do things *Make exercise a part of your daily routine.*

scrutinise *v* to look at or examine sb/sth carefully

short-haul *adj* that involves transporting people or goods over short distances, especially by plane *short-haul routes/flights*

spacious *adj* large and with plenty of space for people to move around in *The hotel rooms are spacious and comfortable.*

squashed *adj* pushed into a space that is too small *There were dozens of us in the room, squashed together like sardines.*

stressful *adj* causing a lot of anxiety and worry *a stressful job/situation*

suite *n* a set of rooms, especially in a hotel

teleconferencing *n* having a discussion at which members are in different places and speak to each other using telephone and video connections

time zone *n* one of the 24 areas that the world is divided into, each with its own time that is one hour earlier than that of the time zone immediately to the east

unwillingness *n* the state of not wanting to do sth

unit 4

access – see unit 3

bankrupt *adj* without enough money to pay what you owe *They went bankrupt in 1999.*

budget – see unit 2

catalogue *n* a complete list of items, for example of things that people can look at or buy *a mail-order catalogue*

chain *n* a group of shops/stores or hotels owned by the same company

chief executive *n* the person with the highest rank in a company or an organisation

collapse *n, v*
(*n*) a sudden failure of sth, such as an institution, a business or a course of action
(*v*) to fail suddenly or completely

competitor *n* a company that offers the same or better goods and services as another and therefore competes for the same customers *This firm is one of our biggest competitors.*

consumer *n* a person who buys goods or uses services *consumer demand/choice/rights/spending*

controversial *adj* causing a lot of angry public discussion and disagreement *a highly controversial issue/topic/decision*

crack a/the market *exp* to enter a new market successfully

dotcom business *n* an on-line/Internet company

downturn *n* a fall in the amount of business that is done; a time when the economy becomes weaker *a downturn in sales/trade/business*

extravagance *n* the act or habit of spending more money than you can afford or than is necessary

findings – see unit 2

funding *n* money for a particular purpose; the act of providing money for such a purpose *There have been large cuts in government funding for scientific research.*

get/have (a) bad press *exp* negative reports that newspapers write about sb/sth *The airline has had a bad press recently*

globalisation *n* a situation in which companies from one country operate in many different parts of the world

high profile *adj* receiving or involving a lot of attention and discussion on television, in newspapers, etc.

in vain *exp* without success

income – see unit 1

invest (in) *v* to buy property, shares in a company, etc. in the hope of making a profit

investor *n* a person or an organisation that invests money in sth

formula *n* a particular method of doing or achieving sth

launch *v, n*
(*v*) open a new store, start an Internet site, start a new service, etc.
(*n*) the act of opening a new store or starting a new Internet site, or starting a business in a new market

lavish *adj* large in amount, or impressive, and usually costing a lot of money

lifestyle *n* the way in which a person or a group of people lives and works

mail order *n* a system of buying and selling goods through the mail *a mail-order catalogue*

majority owner *n* person who owns the largest number of shares in a company

make redundant (be made redundant) *v* to lose your job because there is no more work available for you in a company

market *n* a particular area, country or section of the population that might buy goods *the US/Japanese market*

profit *n* the money that you make in business or by selling things, especially after paying the costs involved *a rise / an increase / a drop / a fall in profits*

quarter *n* a period of three months, used especially as a period for which bills are paid or a company's income is calculated *Sales were up 10% in the first quarter of 1999.*

rural *adj* connected with or like the countryside *rural areas/communities*

site *n* a place on the Internet where a company or organisation puts information

slowdown *n* a reduction in speed or activity *a slowdown in economic growth*

start-up costs *n* the costs connected with starting a new business or project

strategy *n* a plan that is intended to achieve a particular purpose

transformation *n* a complete change in sb/sth

turnover *n* the total amount of goods or services sold by a company during a particular period of time *The firm has an annual turnover of $75 million.*

value retailer *n* a store which sells goods that are not very expensive, but which are good quality for the money they cost

website – see unit 4: **site**

unit 5

abusive *adj* (of speech or of a person) rude and offensive; criticizing rudely and unfairly

appropriately *adv* suitably, acceptably or correctly for the circumstances

benefit *n* an advantage that sth gives you; a helpful and useful effect that sth has *I've had the benefit of a good education.*

channel *n* a method or system that people use to get information, to communicate, or to send sth somewhere

compose *v* to write a letter, etc. usually with a lot of care and thought *She composed a letter of protest.*

confidential *adj* meant to be kept secret and not told to or shared with other people *confidential information/documents*

cyberspace *n* the imaginary place where electronic messages, pictures, etc. exist while they are being sent between computers

data *n*
1 facts or information, especially when examined and used to find out things or to make decisions *the analysis/interpretation of the data*
2 information that is stored by a computer

delete *v* to remove sth that has been written or printed, or that has been stored on a computer *This command deletes files from the directory.*

document *n* an official paper that gives information about sth, or that can be used as evidence or proof of sth

draft *n* a rough written version of sth that is not yet in its final form *I've made a rough draft of the letter.*

flame mail *n* angry or aggressive messages sent by e-mail

flood *v* to send sth somewhere in large numbers *The office was flooded with applications for the job.*

highlight *v* to emphasize sth, especially so that people give it more attention *The report highlights the major problems facing society today.*

illegal *adj* not allowed by the law

imminent *adj* likely to happen (very) soon

impact *n* the powerful effect that sth has on sb/sth *Her speech made a profound impact on everyone.*

in person *exp* if you do sth in person, you go somewhere and do it yourself, instead of doing it by letter, asking sb else to do it, etc. *The director will be there in person to welcome the new staff.*

invaluable *adj* extremely useful *invaluable help/information/support, an invaluable asset/tool*

invoice – see unit 2

legal *adj* allowed or required by law

legislation *n* a law or a set of laws passed by a parliament *an important piece of legislation*

medium *n* a way of communicating information, etc. to people *Television is the modern medium of communication.*

minutes *n pl* a summary or record of what is said or decided at a formal meeting *We read through the minutes of the last meeting.*

PA = personal assistant *n* a person who works as a secretary or an assistant for one person

paperwork *n* the written work that is part of a job, such as filling in forms or writing letters and reports *We're trying to cut down on the amount of paperwork involved.*

proposal *n* a formal suggestion or plan; the act of making a suggestion *a proposal to build more office accommodation*

registration form *n* an official paper on which a record is made of somebody agreeing to attend a course/seminar, or checking in at a hotel

reservation *n* a feeling of doubt about a plan or an idea *I have serious reservations about his ability to do the job.*

review *v* to carefully examine or consider sth again, especially so that you can decide if it is necessary to make changes

revolutionise *v* to completely change the way that sth is done

sensitive *adj* that you have to treat with great care because it may offend people or make them angry *That's a sensitive area/topic.*

snail mail *n* used humorously, especially by people who use e-mail on computers, to describe the system of sending letters by ordinary mail

survey *n* an investigation of the opinions, behaviour, etc. of a particular group of people, which is usually done by asking them questions
A recent survey showed 75% of those questioned were in favour of the plan.

time management course *n* a training course which aims to help people use their time at work more efficiently

trace back *v* to find the origin or cause of sth

update *n* a report, newsletter, etc. which gives the most recent information about sth *The newsletter gives an update on current activities.*

urgent *adj* that needs to be dealt with immediately
a problem that requires urgent attention

unit 6

access – see unit 3

adjustable *adj* that can be moved to different positions or changed in shape or size

admit (be admitted) to *v* to take sb to a hospital, or other institution where they can receive special care *Two crash victims were admitted to the local hospital.*

agricultural labourer *adj, n* farm worker

assembly worker *n* factory worker whose job is to put together parts of a product

awkward *adj* not graceful; not comfortable *I must have slept in an awkward position – I'm aching all over.*

blame *v* to think or say that sb/sth is responsible for sth bad *Police are blaming the accident on dangerous driving.*

break (a rule) *v* to not follow a rule

cable *n* a set of wires, covered in plastic or rubber, that carries electricity, telephone signals, etc.

clearance *n* the removal of things which are not wanted

complain *v* to say that you are annoyed, unhappy or not satisfied about sb/sth

comply with *v* to obey a rule, an order, etc.

construction worker *n* someone whose job involves building roads, bridges or buildings

courier *n* a person or company whose job is to take packages or important papers somewhere

damaged *adj* harmed, spoiled

designated *adj* officially given a particular character or function *The second floor is a designated no-smoking area.*

ensure *v* to make sure that sth happens or is definite *Please ensure (that) all lights are switched off.*

extinguish *v* to make a fire or cigarette stop burning

extinguisher *n* a metal container with water or chemicals inside for putting out small fires

eye strain *n* a condition of the eyes caused, for example, by a long period of reading or looking at a computer screen

fatal *adj* causing or ending in death *a fatal accident/blow/illness*

forearm *n* the part of the arm between the elbow and the wrist

fracture *n* a break in a bone or other hard material

hazard *n* a thing that can be dangerous or cause damage *a fire/safety hazard*

horizontal *adj* flat and level; going across and parallel to the ground rather than going up and down

inadequate *adj* not enough; not good enough

injury *n* harm done to a person's or an animal's body, for example, in an accident *There were no injuries in the crash.*

install – see unit 1

keyboard *n* the set of keys for operating a computer or typewriter

layout *n* the way in which the parts of sth such as the page of a book, a garden or a building are arranged *Are you familiar with the general layout of the hospital?*

legal – see unit 5

legislation – see unit 5

mouse *n* a small device which is moved by hand across a surface to control the movement of the cursor on a computer screen

obligation *n* something which you must do because you have promised, because of a law, etc.

obstruction *n* something blocking a road, an entrance, etc. *It is my job to make sure that all pathways are clear of obstructions.*

procedure *n* a way of doing sth, especially the usual or correct way *emergency/safety/official procedures*

ozone *n* a poisonous gas with a strong smell that is a form of oxygen

posture *n* the position in which you hold your body when standing or sitting *Back pain can be the result of bad posture.*

power point *n* a device in a wall which you put a plug into in order to connect electrical equipment to the power supply of a building

prescribe (be prescribed) *v* (of a doctor) to tell sb to take a particular medicine or have a particular treatment; to write a prescription for a particular medicine

productive *adj* doing or achieving a lot

prolonged *adj* continuing for a long time

protective device *adj, n* an object or a piece of equipment which has been designed to provide protection

reassure *v* to say or do sth that makes sb less frightened or worried *They tried to reassure her, but she still felt anxious.*

recommendation *n* an official suggestion about the best thing to do

regulation *n* an official rule made by a government or some other authority *fire/safety/building regulations*

repetitive *adj* saying or doing the same thing many times, so that it becomes boring *Machines can now perform many repetitive tasks in the home.*

repetitive strain injury *n* muscle pain caused by repeating the same movement frequently

risk *n* a person or thing which is likely to cause problems or danger at some time in the future *a major health/fire risk*

slip *v, n*
(*v*) to slide a short distance accidentally so that you fall or nearly fall *As I ran up the stairs, my foot slipped and I fell.*
(*n*) an act of slipping

slippery *adj* difficult to stand or move on, because it is smooth, wet or polished

standards *n pl* – see unit 2

storeroom *n* a room used for storing things

stressful – see unit 3

subsequent *adj* happening after sth else *This issue will be dealt with in a subsequent report.*

tile *n* a flat, usually square, piece of baked clay, carpet or other material which is used in rows for covering walls and floors

toner *n* a type of ink used in machines which print or photocopy

trailing *adj* hanging downwards over sth or along the ground *Computer wires were trailing all over the floor.*

trap (be trapped) *v* to keep sb in a dangerous place that they want to get out of but cannot *They were trapped in the burning building.*

trip *v* to catch your foot on sth and fall or almost fall *Someone will trip over that cable.*

uneven *adj* not level, smooth or flat *The floor felt uneven under his feet.*

ventilation *n* the state of having enough fresh air entering and moving around a room, building, etc. *Make sure that there is adequate ventilation in the room before using the paint.*

wastepaper bin *n* a container for paper which is not wanted and is to be thrown away

workstation *n* the desk and computer at which a person works

unit 7

access – see unit 3

accountancy *n* the work of keeping written records of money which is owed to and paid by a business, calculating profits, etc.

administration *n* the control and organisation of a company or particular business activity

application *n* a formal (often written) request for sth, such as a job or a place at a college or university

background *n* the details of a person's family, education, experience, etc. *The job would suit someone with a business background.*

bear out (be borne out) *v* to show that sb is right or that sth is true

candidate *n* a person who is applying for a job

careers staff / careers development staff *n* university staff whose job is to advise students about their future career

circulate *v* to send information to all the people in a group *The document will be circulated to all staff.*

commonplace *adj* done very often, or existing in many places, and therefore not unusual *Computers are now commonplace in primary classrooms.*

compensation and benefits package *n* salary and other money, goods, etc. given to an employee by the company he/she works for

consult *v* to discuss sth with sb to get their permission for sth, or to help you make a decision *I need to consult with my colleagues on the proposals.*

correspondence *n* the letters a person or business sends and receives

cost-effective – see unit 3

curriculum vitae (CV) *n* a written record of your education and employment, which you send when you are applying for a job

database *n* an organised set of data that is stored in a computer and can be looked at and used in various ways

ensure – see unit 6

expertise *n* expert knowledge or skill in a particular subject, activity or job *professional/scientific/technical expertise*

external *adj* (coming from) outside the company

field *n* a particular subject or activity that sb works in or is interested in *All of them are experts in their chosen field.*

findings – see unit 2

graduate *n* a person who has a university degree

hire *v* to give sb a job

human resources – see unit 2

internal *adj* (coming from) inside the company

interpersonal *adj* connected with relationships between people *interpersonal skills*

investigate *v* to find out information and facts about a subject or problem by study or research

job board *n* a website on which job openings are advertised

job fair *n* an exhibition at which companies try to recruit graduates

job listing *n* a job advertised on a job board

job swap programme *n* a system in which people exchange jobs with each other, in order to learn more about different parts of the company

liaise with *n* to work closely with sb and exchange information with them

on/at the leading edge *exp* in the most important and advanced position in an area of activity, especially technology *at the leading edge of scientific research*

opening *n* a job that is available *There are several openings in the sales department.*

paperwork – see unit 5

paste *v* to copy or move text into a document from another place or another document

personnel *n* the people employed by an organisation

placement *n* finding and placing someone in a job

post *v* advertise a job on an electronic job board

potential *adj* that can develop into sth or be developed in the future *potential customers/candidates*

prospective *adj* expected to do sth or to become sth *a prospective buyer/client*

qualified *adj* having passed the exams or completed the training that are necessary in order to do a particular job *She's extremely well qualified for the job.*

recruiting *n* – see unit 2: **recruit** *v*

recruitment agency *n* a company which finds and recruits staff for client companies

recruitment fair – see unit 7: **job fair**

reference *n* a letter written by sb who knows you, giving information about your character and abilities, especially to a new employer *We will take up references after the interview.*

requirement *n* something that you must have in order to do sth else *to meet/fulfil/satisfy the requirements*

routine – see unit 3

screening process *n* the process of ensuring that a candidate is suitable for a job

select – see unit 2

set up *v* arrange an interview, meeting, etc.

shortage *n* a situation when there is not enough of the people or things that are needed

skilled *n* having enough ability, experience and knowledge to be able to do sth well *a shortage of skilled labour*

sort through *v* to look through a number of things, either in order to find sth or to put them in order *I sorted through my paperwork.*

state of the art *adj* using the most modern or advanced techniques or methods; as good as it can be at the present time

strategy – see unit 4

submit *v* to give a document, proposal, etc. to sb in authority so that they can study or consider it *to submit a(n) application/claim/complaint*

talented *adj* – see unit 1: **talent** *n*

time-consuming *adj* taking or needing a lot of time

time management course – see unit 5

to their/its full potential *exp* as much as possible, to use completely and fully *Many people don't use their computers to their full potential.*

trainee *n* a person who is being taught how to do a particular job *a management trainee*

turn down *v* to reject or refuse to consider an offer, a proposal, etc. or the person who makes it *He has been turned down for ten jobs so far.*

vacancy *n* a job that is available for sb to do *There's a vacancy in the accounts department.*

website – see unit 4

unit 8

arrest *v* to stop a process or a development *They failed to arrest the company's decline.*

banner ad *n* an advertisement placed on a website, usually running in a strip across the top of the computer screen

billboard *n* a large board on the outside of a building or at the side of the road, used for putting advertisements on

calorie *n* a unit for measuring how much energy food will produce *a low-calorie drink/diet*

campaign *n* a series of planned activities with a particular commercial aim *The advertising campaign that launched our latest soft drink was exceedingly successful.*

charity *n* an organisation for helping people in need *The concert will raise money for local charities.*

commercial *n* an advertisement on the radio or on television

consumer magazine *n* a magazine bought by members of the public that contains advertisements as well as articles

convenience – see Unit 3

copy *n* the written text that appears in a printed advertisement

coupon *n* a small piece of printed paper which you can exchange for sth or that gives you the right to buy sth at a cheaper price than normal

customer base *n* the group and type of people that are a specific company's customers

deadline *n* a time and date by which something must be achieved or completed *When is the deadline for advertising copy?*

delivery *n* the act of taking goods to the people that have ordered them

direct mail *n* a method of selling by sending information about goods and services straight to possible customers

discount *n* a reduction in the selling price of something

display ad *n* an advertisement in a newspaper, magazine or yellow pages directory, which is specially designed and positioned to be easily noticed

evolve *n* to develop gradually, especially from a simple to a more complicated form *The company has evolved into a major chemical manufacturer.*

feature *n* something important, interesting or typical of a place or thing *Teamwork is a key feature of the training programme.*

florist's *n* a shop/store that sells flowers and plants

folder *n* a cardboard or plastic cover for holding loose papers, etc.

food supplement *n* a product which people eat or drink in order to make their diet healthier or more balanced

fund-raising *n* the act of collecting money for a charity or other organisation *The hospice is planning a major fund-raising event for June.*

gender *n* the fact of being male or female

in the market (to buy / for sth) *exp* interested in buying sth *I'm not in the market for a new car at the moment.*

ingredient *n* one of the foods that are used together to make a particular dish

insert an ad *v* to put an advertisement in a newspaper or magazine

investment *n* the purchase of materials, machines, etc. in order to produce goods or offer a service

issue *n* one of a regular series of magazines or newspapers *The article appeared in issue 25.*

launch – see unit 4

listing *n* an entry in a list of people or things *We have a listing in the yellow pages under 'charities'.*

local *adj* belonging to or connected with the particular place or area that you are talking about or with the place where you live *a local newspaper/local radio*

media buying *n* the job or act of booking air time and advertising space

medium – see unit 5

multinational – see unit 1

nationwide *adj* happening or existing in all parts of a particular country

nutritionist *n* a person who is an expert on the relationship between food and health

pay off *v* to be successful and bring good results

point of sale *n* the place where a consumer buys something *A video above the counter advertises the goods at the point of sale.*

poster *n* a large printed picture or notice in a public place, used to advertise something

potential – see unit 7

power drill *n* a tool or machine with a pointed end for making holes, operated by electricity

promote – see unit 2

promotion – see unit 2

proposal – see unit 5

publication date *n* the date on which a specific issue of a newspaper or magazine will be on sale

purchasing preferences *n, pl* the things which a group of people like to buy

rate *n* an amount charged or paid for work done or services provided *Your advertising rates are rather high.*

readership *n* the number or type of people who read a particular newspaper, magazine, etc.

regional *adj* of or relating to a region

reply card *n* a printed card enclosed with direct mail advertising which potential customers fill in and return to the company if they are interested in the goods or services advertised

script *n* a written text of a radio or TV commercial

sound effect *n* a sound that is made artificially and used in a film, play, computer game, etc. to make it more realistic

special offer *n* a product that is sold at less than its usual price, especially in order to persuade people to buy it; the act of offering goods in this way

target *v, n*
(*v*) to aim to sell to a particular group of people, especially by using advertising designed to appeal to this group *These cosmetics are targeted at the teenage market.*
(*n*) the group of people that a product or service is aimed at *The advertising must reach our target market.*

trade magazine *n* a magazine that is published for a particular trade or industry

unique selling proposition (USP) *n* a feature of a product or service which makes it different from other products or services and therefore attractive to customers

validity *n* the state of being logical and true

yellow pages *n* a book with yellow pages which gives a list of companies and organisations and their telephone numbers, arranged according to the type of services they offer

unit 9

agent *n* a person or organisation that buys or sells goods for someone else *our agents in the Middle East*

accountancy – see unit 7

authorities *n pl* the people or an organisation who have the power to make decisions or who have a particular area of responsibility in a country or region

cautious *adj* being careful about what you say or do, especially to avoid danger or mistakes; not taking any risks *They've taken a very cautious approach.*

chamber of commerce *n* an association of local business people, formed to promote and protect their interests

circumstances *n pl* the conditions and facts which are connected with and affect a situation, an event or an action *changing social and political circumstances*

colleague *n* a person that you work with, especially in a profession or a business

commercial *adj* connected with the buying and selling of goods and services *the commercial heart of the city*

commercial attaché *n* a person who works at an embassy and has special responsibility for trade and commerce

contract – see unit 2

costly *adj* causing problems or the loss of sth *a costly mistake/failure*

counterpart *n* a person who has the same position or function as sb else in a different place or situation

counterproductive *adj* having the opposite effect to the one which was intended

deal *n* an agreement, especially in business, on particular conditions for buying or doing sth *to make/sign/conclude/close a deal*

delay *n* a situation in which sth does not happen when it should

distribution – see unit 2

distributor *n* a person or company that supplies goods to shops/stores, etc. *Japan's largest software distributor*

elastic *adj* that can change or be changed *Our plans are fairly elastic.*

embassy *n*
1 a group of officials who represent their government in a foreign country
2 the building in which an embassy works

export *n* a product that is sold to another country *the country's major exports*

gauge *v* to make a judgement about sth, especially people's feelings or attitudes *They interviewed employees to gauge their reaction to the changes.*

golf club *n* a long metal stick with a piece of metal or wood at one end, used for hitting the ball in golf

head office *n* the main office of a company *Their head office is in New York.*

hospitality – see unit 2

hygiene *n* the practice of keeping yourself and your living and working areas clean in order to prevent illness and disease

interpreter *n* a person whose job is to translate what sb is saying into another language

market – see unit 4

metropolis *n* a large important city (often the capital city of a country or region)

on behalf of sb / on sb's behalf *exp* as the representative of sb or instead of them

partner *n* a person or an organisation that has an agreement with another one *a trading/business partner*

permit n an official document that gives sb the right to do sth, especially for a limited period of time

potential – see unit 7

preliminary adj happening before a more important action or event
preliminary results/findings/discussions

promising adj showing signs of being good or successful
The research produced promising results.

prospective – see unit 7

quality control – see unit 2

reception n a formal social occasion to welcome sb or celebrate sth

reliability n the state of being able to be trusted to do sth well

representative of adj typical of a particular place or group of people

requirement – see unit 7

sales outlet n a shop store that sells goods for a particular company

sales subsidiary n an office or company owned by the company whose goods it sells

short list n a list of potential candidates for a job, agents chosen to represent your company, etc.

speed up v to make sth move or happen faster
Can you try and speed things up a bit?

switch v to change or make sth change from one thing to another *The meeting has been switched to next week.*

trade delegation n a group of people who represent their country or company and go to another country to set up business connections

trade fair – see unit 2

translator n a person who translates writing or speech into a different language, especially as a job

vital adj necessary or essential in order for sth to succeed or exist
Good financial accounts are vital to the success of any enterprise.

warehouse n – see unit 2

unit 10

assess v to make a judgement about the nature or quality of sb/sth *We are trying to assess how well the system works.*

attention span n the length of time that sb is able to spend listening to, looking at or thinking about sth
Small children have a short attention span.

boost v to make sth increase, or become better or more successful *to boost exports/profits/to boost sb's confidence*

breakdown – see unit 2

brochure – see unit 1

catalogue – see unit 4

close a sale v to succeed in selling your product or service to a customer

colleague – see unit 9

competitor – see unit 4

complaint – see unit 2

concern n a feeling of worry, especially one that is shared by many people

consistently adv always behaving in the same way *We have argued consistently for a change in the law.*

consultant n a person who knows a lot about a particular subject and is employed to give advice about it to other people

courier – see unit 6

damaged – see unit 6

deadline – see unit 8

dealer n a person whose business is buying and selling a particular product
a(n) art/antique/car dealer

delivery – see unit 8

delivery charge n a sum charged to the buyer to cover the cost of delivering goods that have been ordered

demonstrate v to show and explain how sth works or how to do sth *Her job involves demonstrating new educational software.*

demonstration n an act of showing or explaining how sth works or is done

discount – see unit 8

disparity n a difference

downtown adj in the centre of a city, especially its main business area
a downtown store

effectiveness n the quality of producing the result that is wanted or intended
to check the effectiveness of the security system

efficiency n the quality of doing sth well with no waste of time or money
improvements in efficiency at the factory

enquiry card n a printed form on which visitors to an exhibition stand record their contact details, and which products or services they might be interested in

evaluate v to form an opinion of the amount, value or quality of sth after thinking about it carefully *We need to evaluate how well the policy is working.*

exhibitor n a person or a company that shows their work or products to the public

fog light n a very bright light on the front or back of a car to help the driver to see or be seen in fog

hand out v to give a number of things to the members of a group

headlight n a large light, usually one of two, at the front of a motor vehicle

indicator n a sign that shows you what sth is like or how a situation is changing

investigation n – see unit 7: **investigate** v

invoice – see unit 2

lead n a piece of information that may help to find out more facts about a situation or identify a new potential customer

make eye contact with sb exp to look at sb until they look at you too

on the job training n training which takes place at the same time as sb is carrying out their usual job

place v to give instructions about sth or make a request for sth to happen
to place an order

priority – see unit 2

product literature n brochures, catalogues and other printed information about a company's products

prospective – see unit 7

regardless of prep paying no attention to sth/sb; treating sth/sb as not being important *He went ahead and did it, regardless of the consequences.*

rejection n the state of being refused
Her proposal met with unanimous rejection.

replace v to change sth that is old, damaged, etc. for a similar thing that is newer or better

replacement n a thing that replaces sth, especially because the first thing is old, broken, etc.

rural – see unit 4

sample n a small amount or example of sth that can be looked at or tried to see what it is like

setback n a difficulty or problem that delays or prevents sth, or makes a situation worse

stand n a table or an upright structure where things are displayed or advertised, for example at an exhibition
a display/exhibition/trade stand

staying power n stamina; an ability to keep going despite setbacks or tiredness

suburb n an area where people live that is outside the centre of a city

trade fair – see unit 2

voice v to tell people your feelings or opinions about sth *to voice complaints/ criticisms/doubts/objections*

unit 11

acquire v to gain sth by your own efforts, ability or behaviour *She has acquired a good knowledge of English.*

against the clock exp if you do sth against the clock, you do it fast in order to finish before a particular time

appearance n the way that sb/sth looks on the outside

appreciate v to recognize the good qualities of sb/sth *His talents are not fully appreciated in that company.*

aptitude n natural ability or skill at doing sth
She showed a natural aptitude for the work.

assess – see unit 10

bonus n an extra payment given to employees in addition to their normal wages.

career prospects n the chances of developing your career

challenging – see unit 2

compensate for v, prep to provide sth good to balance or reduce the bad effects of damage, loss, etc.
All the staff got a bonus to compensate for the extra work they did during the office move.

compensation package – see unit 7: **compensation and benefits package**

context n the situation in which sth happens

deadline – see unit 8

dissatisfaction n a feeling that you are not pleased and satisfied

drop n a fall or reduction in the amount, level or number of sth

ensure – see unit 6

estimate v to form an idea of the cost, size, value, etc. of sth, but without calculating it exactly *The deal is estimated to be worth around $1.5 million.*

(sb's) face doesn't fit exp used to say that sb will not get or keep a particular job because they do not have the appearance, personality, etc. that the employer wants *It doesn't matter how qualified you are, if your face doesn't fit, you don't stand a chance.*

flexitime *n* a system where employees can start and finish work at different times each day, provided they work a certain number of hours in a week or month

fringe benefit *n* extra things that an employer gives you as well as your wages *The fringe benefits include free health insurance.*

have sth in common (with sb) *exp* to have the same interests, ideas, etc. as sb else *I have nothing in common with Jane.*

incentive *n* something that encourages you to do sth

influence *v* to have an effect on the way that sb behaves or thinks *The government refuses to be influenced by public opinion.*

inspire *v* to give sb the desire, confidence or enthusiasm to do sth well

in tray *n* a container on your desk for letters that are waiting to be read or answered

job security – see unit 1

layout – see unit 6

leave *n* a period of time when you are allowed to be away from work for a holiday/vacation or for a special reason

maximum potential – see unit 7: **to their/its full potential**

merit *n* a good feature that deserves praise, reward or admiration *We will consider each case on its (own) merits. (= without considering any other issues, feelings, etc.)*

morale *n* the amount of confidence and enthusiasm, etc. that a person or a group has at a particular time *Staff are suffering from low morale.*

motivate *v* to make sb want to do sth, especially sth that involves hard work and effort *The plan is designed to motivate employees to work more efficiently.*

net *adj* final, after all the important facts have been included *The net result is that small shopkeepers are being forced out of business.*

pay package – see unit 7: **compensation and benefits package**

perk – see unit 3

prioritise *v* to put tasks, problems, etc. in order of importance, so that you can deal with the most important first

promotion – see unit 1

recognition *n* public praise and reward for sb's work or actions *She gained only minimal recognition for her work.*

residential *adj* requiring a person to live at a particular place; offering living accommodation *a residential language course*

rumour *n* a piece of information, or a story, that people talk about, but that may not be true *There are widespread rumours of job losses.*

standard of living *n* the amount of money and level of comfort that a particular person or group has

status *n*
1 the fact of whether you are single, married, etc.
2 the social or professional position of sb/sth in relation to others *low status jobs*

strain *n* pressure on sb/sth because they have too much to do or manage, or sth very difficult to deal with; the problems, worry or anxiety that this produces

strength *n* a quality or an ability which a person or thing has that gives them an advantage *The ability to keep calm is one of her many strengths.*

strengthen *v* to become stronger; to make sb/sth stronger

stress *n* pressure or worry caused by the problems in sb's life *Things can easily go wrong when people are under stress.*

tactic *n* the particular method you use to achieve sth *They tried all kinds of tactics to get us to go.*

talent – see unit 1

team building event *n* an event designed to help a group of people work effectively together

unsatisfactory *adj* not satisfactory; not good enough

unit 12

acknowledge *v* to show that you have noticed sb/sth by smiling, waving, etc. *I was standing right next to her, but she didn't even acknowledge me.*

after-sales service *n* the care of a product provided by a supplier after it has been sold *We offer (a) free after-sales service for the first twelve months after purchase.*

aggressive *adj* behaving in a very determined and forceful way in order to succeed *an aggressive advertising campaign*

assume *v* to think or accept that sth is true but without having proof of it *It is generally assumed that stress is caused by too much work.*

assumption *n* a belief or feeling that sth is true or that sth will happen, although there is no proof

at hand *exp* close to you in time or distance *Let's get on with the task at hand instead of worrying about tomorrow's meeting.*

bargain hunter *n* a person who is looking for goods that are good value for money, usually because they are being sold at prices that are lower than usual

call centre *n* an office in which a large number of people work using telephones, for example taking customers' orders and answering questions

chain – see unit 4

chase *v* to try to obtain or achieve sth, for example money, work or a contract *We're chasing a big contract in Saudi Arabia at the moment.*

complacent *n* too satisfied with yourself or with a situation, so that you do not feel that any change is necessary *a dangerously complacent attitude to the increase in unemployment*

contract – see unit 1

dead *adj* not working *Suddenly the phone went dead.*

deal – see unit 9

defective *adj* having a fault or faults; not perfect or complete

diagnostic *adj* connected with identifying sth, especially an illness or a fault in a machine or system *to carry out diagnostic assessments/tests*

disgruntled *adj* annoyed or disappointed because sth has happened to upset you *I left feeling disgruntled at the way I'd been treated.*

eliminate *v* to remove or get rid of sth/sb

engaged *adj* (of a telephone line) being used *I couldn't get through. The line's engaged.*

enquiry *n* a request for information about sb/sth; a question about sb/sth *All enquiries should be addressed to the customer services department.*

established *adj* respected or given official status because it has existed or been used for a long time *They are an established company with a good reputation.*

faulty – see unit 2

guarantee *n* a written promise given by a company that sth you buy will be replaced or repaired without payment if it goes wrong within a particular period *The television comes with a year's guarantee.*

implement (be implemented) *v* to make sth that has been officially decided start to happen or be used *A new work programme for young people will be implemented.*

Internet Service Provider (ISP) *n* a company which connects a computer, or private computer network, to the Internet

interrogation *n* the process of asking sb a lot of questions over a long period of time, especially in an aggressive way

invest – see unit 8: **investment**

irritating *adj* annoying

land *v* to succeed in getting a job or a contract

leave/lay yourself wide open to *exp* to put yourself in a situation where you are likely to suffer sth such as criticism, injury, etc. *He has laid himself wide open to political attack.*

log *n* an official record of events during a particular period of time

loyal *adj* remaining faithful to sb/sth and supporting them or it

maintenance *n* the act of keeping sth in good condition by checking or repairing it regularly

manual *n* a book that tells you how to do or operate sth, especially one that comes with a machine, etc. when you buy it *a computer/car/instruction manual*

menu *n* a recorded list of possible choices that you are given when you call a call centre

mystery shopper *n* a person whose job is to visit retail outlets to gather information about customer service, or competitors' goods and prices, while pretending to be a normal customer

negotiate – see unit 2

point of sale – see unit 8

policy *n* a plan of action agreed or chosen by a political party, a business, etc. *The company has adopted a new policy on product returns.*

product return(s) *n* the process used when dealing with goods which have been taken back to the shop because they are faulty, or specific examples of products which have been returned in this way

promotion – see unit 2

purchase *n* something that you have bought *If you are not satisfied with your purchase, we will give you a full refund.*

query *n* a question, especially one asking for information or expressing a doubt about sth *Our assistants will be happy to answer your queries.*

queue – see unit 3

rate *v* to have or think that sb/sth has a particular level of quality, value, etc. *They rated him highly as a colleague.*

rating *n* a measurement of how good, popular, important, etc. sb/sth is, especially in relation to other people or things

reference number *n* a number that shows where you can find a piece of information *Please quote your reference number when making an enquiry.*

refund *n* a sum of money that is paid back to you because you returned goods to a shop/store *to claim/demand/receive a refund*

repair *v* to mend sth that is broken, damaged or torn *It's almost fifteen years old. It isn't worth having it repaired.*

replace – see unit 10

reputation *n* the opinion that people have about what sb/sth is like, based on what has happened in the past *The company enjoys a world-wide reputation for quality of design.*

return flight *n* a journey by plane to a place and back again

rival *adj* describing a person, company or thing that competes with another in sport, business, etc.

scepticism *n* an attitude of doubting that claims or statements are true *Such claims should be regarded with a certain amount of scepticism.*

secondary (to) *adj* less important than sth else *For some customers, quality is secondary to price.*

service contract *n* an arrangement with a supplier to provide repairs or safety checks for items bought, usually in return for regular payment

service engineer *n* a person whose job is to maintain or repair machinery and equipment

slash *v* to reduce sth by a large amount *to slash costs/prices/fares*

speed up – see unit 9

stage *v* to organise and take part in action that needs careful planning

status report *n* a written or spoken report on the situation at a particular time during a process

support – see unit 2: **support** *v*

take advantage of *exp* to make use of sb/sth in a way that is unfair or dishonest

take for granted *exp* to be so used to sb/sth that you do not recognise their true value any more and do not show that you are grateful

tendency *n* if sb/sth has a particular tendency, they are likely to behave or act in a particular way *I have a tendency to talk too much when I'm nervous.*

user name *n* the identification that a user gives to log on to a computer system *Users have to change their user names regularly for security reasons.*

waterproof *adj* that does not let water through

website – see unit 4

woo *v* to try to get the support of sb *Selected items are being sold at half price to woo customers into the store.*

unit 13

activist *n* a person who works to achieve political or social change, especially as a member of an organisation with particular aims

animal rights/welfare *n* the idea that animals should be treated without cruelty

approve (of) *v* to think that sb/sth is good, acceptable or suitable *Do you approve of my idea?*

bribe *n* a sum of money or sth valuable that you give or offer to sb to persuade them to help you

bribery *n* the giving or taking of bribes

chain store – see unit 4: **chain**

charity – see unit 8

child labour *n* the practice of employing children as workers

close to sb's heart *exp* having a lot of importance and interest for sb

code *n* a set of written rules that state how people in an organisation should behave *the company's code of ethics*

commitment *n* a promise to do sth or to behave in a particular way; the fact of committing yourself *The company's commitment to providing quality at a reasonable price has been vital to its success.*

compromising *adj* if sth is compromising, it shows or tells people sth that you want to keep secret, because it is wrong or embarrassing

consult (be consulted) – see unit 7

co-operative *n* a business owned and run by the people involved, with the profits shared by them *The factory is now a workers' co-operative.*

corporate *adj* relating to a company or group *concern for the environment is a important part of our corporate policy*

customer demand *n* the desire of consumers and customers for goods or services of a particular type *We introduced our low-fat burgers in response to customer demand.*

documentary *n* a film or a radio or television programme giving facts about sth

donation *n* something, often money, that is given to a person or an organisation such as a charity, in order to help them

draw up *v* to make or write sth that needs careful thought or planning *to draw up a contract/list*

enhance *v* to increase or further improve the good quality, value or status of sb/sth *This is an opportunity to enhance the reputation of the company.*

environment *n* the natural world in which people, animals and plants live *damage to the environment*

equal opportunities *n* the same chances of jobs, pay, etc. for both women and men

ethics *n pl* moral principles which control or influence a person's behaviour

foundation *n* an organisation that is established to provide money for a particular purpose, for example, for scientific research or charity

house *v* to provide a place for sb to live

human rights *n* the basic rights that everyone has to be treated fairly and not in a cruel way, especially by their government *The country has a poor record on human rights.*

image *n* the impression that a person, an organisation or a product, etc. gives to the public *The advertisements are intended to improve the company's image.*

impact – see unit 5

in a vacuum *exp* existing separately from other people, events, etc. when there should be a connection *This kind of decision cannot ever be made in a vacuum.*

initiate *v* to make sth begin *The government has initiated a programme of economic reform.*

investigate – see unit 7

issue *n* an important topic that people are discussing or arguing about *a key/sensitive/controversial issue*

labour practices *n* the ways in which a company treats its employees, and the type of employees it chooses

land – see unit 12

legislation – see unit 5

line sb's / your own pockets *exp* to get richer or make sb richer, especially by taking unfair advantage of a situation or by being dishonest

living wage *n* a wage which is high enough for sb to buy the things they need in order to live

make redundant (be made redundant) – see unit 4

media coverage *n* the reporting of news and sport in newspapers and on the radio and television

minimise *v* to reduce sth, especially sth bad, to the lowest possible level

moral responsibility *n* a duty to help or take care of sb or to behave correctly *I think we have a moral responsibility to help these countries.*

offend *v* to make sb feel upset because of sth you say or do that is rude or embarrassing

opt for *v* to choose to take a particular course of action *After graduating she opted for a career in music.*

packaging materials – see unit 2: **packaging**

persuade *v* to make sb do sth by giving them good reasons for doing it

pittance *n* a very small amount of money which sb receives, for example, as a wage, and that is hardly enough to live on

plantation *n* a large area of land, especially in a hot country, where crops such as coffee, sugar, rubber, etc. are grown

point out *v* to mention sth in order to give sb information about it or make them notice it *She tried in vain to point out to him the unfairness of his actions.*

policy – see unit 12

pollution *n* substances that make air, water, soil, etc. dirty *beaches covered with pollution*

press conference *n* a meeting at which sb talks to a group of journalists in order to answer their questions or to make an official statement

pressure group *n* a group of people who try to influence the government and ordinary people's opinion in order to achieve the action they want, for example a change in a law *Greenpeace is an environmental pressure group.*

produce *n* things that have been made or grown, especially things connected with farming.
The shop sells only fresh local produce.

profitable – see unit 1

rainforest *n* a thick forest in tropical parts of the world which have a lot of rain

repair – see unit 12

secondment *n* a short period of time in which an employee is sent to another department, office, etc. in order to do a different job

service engineer – see unit 12

shareholder *n* an owner of shares in a company or business; people who own shares receive part of the company's profits

spinal injury *n* an injury to the row of small bones which are connected together down the middle of the back

stakeholder *n* a person who has an interest, but not necessarily a financial one, in a company

standard – see unit 2

supply chain *n* a network of companies which provide goods or services to other companies which sell to the public

sustainable *adj* involving the use of natural products and energy in a way that does not harm the environment
sustainable forest management

sweatshop *n* a place where people work for low wages in poor conditions

switch – see unit 9

token *n* a round piece of metal or plastic used instead of money to operate some machines or as a form of payment

values *n, pl* beliefs about what is right and wrong and what is important in life
cultural/social/moral values

voluntary work *n* work done by people who choose to do it without being paid
I do some voluntary work at the local hospital.

volunteer *v* to offer to do sth without being forced to do it or without getting paid for it

well-intentioned *adj* intending to be helpful or useful but not always succeeding very well

unit 14

at a keystroke *exp* with one touch of a key on a computer keyboard

base *n* the main place where you live or stay or where a business operates from
I spend a lot of time in Britain but Paris is still my base.

boundary *n* a real or imagined line that marks the limits or edges of sth and separates it from other things or places

challenging – see unit 2

commute *v* to travel regularly by bus, train, car, etc. between your place of work and your home *She commutes from Oxford to London every day.*

concentrate *v* to give all your attention to sth and not think about anything else
I can't concentrate with all that noise going on.

corporate – see unit 13

dedicated *adj* designed to do only one particular type of work; used for one particular purpose only

desktop computer *n* a computer with a keyboard, screen and main processing unit, that fits on a desk

disciplined *adj* having the ability to control your behaviour or the way you live, work, etc. *I'm not sure that he's disciplined enough to telework successfully.*

distraction *n* a thing that takes your attention away from what you are doing or thinking about *I find it hard to work at home because there are too many distractions.*

economical *adj* using no more of sth than is necessary
an economical use of land/space

enable *v* to make it possible for sb to do sth
The software enables you to access the Internet in seconds.

explosion *n* a large, sudden or rapid increase in the amount or number of sth
an explosion of interest in learning Japanese

filing cabinet *n* a piece of office furniture with deep drawers for storing files

findings – see unit 2

guru *n* a person who is an expert on a particular subject or who is very good at doing sth
a management/health/fashion guru

hot-desking *n* the practice of working in an office using whatever desk or computer terminal is available instead of giving each employee a dedicated desk

impromptu *adj* done without preparation or planning *an impromptu speech*

in principle *exp* if something can be done in principle, there is no good reason why it should not be done although there may be some difficulties *In principle there is nothing that a human can do that a machine might not be able to do one day.*

interruption *n* something that temporarily stops an activity or a situation *I managed to work for two hours without interruption.*

intranet *n* a computer network that is private to a company, university, etc. but is connected to and uses the same software as the Internet

isolated *adj* without much contact with other people *I felt very isolated in my new job.*

isolation *n* the state of being alone or lonely

justify *v* to show that sb/sth is right or reasonable *How can they justify paying such huge salaries?*

laptop computer – see unit 3: **laptop**

modem *n* a device that connects one computer system to another using a telephone line so that data can be sent

motivation – see unit 11: **motivate**

on the plus side *exp* used to introduce an aspect of sth that you consider to be a good thing *On the plus side, all the staff are enthusiastic.*

plug in *v* to connect a piece of electrical equipment to the main supply of electricity or to another piece of electrical equipment *Is the printer plugged in?*

policy – see unit 12

population *n* all the people who live in a particular area, city or country; the total number of people who live there *countries with ageing populations*

premises *n, pl* the building and land near to it that a business owns or uses
The company is looking for larger premises.

productive – see unit 6

productivity *n* – see unit 6: **productive** *adj*

psychological assessment *n* a process intended to judge and form an opinion about a person's mind and the way in which it works; the results of such a process

remote *adj* far away

remotely *adv* from a distance
remotely operated

rush hour *n* the time, usually twice a day, when the roads are full of traffic and trains are crowded because people are travelling to or from work
Don't travel at rush hour.

storage *n* the process of keeping sth in a particular place until it is needed; the space where things can be kept
We need more storage now.

strain – see unit 11

stress – see unit 11

subsidiary – see unit 2

tailor (be tailored) *v* to make or adapt sth for a particular purpose, a particular person, etc. *Much of the software is supplied tailor-made for the user.*

team building event – see unit 11

telecottage *n* a building, usually in the country, equipped with computers so that people can work without travelling to an ordinary office in town

telecommuting – see unit 14: **teleworking**

teleconferencing – see unit 3

teleworking *n* the practice of working from home, communicating with your office, customers and others by telephone, computer, etc.

tension *n* a feeling of anxiety

translator – see unit 9

videoconferencing – see unit 3: **teleconferencing**

virtual *adj* made to appear to exist by the use of computer software

working practices – see unit 1: work patterns/working practices

workstation – see unit 6

acknowledgements

The authors and publisher are grateful to those who have given permission to reproduce the following extracts and adaptations of copyright material:

p8-9 'A matter of choice', *The Economist* 22 December 2001. Reproduced by permission of Economist Newspapers Ltd., London.

p8-9 'No more nine to five' by Richard Reeves, *The Observer* 23 July 2000. Reproduced by permission of Richard Reeves.

p24 'The sick truth about flying' by Jim Pollard, *The Observer* 3 December 2000. Reproduced by permission of Jim Pollard.

p32 'The high cost of conquering a new market' by Nicholas George, *Financial Times* 30 May 2001. Reproduced by permission of *Financial Times* Ltd.

p40 'Can snail mail beat email?' by Kate Hilpern, *The Guardian* 27 March 2000. Reproduced by permission of Kate Hilpern.

p56 'Developing the personal touch' by John Crace, *The Guardian* 8 January 2000. Reproduced by permission of John Crace.

p56 'Finding talent on the internet' by Patricia Nakache, *Harvard Management Update*, April 1997. Reproduced by permission of Harvard Business School Publishing.

p72 'Contacts that make or break Turkish ventures' by Sergey Frank, *Financial Times* 17 October 2001. Reproduced by permission of Sergey Frank.

p80 'The tests of a goodsalesperson' by Saul W. Gellerman, *Harvard Business Review* May – June 1990. Reproduced by permission of Harvard Business School Publishing.

p88 Extracts from W H Smith Total Guide to Improving your Career by Ben Williams and Chris Dunkerley. Reproduced by permission of W H Smith, Chris Dunkerley and Ben Williams, the Edinburgh based Chartered Corporate Psychologist.

p104 'Jobs with added value' by Kate Hilpern, *The Guardian* 11 September 2000. Reproduced by permission of Kate Hilpern.

p104 'Ethics on the march' by Eileen Sheridan, *The Guardian* 10 October 2000. Reproduced by permission of Eileen Sheridan.

p106 'Richer sounds. Rich Rewards' by David Teather © *Guardian Unlimited* 5 November 2001. Reproduced by permission of Guardian Newspapers Ltd.

p103 'McDonald's responds to anti-capitalist grilling' by Alison Maitland, *Financial Times* 14 April 2002. Reproduced by permission of *Financial Times* Ltd. p112 Extracts from www.flexibility.co.uk. Reproduced by permission of HOP Associates.

Although every effort has been made to trace and contact copyright holders before publication, this has not been possible in some cases. We apologize for any apparent infringement of copyright and if notified, the publisher will be pleased to rectify any errors or omissions at the earliest opportunity.

The logos are reproduced with the kind permission of the following: p6 Bayer, British Airways, BBC, BMW, The Body Shop International plc, DHL, Hewlett Packard, IBM, ICI, JVC, KLM, Mercedes-Benz, Nokia, Shell, Sky, Tesco, p34 Amazon.co.uk

The 'Coca-Cola' and 'Coke' are registered trade marks of The Coca-Cola Company and are reproduced on p6 with kind permission from The Coca-Cola Company.

The Spring Summer 2002 Collection Directory on p34 is reproduced by kind permission of Next.

The Screen grabs are reproduced with kind permission of the following: p56 Sony, p62 Virgin.

Illustrations by:
Adrian Barclay p48
Mark Duffin pp46, 68, 70, 117
Getty Images/Illustration Works p14 (map)
Nigel Paige pp22/23, 26, 40, 67, 85, 89, 94, 99, 101,117

We would like to thank the following for their kind permission to reproduce the following photographs:
Alamy.com pp54 (picture 1), 102 (industrial site)
Associated Press pp30 (Julie Jacobson/Gap), 62 (Richard Vogel /Budweiser), 93 (Diether Endlicher/rafting), 107 (Claude Paris /apples, DiegoGiudice/Manpower), 30 (Benetton)
John Cleare Mountain Camera Picture Library pp88 (rock climber), 93 (ramblers),
Corbis Images pp14 (Chris Coxwell/pharmaceutical factory), 43 (Yang Liu/woman on phone), 77 (David Samuel Robbins/Indonesia), 115 (LWA-JDC)
Corbis Sygma p64 (Despotovic Dusko)
Getty Images pp7 (Antonia Mo/Japanese man, Darren Robb/man in suit), 8, 10 (Stephen Simpson), 14 (Fisher Thatcher/business presentation, PS Productions/computer training, Australian dollars, David J Sams/pharmaceutical salesman carrying boxes), 16 (Photomondo), 18 (David Paul Productions), 20 (Phil Boorman), 24 (V.C.L./Spencer Rowell), 38 (Michael Malyszko/filing, Crowther & Carter/web browser), 50, 52 (Paul Venning/architects), 54 (Bob Schatz/picture 4), 54 (interview), 60, 72 (Andrea Pistolesi), 76 (Alex McKinsey), 80/81, 83 (Peter Gridley), 86 (Bob Scott/stressed man, Klaus Lahnstein/office workers), 87 (James Muldowney/young woman, David Lees/man, Steven Peters/older woman), 90 (Darren Robb), 91 (Andy Sacks/office block), 93 (Angela Wyant/kayak), 96/97 (Daly & Newton), 98 (David Lees), 110 (video conferencing)
Robert Harding Picture Library p17
H & M pp32, 33
Network Photographers pp43 (Tom Wagner/Saba/hand & mobile phone), 44 (Ed Kashi), 66 (Barry Lewis), 112 (Christopher Pillitz)
OUP pp7 (Photodisc/woman dark hair, man grey hair, woman fair hair), 35 (Photodisc), 38 (Photodisc/business people), 74 (Stockbyte), 76 (Photodisc/Jenny Burns, Stockbyte/Patrick O'Connor), 91 (Photodisc/crowd),
Panos p107 (Karen Robinson/flooding)
Press Association pp34 (EPA/megastore), 78 (left), 102 Barry Batchelor/production line), 108 (EPA)
Rex Features p28
Richer Sounds p106
Science Photo Library p102 (George Lepp/Agstock/battery hens)
The Scotsman p110 (Stephen Mansfield/hot desking)
Topham pp44 (Image Works/hot air balloon), 78 (Star Images/right), 88 (ImageWorks/men)
University of London Careers Service p54 (picture 3) www.careers.lon.ac.uk
Zurich Financial Services p104

Commissioned Photography by:
Steve Betts pp30 (bag), 54 (recruitment agency), 62 (supermarket, realia), 102 (bank, supermarket), 110 (homeworking), 120 (products)

OXFORD

UNIVERSITY PRESS

Great Clarendon Street, Oxford OX2 6DP

Oxford University Press is a department of the University of Oxford.
It furthers the University's objective of excellence in research, scholarship,
and education by publishing worldwide in

Oxford New York

Auckland Cape Town Dar es Salaam Hong Kong Karachi
Kuala Lumpur Madrid Melbourne Mexico City Nairobi
New Delhi Shanghai Taipei Toronto

With offices in

Argentina Austria Brazil Chile Czech Republic France Greece
Guatemala Hungary Italy Japan Poland Portugal Singapore
South Korea Switzerland Thailand Turkey Ukraine Vietnam

OXFORD and OXFORD ENGLISH are registered trade marks of
Oxford University Press in the UK and in certain other countries

Any websites referred to in this publication are in the public domain and
their addresses are provided by Oxford University Press for information only.
Oxford University Press disclaims any responsibility for the content

ISBN: 978 0 19 453197 9

Printed in China